ILONGOT HEADHUNTING

1883-1974

A STUDY IN SOCIETY AND HISTORY

Renato Rosaldo

STANFORD UNIVERSITY PRESS

STANFORD, CALIFORNIA

For my parents,
Betty and Renato

Stanford University Press
Stanford, California

© 1980 by the Board of Trustees of the
Leland Stanford Junior University

Printed in the United States of America
Cloth ISBN 0-8047-1046-5
Paper ISBN 0-8047-1284-0

Original edition 1980
Last figure below indicates year of this printing:

08 07 06 05 04 03 02 01 00

ILONGOT HEADHUNTING
1883-1974

ACKNOWLEDGMENTS

I am most indebted to my Ilongot friends and companions whose names (pseudonyms, for obvious reasons) appear in this book. It has been a pleasure to recollect our conversations and days of walking together along the trails.

The present form of the manuscript owes much to the stimulation of conversations among anthropologists and social historians during 1975–76, when I was a member of the Institute for Advanced Study in Princeton, New Jersey. The field research, during 1967–69 and 1974, was financed by a National Science Foundation predoctoral fellowship, by National Science Foundation Research Grants GS-1509 and GS-40788, and by a Mellon award for junior faculty from Stanford University. A sabbatical quarter from Stanford in the fall of 1977 also provided time for writing.

Among members of the New Tribes Mission who cooperated with our research, Dell and Sue Schultz were particularly helpful. A number of people, including Harold Conklin, Jean Conklin, Robert Fox, Barbara Pringle, Robert Pringle, and Douglas Yen, visited us in the field and made insightful comments on our research. Our institutional affiliation in the Philippines was the Division of Anthropology of the National Museum, and I am most grateful for their generous support.

The manuscript has benefited from extensive comments by Jane Atkinson, Harold Conklin, Jean-Paul Dumont, Genevieve Edwards, Clifford Geertz, Mary Jane Himel, Bridget O'Laughlin, Sherry Ortner, William Reddy, Michelle Rosaldo, William Sewell, Sylvia Yanagisako, and Aram Yengoyan. I have also received helpful comments from Keith Aufhauser, Jens Christiansen, George Collier, Jane Collier, Robert Darnton, Duncan Foley, Hildred

Geertz, Robert Paul, Mary Pratt, Edith Turner, Victor Turner, and Harriet Whitehead. Amy Burce prepared the chronological index.

Together, Michelle Rosaldo and I lived through the pain and joy of research and writing. Our relationship has brought me much that I am grateful for.

R.R.

CONTENTS

ILONGOT PHONOLOGY

Consonants:

p	t	k	'
b	d	g	
m	n	ng	
	l	r	
	s		
w	y		

Vowels:

i		u
	e	
	a	

Note:

' is a glottal stop.

ng is a velar nasal.

r is a voiced velar fricative.

Vowels i and u have context-determined high and low allophones. High tense realizations are obligatory after voiced stops and, in the case of i, before nonliquid dental consonants.

e is a midcentral unrounded vowel that when lengthened (ē) is raised and fronted.

ILONGOT HEADHUNTING

1883-1974

INTRODUCTION

This book should be read as a demonstration that ethnography stands to gain considerable analytical power through close attention to historical process. By now the proven strengths and glaring weaknesses of synchronic studies in anthropology are probably apparent to most practitioners of the discipline. Certainly I and others of my generation find it impossible to fit the results of our investigations into the classic ethnographic mold. In some cases the results would be repetitious, merely a minuscule variation on, for example, a theme of balanced segmentary opposition. In other instances, like that of the Ilongots, one encounters forms of life that are simply unsuited for the set of conceptual tools developed by conventional ethnographic methods. What is less clear, given the current state of the craft, is exactly in which direction to make the next move.

My present stance, that ethnography should now begin to explore so-called primitive societies from a historical perspective, was arrived at by a rather circuitous route, which I shall briefly recount in the pages that follow. I begin by reflecting on the differences between my world and the world of William Jones, an ethnographer who knew the Ilongots late in the first decade of this century; the point is methodological, for just as I view the Ilongots in historical perspective, I must see myself in the same way. Next, I show how and why synchronic studies of social structure are inadequate. Third, I attempt to demonstrate that attention to historical process cannot simply be aggregated to, but rather requires a fundamental reconception of, social structure, and that the reconceiving in turn demands a sharp departure from earlier ways of writing ethnographies. Finally, I shall argue that the image of the timeless primitive is not a finding, but an illusion created by the preeminent methods of anthropological research.

REFLECTIONS ON JONES AMONG THE ILONGOTS

My concern with the Ilongots of northern Luzon, Philippines, began in the fall of 1966 when Michelle Rosaldo and I were given a copy of Henry Milner Rideout's biography of William Jones, an American anthropologist. Jones had done field research among the Ilongots, and the gift was supposed to whet our curiosity about the people and thus lead us to conduct an ethnographic investigation among them. Initially fascinated, as I skimmed over vivid letters and diary extracts, I became at once more intrigued and more apprehensive as I reached the end of the biography and learned that after nearly a year of ethnographic research Jones was murdered by the Ilongots on April 3, 1909.*

In the course of a closer reading, fascination won out. I found myself lured by Jones's characterization of the Ilongots as expressive, "fond of animated conversation," and prone to "use much gesture and exclamation" (Rideout 1912: 171). Writing in an era when American ethnography was younger and more zestfully innocent in its romantic pursuit of the exotic, Jones was evidently euphoric at finding himself among perhaps the "wildest" people in northern Luzon: their habitat, like their character, was "wonderful" and "picturesque." In a letter of April 16, 1908, the day Jones arrived in Ilongot country, he portrayed the natural abundance of his research hideaway in these glowing terms:

Please don't address a letter to me at this place, for it will never get here! It is far up the Cagayan . . . when one gets to it one has to wander in the jungle to find it. It is the most out-of-the-way place I have yet run into out here, and probably the people are the wildest. I have a nice, cool little house to dwell in. It is thatched with palm leaves of the betel nut, and stands off the ground about seven feet. I have a far view in various directions. There is abundant game everywhere around. I wish I had a shot gun. The river is full of fish. (Pp. 146–47)

---

*Jones in large measure brought about his own murder. The entries from his field diaries (1907–9) reveal his utter frustration with Ilongot delays in transporting his collection of material culture to the lowlands. Jones's impatience gave way to verbal abuse of his companions and then a threat to imprison an old man (Stoner 1971).

A cluster of Ilongot houses in Tamsi, 1908. Photograph by William Jones. (*Courtesy Field Museum of Natural History, Chicago.*)

Jones's letters and diary extracts portray a vision of primeval abundance reaped from flowing streams and forested hills. It was in that luxuriant habitat that the ethnographer, well sheltered and well fed, carried on the day-to-day business of dialogue with the Ilongots—fine talkers, to be sure.

Ilongot life, however, was not all palm leaves and fish, and Jones's perception of his hosts turned at times to disgust. In a passage from his field diary dated October 10, 1908, Jones described the state of his Ilongot companions on the morning of the second typhoon within a single week:

Since the foul weather set in, this house has been a general gathering place for the greater part of Tamsi. The people come out of their shelters and lounge about in here till after the morning meal. When their bellies are filled they depart. Their aspect is most repelling. Hands, faces and bodies are smeared with blotches of various kinds of dirt; and their stiff hair is dishevelled. As they sit and scratch their lousy selves they seem more like beasts than human beings. These women suckle puppies. (Rideout 1912: 176)

Where Jones most often exhibited both enchantment and disgust with Ilongot lifeways was in his descriptions of headhunting. In a letter of March 19, 1909, ten days before his death, he wrote: "As I write, a bunch of men have gone out to search for two youths who went for bamboo yesterday and have not returned" (p. 188). The youths had gone for bamboo to make rafts to transport Jones, his belongings, his ethnographic notes, and his collection of material culture downstream toward the lowlands and eventually homeward to the Field Museum in Chicago. Jones went on in the same letter:

You see the weather is growing more torrid every day, and the sun can now shine for a whole day at a time. As a result every Ilongot house is on the watch for prowlers looking for heads, and ambitious youths are off

A group of Ilongots from Tamsi and nearby places, 1908. Photograph by William Jones. (*Courtesy Field Museum of Natural History, Chicago.*)

looking for the same in other districts. As Captain Bowers said at Tamsi when the Ilongots refused to do his bidding because what he wanted involved a taboo: "This may be good ethnology, Jones, but it makes me tired!" (P. 188)

On a deeper level, Jones's ambivalence toward the Ilongots, shifting as it did between a love of their primeval beauty and a hatred of their primitive bestiality, can be traced to the confluence of his own life history and the flow of American history at the turn of the century. The appeal of his Philippine research site seemed to emerge from what George Santayana (who taught at Harvard while Jones was a student there) regarded as the frankly mythic, yet revealing, construct of American social character. Santayana asserted that, for his archetypal American, "great empty spaces bring a sort of freedom to both soul and body" (1920: 197). Jones displayed the preferences of his particular version of turn-of-the-century American character when he wrote, "It is not so much the society of the Ilongots that has enchanted me, but rather the free life in these wild rugged hills and silent gloomy jungles" (Rideout 1912: 198). Indeed, Jones repeatedly invoked, with evident pleasure, what Santayana would have called the "great emptiness" of Ilongot territory in 1908–9.

Yet even Jones's love of the "great emptiness" he embraced in his field research was laced with a yearning for home. In a letter, Jones issued a stern warning that a dot on the map might not represent "a definite locality, at least as definite as an Indian village" (p. 148). What was brought home in that telling detail, the contrast between dispersed Ilongot houses and relatively compact American Indian villages, was that Jones passionately wished that the "wild rugged hills" of Ilongot country could replace the wide open plains of his youth in the Oklahoma Territory.

Jones had romanticized his recollections of an irretrievable time and place, his childhood and teenage years spent largely in Oklahoma. Those years in the Indian Territory, from his birth in 1871 to his eighteenth birthday in 1889, were spent in part with his Fox Indian paternal grandmother and in part working as a cowboy. In fact, before leaving for the Philippines in 1907, Jones had returned to have a "last look" at his native Oklahoma; his impressions of this visit, as recalled in a nostalgic letter of February 25, 1909, are worth recording at some length:

I wish the plains could have remained as they were when I was a "kid" . . . I cannot put into words the feeling of remorse that rose within me at the things I saw. The whole region was disfigured with a most repelling ugliness—windmills, oil wells, wire fences. Go to so and so for drugs, go to another for groceries, and so on. The cowboy and the frontiersman were gone. The Indians were in overalls and looked like "bums." The picturesque costumes, the wigwams, horsemen, were things of the past. The virgin prairies were no more. And now they say that the place is a state! Nevertheless you saw the stars that I used to see. Did you ever behold clearer moonlight nights anywhere else? Did you hear the lone cry of the wolf and the yelp of the coyote? I wish you could have seen the longhorn and the old time punchers. The present would-be punchers are of a different build. (Pp. 200–201)

In that letter from Ilongot country Jones mourned the passing of the wild West, cowboy and Indian alike, in its heyday; he grieved for an era that was at once his own childhood and a slice of time in American history.

In returning to Oklahoma before his departure for the Philippines, Jones was no doubt confirming what had already become evident during his Harvard years (1897–1900). While at Harvard, Jones once took three of his classmates "behind the scenes" at Buffalo Bill's Wild West show; there, in a "green-room open to the sky," they saw "dressing-tents, horses and harnesses, Cossacks, gatlings, buffaloes, Indians, and Rough Riders whom Jones had known in 'the Territory' " (Pp. 66–67). What Buffalo Bill, among others, represented was the metamorphosis from a vital life form to a nostalgic scene, flanked by cossacks and Rough Riders, in the backward-looking Wild West show.

Jones's biographer goes on to recall that at the Buffalo Bill show "we met cowboys who welcomed us, in part as Billy's [Jones's] friends, in part because they had fought alongside Harvard men at San Juan" (p. 67). Indeed, the Rough Rider was the successor of the cowboy. The biographer, writing more than ten years later, remembered that moment of his own college days in this vivid manner:

Men who were at Harvard during that spring term remember well the great wave of excitement which came flooding into college, and swamped all personal or academic questions. At first, as we hurried to late breakfast in Memorial Hall, there came the news that the "Maine" was sunk in Havana harbor. The fact stared out from black headlines on the newspaper stall, which stood on the transept, directly under the torn battle flags of an earlier generation. Before many days, the black letters grew larger and larger. (Pp. 56–57)

Jones, the former cowboy, was especially sought out as a recruit for the Rough Riders. In a letter of that time he said:

Mr. Roosevelt has sent word that he wants ten Harvard men to be with him in his troops of cowboy cavalry. Men have come to see if I would go . . . I do feel it my duty to go . . . You, perhaps, may realize what thoughts come through my mind as I think of being in those troops of cowboys. I would thousands of times rather be with those fellows than in any regiments of college men. (Pp. 58–59)

Jones declined the invitation; but within a decade he arrived in the Philippines, the American colony acquired in the Spanish-American War of 1898, the year the Rough Riders came into being.

Upon reflection Jones seems oddly familiar, at once a kindred spirit and utterly foreign. My preoccupations and his are separated by the peculiar gap between an imagination shaped by cowboy films and a childhood actually lived in the wild West. Whereas Jones reached the field in the exuberant first decade of his country's colonial adventure in the Philippines, I arrived there during the height of protest against our neocolonial venture in nearby Vietnam.

Although foreign war brought a "great wave of excitement" to the Harvard I knew during graduate school days, especially in 1969–70, there was no upsurge in enlistments, but rather a determination to resist, at times violently, the national effort in Southeast Asia. Times do change; and perhaps I found the gulf in the two historical periods especially wide because of certain parallels in the personal histories of Jones and myself. I too had made the move, as immediately disorienting as it was eventually formative, from the west to Harvard; I too identified with another heritage, not Indian but Mexican. Yet these similarities, for me, made the differences between us all the more salient. Jones's memories of his youth in the West seem to me as thrillingly exotic, remote, self-contained, and irretrievable as a novel by Sir Walter Scott.

Although I wish William Jones had been less inclined to shoulder the White Man's Burden in the Philippines, at the same time I admire his rugged frontier character. Like Jones's stance toward the Ilongots, mine toward him is complex, at once in awe, respectful, puzzled, annoyed, and angry. If Michelle Rosaldo and I have, as ethnographers among the Ilongots, been his successors we are, as Jones might have phrased it, "of a different build." In the usual way of latecomers to a scene, we are cast as less heroic figures than were the founding pioneers, who loom larger than life.

Our advantages over Jones were hindsight and the possibility, if we took the lessons to heart, of avoiding the errors of our predecessors. This is much as things should be; at any rate, it is so if one accepts Thomas Kuhn's view (1970: 170–73) that science progresses through a movement, not toward truth, but away from the errors of less adequate theories.

ILONGOTS AND THE RECEIVED VIEW OF SOCIAL STRUCTURE

What William Jones made clear was that the Ilongots appeared to have been cut from a traditional ethnographic mold. They were exotic enough to command interest and sufficiently self-contained to justify holistic analysis.

Nonetheless, Jones portrayed Ilongot society as brute in its simplicity and unintelligible in its lack of structure. When in a letter of July 12, 1908, for instance, he characterized Ilongot lifeways, he rushed quickly from his perception of the sparseness of their social order to the abundant richness of their subsistence. He wrote:

Society is pretty simple, and government is largely according to custom. They raise rice, corn, squash, beans, tomato, greens, tobacco, bananas, gabi [taro], and some other things in timbered clearings. They hunt deer and wild hog with the bow and arrow, and use nets and traps for catching fish. They hunt in parties and with dogs. After a killing the meat is divided equally all around. They raise chickens, and here and there a wild hog is penned and fattened, either under the house or close by. (Rideout 1912: 155)

The mode of subsistence and the sexual division of labor during Jones's time was much as I found it in 1967-69 and 1974. Men hunted, fished, and cleared the timber for gardens; women did most of the labor in the cleared gardens, where rice was most valued and other cultigens included sweet potatoes, taro, yams, bananas, sugar, and tobacco. Ilongots, in other words, were hunters, gatherers, and swidden [slash-and-burn] cultivators (see R. Rosaldo 1979; for other recent works on Ilongots, see M. Rosaldo, M. Rosaldo and Atkinson, and R. Rosaldo).

In other contexts, Jones spoke of how no Ilongot stood in authority over another, and how people were free to live their lives in separate and scattered households, without following the dictates of external agents of any kind. All equally rulers of their separate houses, Ilongot men and women were at liberty, of a morning, to choose whether to sleep, to drink sugar cane wine, or to hunt.

From the beginning, then, the problem was less how to study the Ilongot social order than where indeed to find it. Like other groups with cognatic forms of organization, the Ilongots would probably have proved intractable to the generation of ethnographers who followed William Jones.

The Ilongots simply lacked the standard institutions—segmentary lineages, ranked age-grades, men's houses, dual organizations, matrilateral cross-cousin marriage rules, and the like—that so often have given ethnographies their classical elegance.* Indeed, in the classic monographs later written on the Nuer, the Ashanti, the peoples of the Kachin Hills, and a host of others, social structure was understood, by definition, to be an ordered arrangement among parts that endures, relatively unchanging,

---

*The problem of the relative absence of formal institutions is common to a diverse cluster of societies. In terms of kinship and descent, there is that loose aggregate of social forms variously termed bilateral, nonunilineal, and cognatic. These societies are most frequently encountered in the Philippines, the Indonesian island of Kalimantan, and Europe. In terms of subsistence, there is the band level of organization found among certain pastoralists and non-Australian hunter-gatherer groups. Comparisons with other feuding hunter-horticulturists, such as the Yanomamo, should prove revealing. In terms of culture area, there is the label "loosely structured," as applied to Thai societies as well as the problematic ones of New Guinea. In an unpublished manuscript, Shelly Errington (n.d.) contends that Southeast Asian societies, especially former kingdoms, share certain characteristics that make them resistant to conventional models of social structure. Ilongots are (a) cognatic, (b) hunter-horticulturists, and (c) Southeast Asian.

Two Ilongot men, one with a hunting arrow and the other with a spear for fishing, 1974.

through time. Although they postulated a set of enduring relations, in practice the classic analyses usually worked within a synchronic framework; that is, they attempted to deduce the features of long-term social structure from empirical observations made within a narrow slice in time.

Though the dominant synchronic bias of anthropology has pervaded a number of theoretical orientations, for the moment let one example stand for many. The American school of culture and personality, for instance, all too often assumed both cultural homogeneity and cultural continuity. The doctrine of homogeneity allowed practitioners of this school to posit a basic personality shared by all members of a culture. The assumption of continuity across generations allowed them to sidestep longitudinal studies and instead to study parents and their infants at a single point in time, in order to infer (without asking whether the character of

An Ilongot man fishing with goggles and a spear, 1974.

The burning of felled vegetable debris, late May 1974. This is a critical phase of clearing a garden site for planting dry rice.

An Ilongot woman planting rice with a dibble in her cleared garden, June 1974.

Rice sprouting in an Ilongot garden, late June 1968.

children might differ from that of their parents) how child training practices (which themselves might have changed) had produced adult character. Their assumption that primitive cultures were timeless, as static as they were uniform, grew in large part out of a mistaken perception of the limitations imposed by the short term of field research. They restricted themselves unduly to what they could observe during their brief time in the field; for them, seeing was believing.

In general, the social theories dominant in the human sciences until a decade ago have been similarly one-sided, in the sense that they have stressed the given nature of society. To say that society is given is simply to reiterate the point that Emile Durkheim so relentlessly insisted upon: people born into a society receive a ready-made form of life from their predecessors that may endure after their deaths.

This received view of social structure, to indulge in a half-playful sketch, could be conceived according to three images: the play, the house, and the hidden principle. First, the image of the play suggests that social life can usefully be regarded as a troupe of actors who perform their roles from scripts, rather than as a group of individuals. In this view the social drama always remains the same, even when the actors and the stage props change. Second, the image of the house invokes an enduring structure that stands firmly, like a Durkheimian social fact, before, during, and after the lifetime of any particular actor who happens to strut and fret upon its premises. The house, by definition, never changes, and the actors simply move from room to room as they achieve or are ascribed one normatively regulated status after another until the day they die. Third, the image of the hidden principle postulates that observed social facts can be reduced to a simpler set of invisible structures. That complex social facts are generated by elementary principles is perhaps the most up-to-date of the three images of social structure. All three conventional versions of society, despite their significant differences, resemble one another in their failure to notice that human life is both given *and* actively constructed.

LOOKING INTO ILONGOT SOCIETY AND HISTORY

When, in the early summer of 1967, I looked forward to field research, I did not intend to write an ethnographic history. Even after a short stay among the Ilongots, their lifeways seemed perfectly suited for a synchronic study in social anthropology. They were exotic, relatively isolated, and numbered no more than 3,500. Writing from the field in 1968, I outlined a plan of research called "Alliance and Enmity," in which I proposed to study marital exchanges and patterns of feuding.

Both feuding and marriage often involved groups that Ilongots called *bērtan* (class, kind, species, group). Yet the more I understood how central bērtan were in the workings of Ilongot social life, the more puzzled I became about their nature. Two quite different kinds of groups were called bērtan: first, there were 13 co-residential, predominantly (about 80 percent) endogamous bērtan of about 165 persons each; second, there were 54 residentially dispersed bērtan that never united as action groups. Co-residential groups and dispersed groups—these seemed so widely disparate, sociologically speaking, that I was perplexed to find that Ilongots lumped them together in a single cultural category.

Eventually, the baffling capacity of bērtan to shift from trivial labels to collective identities that were crucial in such life-and-death matters as the feud became intelligible when seen in a diachronic perspective. In time I realized that the long-term developmental process of bērtan followed a trajectory from initial residential concentration through later dispersal to final evanescence. The pieces of the puzzle had fallen together, for the co-residential groups were an earlier phase and the loose categories were a later phase of a single developmental process; therefore Ilongots designated both with the single word (see R. Rosaldo 1975). Not only was it exhilarating to discover the order underlying otherwise disjointed observations, but the results had appeared to confirm the validity of a developmental approach to the workings of Ilongot society.

Thus encouraged, I hastened to study Ilongot social structure conceived as four processes neatly layered within the following hierarchy of containment: (1) families; (2) households; (3) local clusters; (4) bērtan. Perhaps Ilongot society could best be understood by putting time into social structure and thereby moving from a synchronic to a diachronic perspective.* Once I had pieced together a composite picture of the four developmental processes, I attempted to gain further precision, first by collecting case histories, second by determining the temporal span between the phases of actual cases. My initial efforts were crude.

At first I collected much of the material for my developmental studies in the form of stories. In everyday natural settings Ilongots usually spoke in the broad, informal speech style of *beita* (gossip, news), and they often used *tadēk* (stories) to spread reports of both witnessed and rumored events. Stories usually are a series of rela-

---

*In using developmental processes to put time into social structure, I followed the seminal paper of Fortes (1949) plus the classic works on cognatic societies by Freeman (1958; 1970) and Campbell (1964). More recent studies on cognatic forms of social organization in the Philippines and Kalimantan include Eggan (1967), Jocano (1968), Macdonald (1977), R. Rosaldo (1975), Yengoyan (1973), and the collection edited by Appell (1976). Perhaps the major pioneering collection of papers on cognatic forms of social organization in Southeast Asia is the volume edited by Murdock (1960).

tively autonomous episodes that are united, like beads on a string, by the winding thread of continuous movement through space, rather than by a rising plot line that points toward its own resolution in a climax. At their most elemental, Ilongot stories may simply list a lifetime of place names where people have gardened or erected their houseposts. More elaborate stories, often about oratory, fishing, hunting, and headhunting, begin at home, move in gradual step-by-step fashion toward their destinations, and conclude with a quick return to the place of origin. Virtually any kind of information, from lists of names to action-packed tales, can be encoded in this flexible cultural form.

Indeed, in time, and against pleas to the contrary, Ilongots decided to tell us stories. They spoke and I listened as I wrote the stories verbatim and then asked about puzzling phrases and incidents. Soon my notebooks were filled with what I regarded—for I saw only scattered bits of data in them—as disposable texts. Perhaps the most tedious stories were about the flight from the Japanese troops in 1945. While people were moved to tears as they recited place name after place name—every rock, hill, and stream where they ate, rested, or slept—my usual response was to continue transcribing in uncomprehending boredom. Unmoved by the endless, evidently aimless episodes of death and hunger, I failed to see the culturally distinctive sense of history that these tales embodied.

When I returned home to write my doctoral dissertation, I took as my model the studies by Barton (1919; 1938; 1949) on the Ifugaos and Kalingas, two upland Philippine groups living northwest of the Ilongots on Luzon. Thus, my analysis of Ilongot social structure was sprinkled with cases in which intricate human events (for example, a divorce leading to a bloody fight resulting in extended deliberations and substantial compensations) were robbed of all personal names and reduced to the illustration of elementary structural principles. It was impossible, among other things, to discern whether the actors in one case were the same as those in another and which of two episodes came first. In retrospect, it is easy to see why seasoned anthropological readers often skim or even skip such illustrative case materials in order to rush ahead and ponder more seriously what the philosopher of history Louis Mink has pointedly called their detachable conclusions.

When I returned to live among the Ilongots in 1974, I began to refine the case histories collected during our previous stay. Although I hoped only to add precision to the analysis of Ilongot developmental cycles, I arrived at an unanticipated conclusion. My earlier analytical breakthrough, like all others, was not a final resting ground, but simply one more step removed from a point where comprehension had failed. I still had farther to go in understanding Ilongot society. In effect, I was making a transition from a developmental to a historical study of Ilongot social life.*

In treating Ilongot stories and our conversations about these stories as texts for cultural analysis and documents for critical assessment, I followed canonical method in anthropology and history.† Initially I assembled various versions of a single incident, and compared them to discern their cultural form and factual discrepancies. The stories Ilongots told about their lives became documents to assess for their truth value, and cultural forms to appraise for their particular meanings.‡

Ilongot stories not only contained but also organized perceptions of the past and projects for the future. In other words, the only way I could apprehend Ilongot lifeways was by looking through (not somehow around or directly behind) the cultural forms that they used to represent their lives to themselves. Even the most brute of brute facts I found to be culturally mediated. In killing from ambush, for instance, Ilongots demonstrated a de-

---

*Among the field manuals I had with me during my research was the volume edited by Epstein (1967). In addition, I found the application of the extended case method in Turner (1957) and the related work of Geertz (1965) especially instructive. Another source of inspiration in the field was the complete works of William Faulkner; through them I struggled over the intricacies with which the past can live in the present, even in small and remote societies. Finally, I believe that certain peoples of Luzon conceive of their lives in cultural terms that make the methods of biography and history especially revealing, as indicated in Barton's classic works. The shift from a monograph on social structure to a study in culture, history, and society thus grew in large measure from the very nature of the Ilongot form of life.

†The procedures for critical assessment of written and oral documents are relatively well known. Among useful recent guides on method in this area are Carmack (1972), Evans-Pritchard (1962), Lewis (1968), MacFarlane (1977), and Vansina (1965). The classic source of course is Thucydides.

‡The failure to see that documents are more than bits of information and that they embody cultural forms is probably more widespread among historians than anthropologists. Even an ethnographic historian as remarkably gifted as Emmanuel Le Roy Ladurie fails to make explicit the narrative form of the documents he otherwise interprets with such great skill (see Davis 1979).

cided lack of chivalry. But what outsiders often saw as the epitome of cowardice, the raiders themselves perceived as a moral act, an attempt to safeguard the lives of their brethren.* Ilongot statements about their past were embodied in cultural forms that highlighted certain facts of life and remained silent about others through their patterned way of selecting, evaluating, and ordering the world they attended to.

In August 1974 I developed a reliable chronology of the Ilongot past, extending backward from 1974 to about 1920, and with less certainty to 1883. Suddenly I had extended the temporal frame of the ethnographic present from the confines of my 30 months of field research to at least the span of a person's lifetime. The constraints imposed on ethnographic research by the brevity of actual fieldwork were, it now became apparent, illusory; or at any rate, they were so for certain kinds of data. As the shape of Ilongot history began to emerge, my perception of Ilongot social structure started, quite unexpectedly, to shift at its very foundations. Rather than construct composite developmental models from observations made at a single point in time, I followed these processes for particular cases that had unfolded over half a century or more.

In order to elucidate matters further, I used the chronology to situate the case materials within all possible convergent lines of evidence, including histories of feuding, marriage, demographic patterns, household compositions, residential moves, and any available written documents. I discovered, for instance, that Ilongot stories about how the Japanese soldiers had invaded during planting season were fully confirmed by reports from the American army. In a more complex case, I found myself painstakingly threading together diverse strands—stories of arrests in 1940, demographic data, tales of a bumper harvest of rice, household histor-

---

*Representative of the many statements on Ilongot cowardice is the following passage from an otherwise often perceptive report: "From the viewpoint of their morals, the Ilongots are the most degraded beings imaginable. Ignorant of any conception of love for their fellow humans, neither do they hold any humanitarian sentiments nor do their base and miserable hearts have a place for a single generous act. Cowards in the extreme, thirsty for the blood of their enemies, without pity for defenceless victims and vengeful by tradition, they provide hospitality for no one and they even destroy one another" (Jordana y Morera 1885: 69–70). Ilongots, on the other hand, found it beyond their moral comprehension that army officers, as they saw in 1945, could command their troops to move into open fire. Soldiers, they remarked, are men who sell their bodies.

ies, conversations about past headhunting threats, the process of a feud, and present-day observations of the few women who aid in hunting—in order to reconstruct the situation of a local cluster within the larger context of delineating the shape of Ilongot collective memories about the catastrophe of 1945 (see Chapter 4). Throughout this process of reconstituting past lives, I moved from tentative understandings of the larger picture to smaller lines of evidence and back again as I continually revised my interpretation of events.

Moreover, the chronology, a mere point of departure for the historian and a difficult achievement for the ethnographer of a nonliterate people, enabled me at last to see together the relations among the developmental processes that I previously described as autonomous cycles, and the interconnections among seemingly separate events that overlapped in time. Through this increasing historical specificity I was able to discern, for instance, the interpenetration of regularities in the life cycle and the contingencies of the historical moment.*

The scope of my project thus definitively moved beyond social structure to encompass the distinctive ways in which Ilongot conduct is culturally patterned, institutionally grounded, and historically produced. Indeed, it is precisely the simultaneous grasp of contingent happenings, developmental processes, and cultural forms, all seen together as they move through time, that constitutes what W. B. Gallie has called the historical understanding.

So it was that when Ilongot narratives of otherwise disparate cases happened to coincide in time, I began to inquire into how else they were related. Was the direction of a series of marriages related to a residential move? Did a particular couple divorce because of emergent tensions between two larger groups? These questions of course presupposed my knowledge of, or at any rate my capacity to learn about, which came first, the marriages or the move, the divorce or the wider tensions. Although in my dissertation, for example, I had mistakenly asserted that the traumatic fights that often follow marital separations are an important factor in producing the low divorce rate among Ilongots, I now understood that most marital separations I had studied earlier co-

---

*A fine methodological essay on the relations of the life cycle and the historical moment can be found in Erikson (1975: 113–68).

incided with two moments of abrupt political realignment and residential movement. The traumatic quarrels following divorces therefore were related less to the infrequency of marital separation than to the political realignments through which both were precipitated. In this manner I moved from the use of case materials as illustrations of developmental processes to their employment as a means to understand the impact of critical events upon the development of a collection of lives.

A major consequence of my casting Ilongot society into historical perspective is that I depart from conventional anthropological practice by using structural summations as an analytical starting point, rather than as an encapsulating conclusion—for I am convinced that structures, in this case developmental cycles, facilitate as much as they constrain human action. I therefore understand Ilongot conduct to be rendered intelligible within (rather than produced by) cultural typifications of developmental cycles. (See pp. 61–66, 136–52, 177–96, 222–29, for the feud, the life cycle, the domestic cycle, and the bērtan, respectively; see also the Chronological Index, p. 299). To phrase matters somewhat differently, I have inverted the analytical location of developmental processes from final goal to entry point because I have found, at least for this case, that such processes are made up less of binding normative rules than of rules that require cultural interpretation—both by Ilongots and by their ethnographer.

When a single event is interpreted in quite different ways, as so often happens in human affairs, the distinct versions can derive from factors that range between two polar types. Sometimes, like soldiers on a battlefield, people see things from such a restricted angle of vision that they simply do not know the whole story; at other times, like partisans who have taken sides in a dispute, whether or not they know better they use their version of the story as a weapon against the other side. In the latter instance, conflicts of interpretation derive from people's locations within the deeper divergences of local political life. Indeed, among the Ilongots, owing in large measure to the absence of a hierarchical ordering of social life beyond sex and age, no single official version of events is widely accepted, and in this sense their cultural knowledge is deeply perspectival.

In general, I am convinced that the central issues of social thought are not only the conventional ones of cohesion and the normative order, but also the emergent ones of dissension and the politics of persuasion, both artful and forceful. To say that certain rules are not given but require interpretation is to say that the study of cultural processes requires an investigation of the structural position of each particular rule-giver. A number of social processes are thus ordered, less through the simple realization of structural principles than through struggles among people with different stakes in the outcome of events.

My extensive use of narratives in the following chapters may do violence to the expectations of readers who are accustomed more to the conventions of ethnographic than of historical writing.* What I hope to convey through the techniques of narrative is an analysis of the unfolding of complex sociohistorical events within a particular local setting. Along with a number of philosophers of history, I regard the narrative form I use less as a matter of surface rhetoric than as an embodiment of a distinctive kind of knowledge: the historical understanding.† More broadly, I would suggest that ethnographers should attend carefully to compositional modes, for what we have to say is rarely separable from how we say it.

Perhaps the most economical way to convey a sense of how narratives can embody the historical understanding is through the example of a game of chance and skill. Consider for a moment the game of baseball, an often used example of what is involved in

---

*What I have in mind here is that ethnography, like any other verbal genre, is understood in relation to the reader's expectations. Otherwise, for example, one could not distinguish earnest debate from playful parody or an accepted truism from a theoretical innovation (see Culler 1975: 113–60).

†The connections between the historical understanding and the use of narrative are probably best elucidated in the works by Gallie (1968), Hexter (1971), Mink (1965), and White (1973). Crapanzano (1977) has recently urged anthropologists to become more self-conscious in their modes of composition. In writing ethnographies, we rarely use already developed literary techniques for the portrayal of the lives of our subjects. Ranging from the standard experimentalist's format of problem-data-analysis-discussion-conclusion to the more meandering clinical case history, the conventions of prose discourse serve both to collect and to organize ethnographic data in accord with distinct analytical presuppositions. In his analysis of the underlying "poetic prefigurations" in the writings of nineteenth-century historians, White (1973) started the kind of project I would advocate for ethnographic writings.

telling about and following a complex event through time.* As the action starts, the perceptive fan begins to think strategically by considering who is at bat (an often-dangerous pull hitter now in a slump), who is pitching (a fresh reliefer whose knuckleball is as often erratic as it is effective), who is on base (an able base runner, on first), how the fielders are playing (at double-play depth), and what the score is (one out, bottom of the ninth, the tying run on first). Clearly, there is a vast difference between merely knowing the rules of the game and having the knowledge required to follow the game in the manner of an experienced fan of fine judgment.

In addition, a storyteller wishing to achieve a proper sense of proportion and possibility would require a peculiar double vision, focused at once on each unfolding moment and on the totality of the long-term course of action. On the one hand, a sense of proportion would come from seeing the particular game in the context of the entire season. How important, after all was said and done, did this single game happen to be? Was it a turning point? On the other hand, a sense of open-ended possibilities would emerge from the forward-looking vantage point of each significant instant of play. Like the avid fan, the storyteller might plot strategies several moves ahead as she or he thinks about who is in the bullpen, possible pinch hitters, how to play the infield if the batter is walked, and so on.

Similarly, my narratives in this book provide certain facts of local biography, society, and history, so that the reader can follow an episode and determine whether it is a routine developmental phase, a startling chance happening, or a decisive turning point in collective life. Throughout I ask about what it was that people were struggling to make happen. What was at stake? The point is to see how circumstances alter and are altered by the course of human actions. Social life—viewed as a forward-looking struggle among alternative courses of action that certain structures both enable to be and limit—begins to emerge, not as the inevitable playing out of underlying principles, but rather as a complex interplay of political processes. At the same time, I attempt to under-

---

*Gallie (1968) and Hexter (1971) both use baseball as a key example in their perceptive reflections on the close kinship between the telling of stories and the historical understanding.

stand each episode in the context of longer trajectories of change. My purpose is to use narratives in order to delineate as fully as possible the complex orchestration among events, institutions, and ideas as they unfold together through time.

In this book, therefore, I shall develop an analysis of society and history conceived as the interplay of received structures and human activity. Along with others now concerned to bring the historical understanding to bear in social thought, I plan to stress not just the given nature of society, but also the ways in which human beings continually construct, manipulate, and even recast the social worlds into which they were born and within which they will die.*

Indeed, one of the most deeply held Ilongot values is that their lives unfold more through active human improvisations than in accord with socially given plans. They often insist, for instance, that in marital choice they follow the desires of their hearts rather than prescriptive rules or the dictates of their elders. Thus they prefer to think that their conduct is guided but not governed by rules that they more or less make up as they go along. Their received traditions, then, are not mere survivals, inert remnants of a bygone past, but instead they constitute an active force in the lived-in present. This at once theoretical and indigenous sense of what Ilongot social life is most significantly about—that it is more actively constructed than passively received—is now central to my conception of how to understand it in historical perspective.

What I hope to achieve by bringing history into anthropology is a method for dissolving such hapless analytical dichotomies as structure and process, cultural pattern and cultural transmission, life cycle and biography. The trick, of course, is to perceive the active interplay of structures and events. Although a composite life cycle, for example, says nothing about how any particular life was lived, personal biographies are not intelligible without a sense of the expectations, constraints, and hopes that frame any life trajectory as it unfolds.

Thus by exploring a feud, by following a collection of biogra-

---

*The theoretical bases for this shift away from the once-dominant view are perhaps best articulated, with reference to a broad range of writings in social theory, by Bernstein (1976), Giddens (1976), and Williams (1977).

phies, and by reaching back into local history, as I do in the three parts of this book, I intend to show the deep sense in which Ilongot lives are a series of improvisations on certain social forms and cultural patterns. First, the feud embodies much of Ilongot historical consciousness and often motivates marriages and residential moves. In this sense the process of feuding is a central moving force for both the conduct and perception of history. Second, in following a collection of biographies the reader should gain a grasp of the patterns that can be seen only as they unfold in processes of change. What does it mean to say that men, for example, take heads or marry in quick succession, like people walking along a path? How is this episodic chain related to peer envy and the violent tenor of an epoch? Such questions about underlying mechanisms can be explored only through the study of particular lives. Finally, by reaching back into early local history I can show how bērtan, far from being changeless units of enduring social structure, actually undergo continual fluctuations and changes. At the very least I hope to show that Ilongot society can best be understood as it unfolds through time rather than as a set of eternal structures.

THE INVENTION OF THE TIMELESS PRIMITIVE

The ethos of anthropology has made it particularly difficult to perceive the consciousness and workings of historical change among our subjects of investigation. Many of us have been drawn into anthropology through romantic yearnings to discover a primeval form of life. William Jones, for instance, in a letter of February 25, 1909, said that one reason he had "made a bee-line" for Ilongot country was that it was not then subdued, and the people still hunted heads "as they've done since days far back in time" (Rideout 1912: 199). When Jones wrote, he did so with a sense that he was a witness to the end of an era. "The point," he said in a letter of March 19, 1909, "is this—warfare among the wild men of Luzon is rapidly being checked, and this is practically the only territory where the mice have free play"(p. 189). Thus Jones savored a corner of Luzon, a place not yet, but (he believed) soon to be, devoured by an omnivorous civilization.

Jones was not alone in constructing his personal romance.* I too wanted to preserve, at any rate record, a vanishing lifeway in the *tristes tropiques*. I tried to ignore my predecessors who had been with the Ilongots, from the Spanish friars of more than 300 years ago to the anthropologist Jones of nearly 60 years before—pretending that before I, the ethnographer, happened along, Ilongot society was as pristine as the Garden of Eden. The extent to which the fiction of the timeless untouched people has guided anthropological research, especially of the so-called primitive variety, can be judged by the number of ethnographies that begin with prefaces designed to establish that a particular group of people has long lived in remote isolation. Their isolation is often attributed to resistance, either of the passive sort or the once-fierce-and-only-yesterday-pacified kind.

As I now see it, my initial failure even to perceive, let alone grapple with, the problem of Ilongot history was a result of my having taken to heart a romantic impulse that had become hardened into an ancestral prohibition against the use of history in anthropology. It was, at least as I have rediscovered the anthropological past, A. R. Radcliffe-Brown who made the classic pronouncement on how the discipline of necessity must abuse historical explanation. In his attack on those who indulged in "pseudo-historical speculations" as opposed to his version of scientific method—systematic synchronic comparativism—he wrote:

The acceptability of a historical explanation depends on the fullness and reliability of the historical record. In the primitive societies that are studied by social anthropology there are no historical records. We have no knowledge of the development of social institutions among the Australian aborigines for example. Anthropologists, thinking of their study as a kind of historical study, fall back on conjecture and imagination, and invent "pseudo-historical" or "pseudo-causal" explanations. (1952: 3)

---

*The literary convention of the omniscient narrator should only be used selectively in ethnographies, not as a matter of course. One first should ask about the situation of field researchers. Did they hear all major sides of a story, or witness an event from all important angles of vision? If not, they mislead their readers when they speak through a narrative persona who sees all and is located nowhere in particular. Throughout what follows, my first-person interventions should be read as a consciously chosen analytical method, not merely as a literary device.

Inspired by polemical motives, Radcliffe-Brown marshaled forth what he called the proper concept of history: the pursuit of institutional origins through the use of written documents. In so restricting his definition he misrepresented a much wider form of inquiry, and thereby rendered history useless for the study of most so-called primitive societies, including the Ilongots. Though successful in ferreting out its abuses, Radcliffe-Brown utterly failed to see the uses of history in anthropology.

More recently, in many fashionable quarters, the label "primitive" has become synonymous not merely with the notion of a society that has an ancient history beyond recovery, but with the notion of a society that is designed to suppress the consciousness of change through time. One articulate spokesman for "timeless" societies, Mircea Eliade (1971), describes "primitives" as people for whom the only meaningful action is the repetition of deeds performed by the ancestors or gods, hence their sense of the eternal recurrence of human actions. Such societies are characterized, for Eliade, by their cyclical rather than linear views of the passage of time. Similarly, Claude Lévi-Strauss (1966) speaks of primitive or "cold" societies that, unlike their opposites, the "hot" ones, deny the effects of time on their fundamental structures. Although members of cold societies may experience demographic and other changes, they fabricate and supposedly believe static versions of their societal structures.

Lest it be thought that this vision of primitives enmeshed in a web of eternal recurrence is dated or perhaps a purely Parisian fantasy, Marshall Sahlins has recently elaborated the same viewpoint in this manner:

And to this gross difference in design correspond differences in symbolic performance: between an open, expanding code, responsive by continuous permutation to events it has itself staged, and an apparently static one that seems to know not events, but only its own preconceptions. The gross distinction is between "hot" societies and "cold," development and underdevelopment, societies "with" and "without" history—and so between large societies and small, expanding and self-contained, colonizing and colonized. (1976: 211)

One burden of this book is to show that those who are refining the gross distinction between societies with and without histories have embarked, not on a difficult conceptual journey, but along the wrong track.

The presumption that so-called primitive societies are timeless, as I think this book shows, reflects less about their basic nature than about a systematic bias in anthropological method that inhibits access to their histories. My point is that the analytical method of freezing time in order better to perceive the relations of a structural-functional societal whole has itself produced the illusion of "timeless primitives." In most anthropological studies the whole question of history, both as process and as consciousness, has been neither refuted nor confirmed, but simply ignored. It is surely no accident that historians study so-called hot societies and anthropologists study so-called cold societies. Thus the sense in which the celebrated contrast between hot and cold societies can be understood is as an artifact of ethnograhic method, not as a reflection of the human condition.

I have chosen a different tack in that I begin with the broadest definition of history, as the study of change through time, and then gradually develop a conception of the term appropriate to the study of Ilongot society. My task is to work between the Ilongots' concept and ours, both broadly defined, and so to try to bring their history into focus. The trick is to avoid the example of Edmund Leach's butterfly collector, that fellow who pins each social case with its own unique label, and instead to use the concept of history in its full range of meanings, at once showing what is culture-specific without losing sight of potentially illuminating comparative juxtapositions (see R. Rosaldo 1975).

What is most difficult to discern in the study of so-called primitives is the extent to which anything of significance has changed. In such communities, so remote and perhaps alien from our own, the problem is to determine precisely the kinds of change that in fact do take place through time. For those of us rather coarsely attuned to more strident movements—the rise and fall of massive totalitarian regimes, the widely resounding booms and busts of the stock market—Ilongot history must appear comparatively silent, even immobile. Relative to our own, the Ilongot past has been inscribed in miniature, written in such a low key that its moving rhythms are all too likely to elude us. Our moral imperative, in attempting to comprehend Ilongots, should be that we take their lives nearly as seriously as we take our own. The perception required of us is that seemingly small changes, many of them phrased in an unfamiliar cultural idiom, can have vast reverberations in the lives of people.

PART I. THE PAST MADE PRESENT

CHAPTER ONE. PERSPECTIVES ON ILONGOT HISTORY

Received anthropological wisdom warns against using statements that people make about their past lives in reconstructing their histories. Even genealogies, we are told, can be manipulated, distorted, and blatantly invented as suits the needs of political disputes of the moment.* Once current disputes intervene, it would seem, historical memories are shredded and rewoven until the designs they display are shaped more by invention than by recollection. Such wisdom does not apply to the Ilongots.

Although Ilongot recollections often are used as a political idiom, they retain a specific historical value. They derive their impact more from the astute selection of earlier episodes than from sheer invention. To recall a kin relation from earlier times, for example, is both to remember correctly and to justify a developing marriage alliance; to recount how one's uncle was beheaded is at once to revive a painful memory and to urge one's children to retaliate. Thus the tales Ilongots tell must be understood both as a moving force in the lived-in present and as an accurate depiction of episodes from bygone days. Indeed, for Ilongots, a story is most persuasive as a charter for conduct if it is an accepted, eyewitness account. What is contestable is less the veracity than the choice of historical incidents to be used as a guide for projected action. Even the most partisan of Ilongot narratives can be used in reconstructing a wider sense of their historical past.

*L. Bohannan (1952) and Leach (1954), among others, have argued that genealogies are often fabricated to justify positions taken in present-day political disputes. Fox (1971) has shown, on the other hand, that certain dynastic genealogies are quite accurate. Midway between the extremes, the Ilongot past often persists into the present as a political idiom, yet historical tales are selected rather than invented to suit present purposes.

The progression of this chapter, from an external history (1565–1974) through a more internal history (1919–44) to an initial delineation of Ilongot conceptions of the past, recapitulates the phases of understanding social processes in their local setting. The initial sketch is based on published ethnohistories that situate the peoples of northern Luzon in the context of a division between lowlanders and uplanders. I then describe how I gained access to Ilongot history by piecing together the oral narratives of the people themselves. Drawing upon that assemblage of indigenous stories, I next outline a preliminary history of the quarter-century before 1945. Finally, I present a number of the cultural conceptions through which the Ilongot past has been constructed and through which it must be understood, by both Ilongots and their ethnographers.

AN ETHNOHISTORIC SKETCH, 1565–1974

The mountainous sector of northern Luzon, like comparable areas of mainland Southeast Asia, appears to be divided between the majority cultures of the lowlands and the cultural minorities of the highlands.* Indeed, most ethnohistoric studies on the region take as their central problem the explanation of the ethnic boundary that divides people living in the valleys from those who live in the hills. In his classic study, *The Ethnohistory of Northern Luzon,* Felix Keesing wrote:

The principal ethnohistorical problem here is whether the differences between the lowland and the mountain peoples can be traced, through historical documents of the long Spanish period or through other evidence, to ecological and cultural dynamics operating upon an originally common population, or whether some theory of separate migrations is called for. (1962: 4)

*A useful general statement on hill and valley peoples in Southeast Asia can be found in Burling (1965). In the context of northern Luzon, two papers by Eggan (1941; 1954) set the stage for Keesing to overthrow definitively the view that upland/lowland differences developed from two separate waves of migration. Studies of Agta hunter-gatherers and the pagan Gaddang, both to the north of Ilongot country, have been made in the context of the hill/valley contrast (see Peterson 1978 and Wallace 1970, respectively). For studies of lowlanders in Luzon, the local histories by Ileto (1975) and Larkin (1972) should be consulted; the best history of uplanders to the northwest of the Ilongots is the work of Scott (1974).

Keesing rejected the hypothesis of separate migrations and concluded that the lowland/upland division in northern Luzon resulted from the Spanish colonial practice of achieving dominion over the valleys while leaving the hills beyond their direct political and religious control.

Though largely correct in saying that Spanish colonization created the cultural separation of lowlanders and uplanders on northern Luzon, Keesing mistakenly surmised that the present Ilongot population derived from an earlier amalgam of refugee groups from the surrounding valley flatlands. His hypothesis was speculative because at the time it was fair to say, as he did, that the Ilongots "have not been described in the ethnological literature, so that the problem of their origin and relationship must remain in abeyance" (p. 296). Keesing's incorrect view was based in part on erroneous reports, beginning with Spanish missionary friars in the eighteenth century and filtering into the ethnological literature of the twentieth, indicating that Ilongots were divided into a number of subgroups based on marked differences in language and culture.* Our research among the Ilongots called into question earlier views. We found no mutually unintelligible dialects, relatively little internal variation in culture, and a strong sense of shared ethnic identity among the people as a whole. Moreover, written documents from as early as the mid-seventeenth century place the Ilongots in their present location. Linguistic evidence that we collected confirms the documentary sources and suggests an even longer span of residence in or near their current homeland at the headwaters of the Cagayan River, some 80 miles northeast of Manila (see Map 1).†

Although Ilongot country is close to Manila as the crow flies, it

*Multiple names for Ilongots reflected not the number of ethnolinguistic subgroups, but rather the paths by which reporters entered the land at the headwaters of the Cagayan River (see R. Rosaldo 1978c). The two self-designations for Ilongots are *bugkalut* (untranslatable) and *'irungut,* in certain dialects *'iyungut* (from the forest). Derived from the latter self-designation and already known in the ethnograhic literature, "Ilongot" perhaps is preferable as a name for the people.

†Though lexicostatistical studies from the early 1960's seem to indicate that the Ilongot language split from the Philippine superstock about 1100 B.C. (see Thomas and Healy 1962; compare Dyen 1965), my linguistic data show that Ilongot is closely related to the languages of its neighbors to the west, that is, Pangasinan, Kallahan, Kankanay, and Ibaloy (Harold Conklin, personal communication).

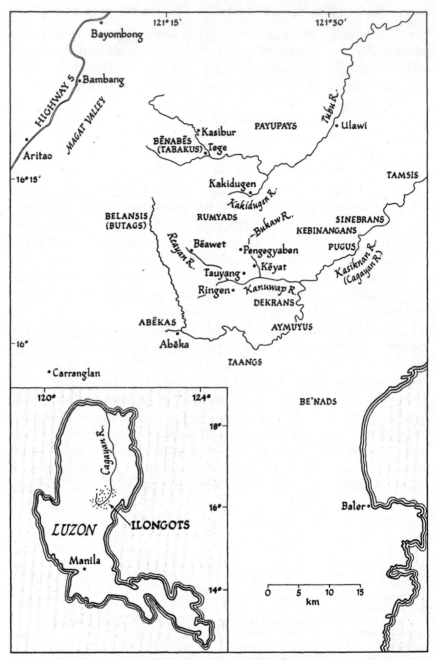

MAP I. Ilongot country in northern Luzon, Philippines. (*Bērtan* names are in capital letters.)

remains relatively inaccessible because the lowland metropolitan centers usually use water and valley routes as their main lines of communication. Frequent heavy gales and steep slopes have hindered the approach to Ilongot territory from the east. The primary protection afforded by the Cagayan, the major waterway into the area, is its length, for it runs more than 400 kilometers from its mouth on the northern tip of Luzon to its source in the Ilongot heartland.

Land travel toward the Ilongot region during the Spanish period (1565–1898) usually started from the plains of Pampanga to the south and followed the route of the late sixteenth-century Spanish explorers and missionary friars through the Magat Valley, west of the Ilongot homeland.* Throughout the period of contact during the Spanish colonial dominion, Christians made no efforts to take their lowland towns and wet rice agriculture into the Ilongot hills. Instead, they attempted by various means to persuade the Ilongots to descend to the valleys, take up the plow, and live near the mission. In fact a number of Ilongots did convert, and some of them eventually became assimilated as lowlanders. Other Ilongots, however, raided, tooks heads in mission towns, and led some of their brethren, called apostates by the Spanish, back to the hills. Their colonial policy long one of the sword behind the cross, the Spanish often responded by sending punitive expeditions of soldiers, who themselves sometimes collected Ilongot heads. By the end of this period, a band of lowland towns along the Magat had effectively removed the Ilongots from frequent direct contact with most other non-Christian hill peoples except for scattered groups of Agta hunter-gatherers on the Ilongot southwestern and northeastern margins.†

* Ilongot documentary history is richest for the eighteenth and twentieth centuries. Dominican, Augustinian, and Franciscan missionary friars are the main reporters for the eighteenth century, and the most valuable local histories for the area, aside from the work of Keesing (1962), are by the Dominican scholars Julián Malumbres (1918a; 1918b; 1919) and P. Fernández and J. de Juan (1969). American colonial officials have provided valuable but little-used materials for local history in the first half of the twentieth century.

† In a reflective note on the work of Keesing (1962), William Henry Scott suggests that the Ifugaos may have lived in the Magat Valley until about 1600, when they fled upland, to the northwest, toward the present location (1975: 46). Ifugaos, in other words, were probably neighbors of the Ilongots until nearly 400 years ago, when they were separated by the Spanish. Ifugao settlers who reached Ilongot country in about 1960 made precisely the same claim as Keesing and Scott, based, they said, on the authority of their oral traditions.

After the Spanish-American War of 1898, the United States, in a burst of imperialist fervor, took the Philippines as its colony. Initially, the Bureau of Non-Christian Tribes was the colonial agency most directly responsible for the Ilongots. By 1908 a province, Nueva Vizcaya, had consolidated political jurisdiction over the region, and schools as well as constabulary units were set up on the margins of Ilongot territory as instruments of civilization. The impact of colonial policies on the Ilongots diminished after 1931, when the lack of funds as a result of the world depression led to the removal of both schoolhouses and constabulary units. During the same decade, increasing numbers of land-hungry lowland Christian settlers, primarily Ilokanos, moved into the Cagayan Valley and began to press south, upstream toward Ilongot country. The 400-kilometer length of the river no longer afforded the protection it had during the Spanish era.

In December 1941 the Japanese invaded the Philippines. The Ilongots immediately retreated toward the interior of their territory. Nearly four years later, however, in June of 1945, a flood of Japanese soldiers was forced into the Ilongot hills by American troops. A third of the Ilongot population died during that month of June.

The impact of direct colonial policies on the Ilongots came to an end on July 4, 1946, with the declaration of Philippine independence. Ilongot society in the postwar years, nonetheless, was to be more deeply transformed than before. After four years of calm (1946–49), Ilongot headhunting began once again as an indirect result of violent battles in the lowlands between members of the Hukbalahap guerrilla movement and counterinsurgency forces called Battalion Combat Teams. Angered because two of their men, a father and his son, were murdered by a member of the constabulary, the Ilongots reached a peak of headhunting intensity in 1959–60, when they went on a rampage that made them banner-headline news items in the Manila press. Headhunting, a practice at once central and problematic for both Ilongot raiders and lowland victims, became even more clearly than before the dominant symbol for Ilongot identity in the context of lowland/upland relations.

The late 1950's and early 1960's were a yet deeper turning point in the long-term development of the region. Land pressure on the margins increased with an influx of settlers who some years earlier, in the mid-1950's, had been displaced from their homes to the northwest by a hydroelectric dam project. Ilongots began to find that such other hill peoples as Kallahans, Ibaloys, and Ifugaos were their new neighbors. Outside influence also began to be felt for the first time directly in the center of Ilongot country, as the New Tribes Mission, an American-based evangelical Protestant group active in the area from 1954, began to use a Piper Cub to transport missionary families and supplies from their lowland airbase to their stations in the interior. Michelle Rosaldo and I flew by missionary plane when we first reached Ilongot country in October 1967.

My ethnohistorical sketch based on literary sources has both revealed and concealed the reality of Ilongot history. It has provided, in the first instance, a valuable corrective to the frequent anthropological fiction of the untouched primitive by showing that Ilongots have lived in the context of the colonization process since at least the eighteenth century. Yet, at the same time, an exclusive reliance on the documentary record can suggest that Ilongots have lived through a chain of reactions as the passive receptors of events originating in metropolitan centers.

In my view, social history done on the local level should break down the false dichotomy between internal studies of oral traditions and external studies of written documents. By moving more deeply inward and investigating Ilongot history from within indigenous conceptual frameworks, I hope to show that the lives of Ilongots become more fully intelligible when followed over a series of events, whether internal or external in source, that are mediated through social processes and cultural forms in the local setting. When, for instance, American colonial officials tried to pacify the region, the impact of their actions—unlike what they imagined it to be—was thoroughly filtered through local histories and patterns of feuding. Hence the sense in which Ilongots, even in reaction to colonial forces, have made their own history.

METHOD: HOW I LEARNED ABOUT
ILONGOT HISTORY

Almost by accident I began to discover the Ilongot past. The entry in my field journal from January 9, 1968, says, "Some kind of history looks possible." This was a scant three months after arrival in Illongot country, and I was still struggling with elementary phrases in the language. At the time I had no intention of embarking on the present project. Somehow I managed to understand enough that day to discover that a 73-year-old man named Lakay had lived both in the center and on the margin of Ilongot territory. I was beginning to see what was confirmed later, that movement is an integral part of the Ilongot way of life.

My inquiries were triggered by an incident of that morning. A group of Ilongots and I were clearing an overgrown area of secondary forest in order to make an airstrip for the missionary's Piper Cub. We had unearthed a number of potsherds and a liquor bottle. Excited by the possibility of an archeology of the recent past, I asked Tukbaw, my Ilongot "brother" and Lakay's son-in-law, whose bottle it could have been. Tired from work and sick of my uncouth questions, Tukbaw answered laconically, "It belonged to grandfather—yeah, grandaddy turd." When I pressed further, Tukbaw grumbled, "How should I know anything about that bottle? Do you think I lived here in this place long ago? Did I stand here and watch the man drink that liquor?"

Through this and numerous later conversations, I learned two things. First, Ilongots make a sharp distinction between what they have witnessed and what they have not. And the former is given credence over the latter. In another context, for example, Tukbaw, speaking about heaven said, "They say it exists, but they have not seen it." Second, the very bedrock of historical knowledge, the conception of factual evidence, is different from our own and specific to Ilongot culture. Sherds and bottles, for me, epitomized hard data for reconstructing the past, and I was deeply puzzled that Tukbaw could have been so cavalier in dismissing their significance.

What more readily became apparent was that Ilongots divided their history into two major periods: before 1945 and after 1945. I heard one tale after another about the events packed into that fateful year of 1945. There were stories about taking Japanese heads; stories about hunger while fleeing through the forest; stories about sudden death and weeping over lost family members; stories studded with the names of every brook and hill and craggy cliff where people walked or ate or spent the night. At the time I found these stories exasperating, but they were impossible to fend off. Almost as trying as being processed through an immigration office, listening to the stories seemed a necessary ordeal that I had to endure before beginning investigation of the Ilongot form of life. I perceived no relation between fleeing through the forest and anything that could be inscribed in an ethnography. Moreover, I thought the stories had been designed—as indeed they in part were—more to conceal than to reveal, for they usually claimed, contrary to fact, that no Ilongot took a head after 1945, when they aided, they said, the American armed forces by decapitating Japanese soldiers.

The stories of 1945 were so numerous, so vivid, so detailed, so often told that it took me over a year to realize that they represented but a narrow strip in time. The nature of the problem became clear to me when a man listed the names of all the places he had ever lived from the time of his birth. Unlike everybody else, he included every place he had stopped as he fled through the forest in 1945; his list, an objectification of human time, lent greater significance to that moment of flight than to the rest of his lifetime. I compared different stories and cross-checked how many days people had spent at each place along the way, and in the end I found a high degree of agreement. Many Ilongots fled to the lowlands after three or four weeks of scrambling through the forest, and at most the period of hunger and deprivation was 14 months. As never before, not even from reading Thomas Mann, I understood the pervasive cultural impact of human experiences so laden with significance as to be protracted in retrospect. How sharp the contrast with events measured in standard units by the clock and calendar.

That year of 1945 was certainly the most amplified moment in the Ilongot remembrance of things past. Their stories, along with genealogies that I collected, government census records, and a written history of the American thirty-seventh Infantry Division, all indicate that at least a third of the Ilongot population died in June 1945 or immediately thereafter. It was in June that the re-treating Japanese troops were driven into the supposedly uninhab-ited hills of Ilongot country, where they would find themselves forced either to starve or surrender. This brief period, called *kaka-pun*, "the time of the Japanese," was so packed with matters of life and death that, for Ilongots who lived the events of that time, it was the great divide that separated a bygone past from one that merged into the present.

Ilongots, I found, had a word, *pistaim*, that designated the era before 1945; people glossed the words as "before the Japanese ar-rived," or "long ago" or "very long, long ago." Then one day I was struck by the obvious. Pistaim, of course, was an Ilongot ren-dition of the English "peacetime," the time before World War II.

When Ilongots characterized the quality of life during peace-time, their past seemed either very good or very bad. Some told me that they used to wait until their houseguests were asleep and then behead them. Worse, they used to go out with the children of neighbors, only to behead them by treachery. The stories of other people clustered at the opposite polarity. In those days, they said, game was abundant and the rivers were filled with fish. Nobody ever had to take a head before marriage; that story, they said, was just another lowland Christian lie. And they cited one man after another who had come of age in that more pacific era of pistaim, without taking a head. How was I to interpret the contradictions between Ilongot versions of their past?

During the initial 21 months of field research, I thought that the present situation of the storytellers was the sole determinant of their disparate versions of the character of peacetime. New Chris-tians were eager to tell me incidents that highlighted the violent tenor of their bloodthirsty past lives. Indeed, the savagery of their past was a central justification, they said, for converting to the reli-gion of the New Tribes Mission and accepting Jesus Christ as their personal savior. One man even told me that I had less need than he to convert because I had not taken a head. Ilongots, who were still pagans, on the other hand, constructed a rendition of their past that—in the eyes of new Ilongot converts, lowland Christians, and secular anthropologists—made them appear, not like crazy head-hunters, but like the sensible human beings they thought they were. When I asked them directly, they simply denied that they had taken heads. How, they replied self-righteously, could I imagine such a thing when they had cared for me so kindly? They had fed me, taught me their language, held my hand on the trail. I felt ashamed and decided they must be right.

It was not until August 1968 that Tukbaw first told me about a raid in which he had participated. On a visit to Manila, we flew in the missionary plane over a spot where he and a group of raiders had once attacked a house; he pointed to where the house used to be and began to tell the story of the raid. Others later followed suit, at first giggling nervously and speaking in a high pitch as they told similar stories. This news was as disorienting for me as it was unsettling for them. I felt compelled, among other things, to try to piece together the Ilongot past, for I could not understand why I was being told two different stories of peacetime. One tale, about high violence, was unchanging; another version, of peace and harmony, was being revised before my very eyes. My crude sociology of knowledge, that new Christians say they used to be bad while everyone else says they used to be good, was not entirely wrong, but it was much too simple as an account of the Ilongot sense of history.

My discovery of the Ilongot word pistaim had led me to discover conflicting views of its nature. I had stumbled upon more problems than I could resolve, for the past seemed too shifting for analysis. The sheer task of developing an accurate chronology appeared overwhelming, because Ilongots where we lived were not literate and simply had no idea of the western calender. How could I even discover the relative sequence of past episodes? Beyond that, Tukbaw's discourse on the bottle of grandaddy turd indicated perhaps that Ilongots had little interest in the unseen past before their lifetimes.

Though I still did not plan to study Ilongot history, I began in June 1968 to push backward in time on routine census materials concerning household composition and the like. People, I found,

had reasonably good recall of the relative sequence of events during their lives. All could remember, for instance, the succession of
places they had lived, and a few could even reconstruct how many
years they had gardened at each site. I tried to determine people's
ages by asking about birth order within and between sibling
groups, and by inquiring about each individual's size at the time of
the Japanese. Throughout my investigations I used 1945, among
other known dates, as a reference point in charting what to me
was the unknown Ilongot past.

Movement, it became more apparent than ever, was an integral
part of Ilongot biographies. People readily listed in succession the
names of the places where they had "erected their houseposts" and
"cleared the forest." This task was as culturally appropriate for
them as listing the place names along any walk they took, whether
to visit, hunt, raid, or flee from the Japanese. Starting with lists of
place names and crude sketches on pieces of paper, I began my effort to reconstitute the past by using 1:50,000-scale maps, along
with cruder but often more useful contour maps improvised from
mud and dotted with wooden chips representing houses and gardens. I also walked with people and looked at as many former
house and garden sites as possible. To coordinate one household
history with others was vexing because clusters of houses split,
then joined and split, then joined again. In addition to the problems posed by phases of gathering and dispersal, the place names
attached to the sites of houses and gardens were variously given as
the names of a nearby craggy rock or the closest hill or the brook
for drinking water or the closest major stream. The task before me
required time, patience, and endurance.

On my return to the field nearly five years later, in March 1974,
Ilongots said that they perceived a qualitative change in my developing understanding of their language and way of life. They said
that when I had been among them before, they simply told me
stories; but now we had reached a point where we could engage in
the give-and-take of conversation. The discontinuity they saw was
that in 1974 I participated in lively conversations with them because I was able to grasp more complex accounts and raise hypothetical cases or actual counterexamples that challenged what they
told me. In addition, I often put forth my own interpretations of

beliefs and events, and they confirmed, modified, or rejected my views as part of our growing dialogue.

Though the conversational mode of inquiry was increasingly rewarding, the course of its development was perhaps more gradual than Ilongots said. During the entire research period, I often worked with spontaneous and elicited stories and then interviewed about them in an open-ended and extensive manner. All of the narratives and interviews were in the native language and, as would be hoped, they increased in complexity over the course of my investigations. Whether abrupt or continuous, the unfolding change that Ilongots identified (like the progression of most fieldwork) reflected the threefold interaction of greater human trust between us, my increasing competence in their language, and my deepening knowledge of their culture and history.

During the four and half years that had passed since our departure, several things had changed. All the people we lived among before had moved their houses, as people do every five years or so, from previous locations. The house where we had lived with three Ilongot families was blown down in a 1970 typhoon. After that house was destroyed, Tukbaw and his wife, Lakay's older daughter, moved upstream. The family of Lakay, who was by then 80 years old, along with his younger daughter's family, moved across the river. The house divided in part because of heated quarrels—a number of which we witnessed—between Lakay's second wife and his older daughter; the other factor in the split was the cultural expectation that the youngest married daughter reside with and care for her aging parents. Thus, the bitter family fights hastened the arrival of a regular phase in the developmental cycle of domestic groups.

When I actually did walk by our old housesite, sometime in April 1974, the only traces I could see of our former life were the rotting remains of a post and a cluster of bamboo once planted for convenient household use. The rest was emerging secondary growth of the monsoon forest. Clearly, Tukbaw's scolding discourse had been well founded; neither bottles nor potsherds were anywhere to be seen, and the most visible evidence to recall our lives there was the cluster of bamboo. Indeed, when Ilongots wished to underline the veracity of their narratives of bygone days, they pointed to their documentary sources, the bamboo and the distinctive secondary growth that covered former gardens. Little children, we were told, were shown the bamboo where Michelle and I—their Aunt Sili and Uncle Natu—had lived. Baket, a woman feeble with age, pointed with pride to the stretch of secondary growth along a river where she had gardened over the course of a lifetime. By then it was clear that the residence histories I was collecting were built upon precisely this Ilongot sense of the past as an ordered sequence of inhabited and cultivated places, each one named and most marked by living trees. The trees themselves bore silent, yet culturally incontrovertible, testimony to the truth of the tales of past residence.

Aside from our fallen house and its bamboo remains, a number of more significant changes had come to that sector of Ilongot country. Three were dramatic: a primary-grade schoolhouse had been built in 1972; a new pan-Ilongot political federation had emerged about the time of martial law; and martial law, declared in September 1972, had, because Ilongots feared rumors of firing squads, abruptly ended the already declining practice of headhunting. Three more changes represented a continuation and intensification of earlier trends: the buzz saws and bulldozers at work on logging roads were within hearing distance; settlers had more than doubled their numbers and were newly interspersed between Ilongot houses; and, finally, the majority of Ilongots had become new Christians.

A teacher, people politicking, an end to headhunting, stripping the forest, more settlers, and evangelical Protestantism—that the changes taking place were relatively sudden and deep was evident. What remained more opaque was how to characterize their impact. Standard concepts offered little illumination. Modernization was simply too grand a word for a one-room schoolhouse with a corrugated tin roof. Acculturation seemed a capricious choice when people were becoming evangelical Protestants in the hills of a Roman Catholic country. My own view, not to discard summary labels altogether, was that these social forces in combination added up to increased local-level control and domination by the nation-state. But that is another story. For present purposes, I should like to consider how the impact of such forces on Ilongots was perceived by the people themselves.

Ilongots in 1974 often told me that they "no longer" were Ilongots. Instead, they said, they had become lowlanders or decided to follow the word of God. They described having given up a range of practices, from magic through oratory to headhunting; their old ways, they said, had been replaced when they started to "follow" such newly available alternatives as the New Tribes Mission, lowland law and order, wet rice agricultural techniques of neighboring settlers, and the reading, writing, and arithmetic of the schoolhouse.

This cultural perception of the discarded past was stated in its most extreme form by a woman who was exactly my age, then 33. She told me that in her childhood she had seen with her own eyes a cultural practice that had since been given up. In the old days, she

Baket telling the story of the places where she has gardened, 1974.

said, people used to place the jawbones of deer and wild pigs in rows along the inside roofs of their houses. I was astounded. I had seen such jawbones myself, on the roof of our earlier house. How could people release their traditions so absolutely and with such apparent ease? They seemed to think that many of their former practices—sometimes their very identity as Ilongots—had been thrown overboard as if they were excess cultural baggage. New Christians appeared to feel that they were riding the wave of the future, and the poignant nostalgia of many others indicated that for them the world was grayer.

Like William Jones, I felt that I was bearing witness to the end of an era. Yet no one would have been more surprised than Jones to learn that nearly 60 years after his death I would be meeting Ilongot young men who still walked about in G-strings and red hornbill earrings (a sign of having taken a human head). Moreover, in the three-score years that had intervened between our stays in the field, headhunting had flourished and then ceased altogether three different times. The dilemma of trying to understand shifting Ilongot perceptions of their lives in transition was that I myself stood knee-deep in the rapid flow of change. I could not perceive the shape of change because I could not, of course, foretell the future. I had no idea whether the Ilongot political federation would fizzle out or prosper: it could clash with the mission, wither away for lack of funds, or become a top-priority project under martial law. And what would happen when, as was planned, the New Tribes Mission withdrew from the Ilongot field and left their churches in the hands of indigenous congregations? An ethnographic history that seeks to follow a collection of lives as they unfold through time should conclude, not start, with the period of actual field research; for the contingencies that enliven the past become imponderables when projected onto the future.

I realized that to understand Ilongot perceptions of their changing lives I should study their past from the perspective we knew together. I had no choice but to confront, once again, the puzzle of peacetime. And the pieces of the puzzle did not fit together until I had developed a reliable chronology for the period. Seeking a more textured account of peacetime, I spent an afternoon in early August 1974 with Kadēng, Tukbaw's older half-brother. During the period 1919 to 1944, Kadēng was between the ages of 10 and 35. To my delight, I found that he had an extraordinary memory. His recall of the past sequence of events and inhabited places was certain and quick. I checked his account against the large number of others I had collected, and at last I could determine: (a) how many years people had lived in each place of residence; (b) which place names were alternative labels for a single household and which ones designated different locations; and (c) how to date the length of stays and the timing of moves with enough precision so that the separate household histories could be mapped onto a single chronology. Ilongots, I saw more than ever, are conscious of the relative sequence of events, even in different places; indeed, their narratives often follow a relentlessly chronological sequence not unlike the varieties of history that are parodied as being about just one damned thing after another.

The problem of the opacity of the Ilongot past was thus more mine than theirs. The key to understanding it was to gain access to what was common knowledge in the local context.* For Ilongots to say where they were living when an incident took place was to tell their listeners how to fit that incident into the larger sequence of past events.

In order to enable the reader to follow my presentation of Ilongot histories throughout this book, however, I have adopted an obvious convention. I often label events by their calendar dates: for example, the arrests of 1923. In talking about such an event, Ilongots, of course, would never mention a calendar date; instead they might refer to the name of the person arrested, or the name of the place where the speaker or the person arrested was living at the time or perhaps where the arrests were made. And the place itself might be given any of a number of alternative names, or located relative to nearby points (as speakers show off their knowledge of

*Haviland (1977) has nicely developed, for the topic of gossip, the notion that certain cultural phenomena become comprehensible to outsiders only through systematic efforts to make explicit what is assumed and therefore usually left implicit by members of a local community. A tale of scandal makes sense, Haviland says, only if the listener is already thoroughly conversant with the reputation of the subject of the story. Is the person a prominent, upright citizen? or a well-established debaucher? The problems of acquiring necessary background knowledge are comparable in the attempt to understand Ilongot stories about the past.

the lay of the land), or perhaps even referred to as the place where the father of so-and-so was buried. Indeed, as people walk along paths they often tell stories of the past as they point to the various places where a house or garden was located, a deer or wild pig killed, a head taken, or whatever.

Ilongots in fact care intensely about the relative sequence of a succession of events, but these excursions into the past are meticulously mapped onto the landscape, not onto a calendar. A reader without detailed knowledge of the local landscape and its myriad placenames would surely infer that Ilongot narrative lacks a historical dimension. This is a problem as basic as it is vexing in the translation of culture. Were I to use their multiple ways of speaking about places, I would capture the tone of their texts but lose their historical sense. Through my use of our calendar dates I have instead chosen to sacrifice a feature of the idiom through which Ilongots represent their past, in order to convey the sense in which an event placed in space is also intelligibly located in time.

THE SHAPE OF PEACETIME, 1919–45

Once my chronology of Ilongot history had fallen into place, I was prepared to explore more deeply than before the character of peacetime. Although it was labeled by a single word, pistaim, I found that the period was by no means uniform in its shape. Before I give a narrative account of pistaim, I can summarize it as characterized by at least two major types of change:

1. Peacetime consisted of movements starting from an initial concentration of population in the center (1919–23) through a dispersal toward the lowland margins (1924–35) to a gradual (1936–41), then sudden (1942–45), return toward the center.

2. Peacetime was marked by phases of intense headhunting (1919–28), no headhunting at all (1929–35), and a more gradual return (1936–41) to the earlier intensity of headhunting (1942–45).

As is probably apparent from the dates cited, social forces located in the world system (most notably, the depression and World War II) shaped the pace, direction, and timing of local-level population movements and headhunting activity.

Ilongot recollections of peacetime were conditioned, not only by whether the speaker had converted to Christianity, but also by headhunting and population movements, both of which in turn were influenced by world events. Whether people resided, at a particular moment, on the margin or in the center of Ilongot country located them at different positions within a system of feuding, hence the centrality of headhunting in people's subjective experiences of peacetime. I shall now describe, as I have pieced them together, the events of 1919–45.

A time of violence, 1919–28. Following a decade or so of relative calm, Ilongot headhunting began a resurgence in 1919. Initially, most decapitations were internal, cast in the idiom of the feud, resulting less often from ambushes set by raiders than from the opportunistic deceptions of feigned friendship in which, for example, a man can behead his companion on the trail, or his host or guest while inside a house.

In 1923 soldiers entered the "navel" of Ilongot country for the first time in over ten years. The troops, of course, were bent on pacification; but the Ilongot informers who guided them, men from the margins, sought vengeance for beheadings by men from the center almost 20 years before. The men from the center were innocent of the crime they had allegedly committed, but because none of them knew a lowland language, they could not answer their accusers. The troopers on the punitive expedition burned houses, destroyed crops, and arrested 11 men. Ilongots living in the center immediately scattered: some sought refuge in the forest, others fled to the homes of relatives on the margins toward the lowlands.

Lakay, who was 29 at the time, was among the 11 men arrested. They were briefly imprisoned in the lowland town of Bayombong and then held under house arrest in a place with a schoolhouse on the northwestern margin of Ilongot territory. There Lakay was fortunate to find two brothers whose paternal grandfather was from the central area where he had been raised. When Lakay and the two brothers met, they wept and told one another the story of their common origins in the center. Long, long ago, in the time of the Spanish, the story went, a woman from the margin went to visit the center, where she was literally grabbed and married. One of her two sons later married and settled in her former home on the margin. There he in turn fathered two sons. His two sons were the two brothers whom Lakay met in 1923.

Ilongots regard such stories from the unseen past as plausible, but not necessarily true and certainly not binding in the present. In order for a story of earlier kin ties to become regarded as factual, it must be invoked to legitimate an ongoing process of marital union. Lakay, who was under arrest in an alien place, lost no time in transforming necessity into virtue: the story of common origins became a charter for a series of intermarriages that took place from 1923 onward. The notion was that the alliance would be stronger if the marital unions were seen as a renewal, rather than an initial creation of kinship relations.

At the same time that he was building union in one place, Lakay had scores to settle elsewhere. One of the men who had guided the soldiers who arrested Lakay was from another place on the margin named Payupay. Hoping to mount a raiding party against the Payupays, Lakay began to gather a group of men who could—out of disparate motives—act in common cause. There were three main explicit reasons that the various people joined to raid. First, the Payupays had guided the arresting soldiers in 1923. Second, a kinswoman of Lakay was beheaded in 1924 by a kinsman of Lakay; the killer said that he wished to make amends, and he pledged to give Lakay a victim to behead as a form of covenant between them. Third, a man from the center had been beheaded in 1920 by the Payupays, and his surviving kin were determined to display their wrath in return.

It was 1927 when Lakay and over 20 others went on a successful raid, in which they beheaded five Payupays. This act of vengeance in turn played upon internal divisions within Payupay, and 11 more of their people had been decapitated by 1928. When the Payupays called in the troops to retaliate against those from the center, two more people were killed by soldiers, and four more were beheaded as an indirect result of this punitive incursion. (These events will be analyzed at length in Chapter 8.)

Ilongot informers from the margin had used soldiers for their own ends in 1923, and their victims from the center had by 1927 retaliated in kind. Kadēng characterized this decade of 1919–28 as years of "killing and killing," when men were "cutting and cutting because they were fierce with anger." The situation had spiraled beyond control.

A time of peace, 1929–35. That horrifying year of 1928 marked the end of the period when violence set the tenor of Ilongot life. "People," Kadēng said, "became very, very quiet." The Payupays split into two separate camps; one of the warring factions moved upstream and the other downstream, thereby quieting the feud between them.

Other groups from the center moved closer to the margins and the relative safety of schoolhouses and troops. A half-brother of Tukbaw moved where a school was to be built. A government official had already taken a census and named a number of Ilongots there barrio captain, counselors, police, and so on. Ilongots described this process of entering governmental jurisdiction with the simile of step-by-step movement toward a person. Their notion was that gradual movement represented high decorum in situations where people at once feared danger and hoped to build a new relation, as in courtship or formal friendship. Using the term they apply to enduring personal relations, Ilongots said they expected to *tagdē* (become used to, grow fond of) lowland law and order.

These hopes, however, led to disappointment, for the schoolhouse was never built and the barrio never formed. The brother of Tukbaw's wife, a man named Tepeg, attributed false promises to lowland officials. They were really, he said, after the venison and wild pig that Ilongot huntsmen could provide for them. When I pressed, he said that the lying officials claimed there was no money for schools. The morning after he told me this, I realized that the place in which they had been living at the time indicated the year 1931. Indeed, by 1932 the annual report of the Department of the Interior and Labor fully recognized the extent of the calamity and spoke of "greatly reduced appropriations and decreased revenue collections due to the general economic depression" (Sison 1932: 167). It was the world depression that resulted in the closing of schools and the removal of troops from the margins of Ilongot territory.

In those seven years, from 1929 to 1935, it seemed that Ilongot headhunting had come to a definite end. Among other things, troops were no longer called in, and their destructive incursions no longer escalated feuds between center and margin. During those days a number of Ilongot men married without taking heads, and a whole generation of schoolboys from the margin did not take heads in their lifetimes. People who resided near schools had already given up raiding for some years, not because—as I had mistakenly surmised—of the moral value of education, but rather because parents feared that their schoolchildren might unwittingly inform on their fathers. People who never lived near schoolhouses, however, claim that their hearts were pounding in anticipation of beheading even during those years of quiet. What they lacked, as they saw it in retrospect, was not so much the desire but the opportunity to take heads.

A gradual return to violence, 1936–41. The year 1935 was a turning point. Not only were the Philippines declared a commonwealth but, more important for Ilongots, the Sakdal peasant rebellion broke out in the lowlands to the south. Kadēng described this as a time of war in the lowlands. Ilongot groups that had earlier moved toward the margins now made major moves toward their former homes in the interior.

Raiding began gradually. From the whole of Ilongot country, there were two raids in 1936; two in 1937; one in 1938; another in 1939; two more in 1940. This time Ilongots took advantage of the chaos of the times and raided against lowlanders to the south, rather than attempting to catch their Ilongot companions off guard and beheading them. Insan, a son of Lakay and the brother of Tepeg, said that after their moves of 1935 the Ilongots felt that they could raid with impunity because "they thought that the soldiers could not reach them." But late in 1940 troops hiked all the way from the lowlands to the center of Ilongot country. Once again the soldiers were guided by informers from the margins—the Butag people—who were about to precipitate a feud. The soldiers, as was their custom, burned houses and crops. The eight men they arrested this time were sent by ship to a prison farm on Palawan, a distant southern Philippine island. Kadēng was among those imprisoned, and he did not return to his Ilongot brethren until 1955. In 1940 there were other incursions by soldiers, other arrests, and more burning.

A peak of violence, 1942–45. In December 1941 the Japanese landed in the Philippines. Large numbers of Ilongots retreated into the interior. All those who had lived in the center before 1923 returned to their former homeland, their numbers swollen by many of their neighbors from the days when they lived on the margins, especially from 1929 to 1935. They had, they said, *'upug* (collected, gathered together, concentrated) in the center in order to gain the strength of numbers to defend themselves against intruders from the periphery.

This was a time of fear and rampant internal violence. Feuding within Ilongot society had been abruptly revived by the incursions of troops. By this time the soldiers themselves were under attack and had been defeated or were in hiding as guerrillas in the hills.

Raiding grew more intense during 1942–45, but the target shifted from lowland victims to other Ilongots. Things became even more extreme in the southern region of Ilongot country, where old grudges were unleashed as neighbors beheaded neighbors in their houses.

Peacetime. I now understood that when missionized Ilongots referred to their violent past, they usually selected their illustrations from the period 1942–45. In the narrowest sense, they had not distorted their past because each of their stories was accurate. Similarly, people who told me how tranquil things had been during peacetime were speaking about the years 1929–35. During that period a number of men did in fact marry without taking heads, and things were generally calm.

The contradictory violent versus peaceful accounts of the quality of life during peacetime were beginning to fall into place at the intersection of headhunting, population movements, world events, and missionization. The various stories of life in those days were settling into the concrete social experiences of people in specific places at particular times.

Stories about peacetime, I should add, were tales told to someone in particular, namely myself. It was clear that shortly after my arrival among the Ilongots, I was identified primarily as an American who was not a missionary. At the time, for Ilongots, I was an anomaly, for they assumed that all Americans were evangelical Protestants. My very presence asked them to reconsider their past, their present, and the New Tribes Mission. In response to my questions, neither new Christians nor traditional Ilongots simply invented the past tenor of their lives. Instead, distortion entered their accounts of the past when they allowed a brief period to represent the enduring character of the whole of peacetime. By overgeneralizing, Ilongots transformed their past in an attempt to justify their present life choices.

THE PROBLEM OF ILONGOT HISTORICAL CONSCIOUSNESS

We need now to examine the idiom of Ilongot historical perceptions. This exploration of history as a cultural construct will be confined to a preliminary sketch of certain key concepts that will be elaborated in later chapters as they recur in distinct contexts, ranging from the chaos of flight from the Japanese to the regularities of marriage.

The reader should keep in mind that a focus on historical consciousness can yield ethnographic depth for some societies, like the Ilongots, but not for others. Cultural conceptions of history, in other words, vary in their degree of symbolic elaboration, their ability to pervade multiple contexts, and their capacity to capture people's imaginations. Beyond these variations in texture, scope and intensity, forms of historical consciousness (though notoriously elusive and little studied among so-called primitives) can be conceived in widely varying idioms from one culture to the next.* It makes a great deal of difference, to take a number of examples, whether one speaks about history as a river running slowly to the sea or as the fierce gales of change, an irretrievably lost moment, a seed grown into a blossoming flower, the good old days, an ugly

---

*Distinctive forms of historical consciousness have been little explored in either ethnography or history. Among the anthropological works that I have found most stimulating are: P. Bohannan (1953), Errington (1979), Evans-Pritchard (1941: 94–183), Leach (1961), Ossio (1977), and Pocock (1964). I have studied the culture-specific sense of history in the Spanish Golden Age theater of Lope de Vega (see R. Rosaldo 1978b).

duckling become a swan, a green betel quid chewed into red saliva, a walk along the path of life, or an oscillation between the focus of inward movement and the diffusion of outward dispersal. These differing cultural idioms embody attitudes as distinctive as soulful nostalgia versus equally deep indifference, and conceptions as divergent as cyclic repetition versus linear change for the better or the worse.

To summarize briefly, Ilongot conceptions of history are embodied in stories. People whose past lives have overlapped tell stories about myriad everyday events. Tales that older men and women tell members of younger generations, on the other hand, are narrower in their range of topics and usually describe the places they have lived, where they have gardened, and how they have feuded. As older people speak, they cite living trees as the significant remains that attest to the historical veracity of what for their listeners is the unseen past. Stories from the unseen past, however, are rarely handed down yet another generation; they tend not to be repeated by those who heard them secondhand. In general, Ilongots are unlikely to accept as true any narrative about events they neither saw for themselves nor heard about from an eyewitness. Hence the Ilongot remembered past, even at its greatest temporal depth in memories of gardening, residential movement, and headhunting feuds, fades out rather abruptly with what the oldest living people recall having heard from their parents and grandparents.

Whether about the shared or the unseen past, Ilongot recollections are located intelligibly through what could be called the spatialization of time. When people speak of peacetime or any other era, it is essential to know exactly where the episodes took place. The knowledge, for instance, that beheadings were provoked by the theft of sweet potatoes gains depth in relation to earlier episodes of how the victims themselves had just raided in the lowlands, then entered the region as fugitives from the law who were doubly vulnerable because they were hungry and far from their closest kin. Though they were told as separate stories, I was able to piece together the temporal sequence of this and other chains of events by conjoining specific incidents with residence and gardening histories. Thus for the outsider to penetrate Ilongot

history it becomes crucial to work through the often vexing prolif-
eration of place names associated with past events. The background against which narrated episodes from the past make sense
is the culturally implicit knowledge, shared by storytellers and
their audiences, of how locations in space can be mapped onto a
temporal framework.

Where a collective sense of the past emerges is through the cumulative effect of personal histories that have intertwined during
significant periods of time. People who have shared a period of co-
residence are described as having " held one another's hands," in a
phrase that suggests mutual support through a difficult life passage. In this manner, personal histories become at least partially
interwoven into the broader collective fabric of shared residence
and the common experience of wider events.

Perhaps this consideration of Ilongot historical consciousness
should now turn to what I learned in late July 1974. By then my
chronology of residential histories was nearing completion, and I
was looking forward to spending a long day with Tukbaw. We
discussed a range of topics about peacetime; he was in a good
mood, at once alert and whimsical, so we both delighted in his gift
for words. In his rendition, people's step-by-step downhill movement—their houseposts were erected here, there, the other place,
and so on—was condensed into one continuous motion so that, at
least verbally, their homes glided along the line connecting the series of points and landed, like a bird from flight or an airplane
touching ground, at the bottom. In his witty manner Tukbaw had
epitomized the Ilongot sense of history conceived as movement
through space in which (and this is the usual analogy drawn)
people walk along a trail and stop at a sequence of named resting
places.

When I sought for the underlying structural regularities that had
shaped people's movements from place to place, Tukbaw scoffed
and said, "Once we lived like wild pigs." Once again he was telling
me that I was way off. When I probed further, he went on: "Sometimes people used to disperse. There were those who separated to
go to Ma'ni. At other times they all came and met again. They
were like wild pigs; they fucked together for a while and then they
dispersed again." The notion was that during peacetime Ilongot

households moved in roughly coordinated ways, as if running in packs like wild pigs, shifting between relative dispersal and relative congregation, perhaps associated with intermarriage. Tukbaw's comments on his ironic sketch displayed feelings divided between the unknowing animality of being unleashed from lowland political jurisdiction, and the intensity of joyous freedom of movement so deeply valued by Ilongots.

Tukbaw's accounting of population movement, alternating between dispersal and concentration, aptly represented the Ilongot sense of sociohistorical process as unpredictable and improvised; social order was conceived of less as eternal form than as a number of persons walking single file along paths that shift in direction. At the same time that it revealed a deep Ilongot cultural pattern, Tukbaw's narrative was also "a mere story." For Ilongots, the most believable stories from the past are eyewitness accounts by people who were at least teenagers when they saw the reported events. Tukbaw's tales were about the first 21 years of his life, from 1923 to 1944. Hence his global characterization of peacetime—that of leading the life of wild pigs—was grounded less in particulars than in a cultural notion of how life must have been before one's birth.

When a couple of weeks later I spent an afternoon with Kadēng, Tukbaw's older half-brother, I discovered that for him the era when Ilongots lived like wild pigs was projected onto the period before 1909, that is, before his birth. He stressed, however, not the image of people moving in packs, but rather the lack of governmental jurisdiction over the Ilongots. He explained that no mayor was in authority over them during that era, and that they heeded only the advice of their elders. In those days, he said, when Ilongots visited one another they were ever on guard, carrying spears, shields, and bolos (the Philippine term for long knives or machetes); they scarcely slept at night for fear that they would be beheaded in their sleep. In this case the time when the dominant tenor of Ilongot life was violent was defined relative to the speaker's date of birth.

Individuals have thus borne witness, from the limits of their own perspectives, to what they know about the past, and they do not attempt to fit their knowledge into a uniform collective history. The perspectival sense of the past held by Ilongots is consistent with their view that social life is determined by what people make up as they go along; societal processes, in other words, are seen more as improvised than given, more meandering than linear, more mobile than stationary. Often imaged as spatial movement, the Ilongot sense of history can be represented, on the one hand, as a group of people walking in single file along a trail and, on the other, as an alternation between the focus of inward concentration and the diffusion of outward dispersal.

The conception of change through time embodied in the image of people walking in single file is rooted in the social fact that peers in age, especially if they live in the same place, tend to undergo more or less coordinated crises of coming of age. Within a single peer group the cultural ideal is for each person in turn to arrive at a certain desired status. In talking about headhunting, for instance, people use the term *tabi* (arrive, reach, come to), and they say, *simabi* (he arrived), meaning that one has taken a head. Peer groups often did in fact take heads, one young man after the other in quick succession. In addition, young adults of both sexes often accompany one another—hugging, blushing, giggling together— as they visit and, in a gesture as flirtatious as it is shy, exchange betel quids. These visits can be a prelude to a series of direct exchange marriages through which peers marry at about the same time and in the same direction.

Whether referring to the headhunter's dangling red earrings or to the imagined pleasures of marriage, Ilongots claim that they feel envy and that they covet what the other person has. Motivated, they say, by jealous rivalry, they all race in a contest where the spoils go ideally in equal portions to each person who ran. In this pattern for conduct, everybody should move in loosely coordinated fashion so that each one, energized through healthy competition, will arrive at his or her equal share.

The Ilongot sense of social change as a quick succession of moves in the same direction by a group of peers is the product of the activities of human actors, not of the automatic unfolding of structural principles. What can happen when politics fail and brittle unions shatter beyond mending was amply illustrated by the events of 1927–28 and 1942–45, when people repeatedly beheaded their neighbors rather than raiding away from home. Because amicable relations require constant cultivation, Ilongots cannot afford to take their alliances for granted. When Lakay was under house arrest on the margin, he and his companions worked hard and were fortunate in being able to negotiate the succession of intermarriages with their new neighbors—for things might have turned out otherwise.

Lakay's case makes it clear that the marital freedom of movement experienced by the junior generation must be seen in relation to the political struggle of the senior generation to create a viable alliance in what otherwise could be a world of strangers. Indeed, the very process of intermarriage was the social foundation for the story about the common origins of Lakay and the people from the margin. The story about the captured bride at once provided grounds for the initial marriage (thus seen not as a union but as a reunion), and then it became accepted fact through the series of intermarriages.

To conclude this chapter on a reflective note, let me make explicit what has only been hinted at concerning the origins of the Ilongot sense of history. The Ilongot notion of their improvised social order, that people shift their directions as they walk the path of life, is thoroughly grounded in their marriage practices, in which children are unlikely to marry the close kin of either parent and hence must, as Ilongots say, walk in another direction when they seek their spouses. The cultural conception of shifting directions as one walks along a path is at once a pattern, reflecting past experiences, and a charter, guiding future projects.

During peacetime, the rhythms of the world political economy were superimposed on the already existing Ilongot sense that the experiences of one generation rarely prove reliable guidelines for the next generation to chart a course during such critical life passages as headhunting and marriage. From the Ilongot perspective, the impact of the outside world shifted in ways as overwhelming as they were inexplicable, from moments of withdrawal and relative calm (1929–35) to times of wrath and destructive invasions (1923–28 and 1942–45). Indigenous responses to world events, however, were not simple reflex actions, but rather were complex in their cultural mediations. First, intrusions of troops were incorporated into the processes of local feuds. Second, population movements that were related to perceived threats embodied cultural conceptions concerning the strength of concentration in a center and the weakness of dispersal toward a margin. Third, the men of one peer group, regarded as walking along a path together, took heads as a prelude to marriage, although their successors did not. Times indeed changed from one historical moment to another, and Ilongots had ample reason for perceiving that their social order was based on processes ever improvised anew.

Though Ilongots see most changes as a shift in directions, they at times perceive deeper ruptures and discontinuities. Historical disjunctions are breaks in the links between successive generations. In the absence of property and offices to transmit, the matrimony and patrimony that most significantly connect the different generations are a cluster of culturally necessary skills, ranging from knowledge of subsistence tasks to the skilled speech of adult social relations. When these skills are abandoned, Ilongots perceive that the social fabric has been torn asunder. To give up dry rice horticulture and take up wet rice agriculture, for instance, is to surrender Ilongot ethnic identity for that of a Philippine lowlander. In this vein, Insan said that certain of his ancestors stopped dry rice cultivation and instead "took the plow in their hands and became lowlanders." In 1972, martial law brought the painful rupture in the transmission from father to son of the elaborate techniques of headhunting, and Ilongots, by the time we were again living among them two years later, sometimes said that they no longer were Ilongots.

CHAPTER TWO. STORIES OF THE BUTAG-RUMYAD FEUD, 1923-1956

My purpose in this chapter and the next is to present the case history of a feud between the Butags and the Rumyads. The feud is the starting point in this phase of analysis because, as an enduring relation of mutual hostility, it is a socially complex event that must be understood in historical perspective. Indeed, I would go further and assert that other major Ilongot social processes, such as marriage and residential movements, are best interpreted in relation to the politics of feuding.

The chapter begins with an outline of the cultural typification of the feuding process, and goes on to identify the covenant as the usual context in which people tell feuding stories—using the past as a social force in the living present. Second, the two bērtan, the Butags and the Rumyads, are briefly sketched, as is my relation to them. Next, a number of tales about insults that were putatively sources of the feud are critically assessed, and the differences among them are located in the structural positions of the story-tellers. Finally, I describe the beheadings and cruel twists of fortune that led irrevocably to the lasting enmity that was the feud.

THE CULTURAL SHAPE OF THE FEUD

Ilongot feuds tend to move through the following four phases: (1) insult or wrong; (2) beheading; (3) covenant; (4) intermarriage or truce, or renewal of feuding. The four phases of feuds resemble the social dramas outlined by Turner (1957: 91–92), except that they do not necessarily occur in succession. Indeed, all feuds begin as public events, not with insults but with a beheading. It is primarily in retrospect, from the vantage point of a beheading, that the source of a feud is identified in an initial insult or wrong. At the same time, a covenant can take place only after a beheading, but a beheading is not necessarily followed by either a covenant or an intermarriage. Furthermore, if intermarriages do take place, they may follow directly from beheadings without an intervening covenant, and in such cases the marriages themselves are viewed as a form of covenant. Ilongots nonetheless are inclined to speak as if the most fully realized feuds are those that move in succession through all four possible phases.

Insult or wrong. In retrospect, Ilongots trace feuds back to their sources (*rapu*) in insults (*bēngen*) that one party perceives it has suffered at the hands of the other. Among such insults are instances where one man has denigrated another by saying, for example, that his bolo or its scabbard is uncouth and poorly crafted, or that he has never worn the dangling red earrings of the proven headhunter. In other instances the affront has grown out of a situation where two men were in contest over the heart of one woman. The man whose courtship began earlier felt insulted when the latecomer "jumped over" him (as if they were in single file) and "grabbed" the woman for himself. All insults, whether over personal adornment or women or both, imply that the target is a *depyang* (most commonly, a man who "fails to bag game" but also one who is generally "incompetent"). To be so insulted constitutes possible grounds for a beheading.

In yet other cases, feuds are traced back to their source in a particular wrongdoing. The minimum there is what people have interpreted as a direct "threat on their lives" (*kaniyaw*). Perhaps somebody was seen stalking with a weapon by the campsite or by the garden or house; or maybe two men were whispering about deceiving their guests and beheading them once they had fallen asleep. In more extreme cases, feuds have been started by beheadings that themselves were interpreted as insults. Ilongots explain that in such cases it mattered less that the victims were at fault (for indeed they may not have been) than that they were in a vulnerable state. Their vulnerability may have been a result of crop failure or the torches of lowland troops, or rapid clusters of deaths caused by epidemic illness or the slashing blades of other Ilongot marauders. These weakened and blameless persons, in the Ilongot view, have fallen victim to youths with characteristic relentless zeal to take heads as they grow into manhood. The youthful impulses to raid, however firmly rooted, would not have grown to fruition without older men who "egged on" their juniors to do as they themselves had done in their youths. Provocations by elders, I hasten to add, would not have been heeded, were it not for the coincidence of male peers coming of age during historical moments when feuds flared up inordinately.

Beheadings. At first glance this phase appears simple enough, for it can be viewed as a series of beheadings that follow one upon the other as if they were a chain reaction sparked by a primal incident in the past. At any particular moment in the feud, and from the perspective of one side, the last killing by the other side constitutes an insult that must be avenged. When an opportune moment arrives, a raiding party is recruited along the lines of personal networks. Centered in a given ego, often the victim's father or brother or son or grandson, these networks are shaped by close ties of kinship and marriage that radiate outward in the form of a bilateral kindred. People differ, of course, in their inclination to raid, and those who organize raiding parties seek out men with known grievances as they attempt to recruit a force of from 4 to 40 raiders.

The raiders strive to wreak vengeance upon any member of the previous offender's bērtan. Retaliation need not be specific to a particular person or family, but can encompass a wider target population, including men and women and adults and children, all equal in their shared liability as victims. In order to minimize the risk to oneself and one's kinsmen—for no Ilongot man would ask his brother to "sell his body"—the victim is killed from an ambush set by a trail or perhaps near a source of water or food. Though the act is impersonal insofar as the victim may be the first person who happens along, it is construed, Tepeg said, as a way of having "the others see what has been severed in two so they will be frightened." In other words, the offender cannot fail to grasp the point of the beheading, regardless of whether he or somebody else turns out to be the victim. The only cases where vengeance is specific to the previous offender are those in which a victim is caught unawares, say on a path or during a visit, and then killed and decapitated, rather than in a raid.

Covenant. Covenants are often held long after the beheadings that sparked a feud. The delay, usually of more than a decade, allows enough time to pass so that hostilities can cool and amends be made. Just as there are opportune historical moments for headhunting, so there are times that stimulate a rash of covenants. In the case at hand, the intrusion of settlers and the New Tribes Mission, plus a decade without guerrilla warfare in the surrounding lowlands, made the late 1960's a period more for the celebration of covenants than for headhunting.

Covenants are celebrations in which, as on no other social occasion, virtually all members of one bērtan gather as an action group and make visible their unity, in opposition to another like unit. In such celebrations, first one side is the host and the other the guest, then the positions are reversed so that the former indemnity givers become the new indemnity takers. Exchanges are reciprocal, the form of the covenant is cast in the idiom of Ilongot formal friendship with its mutual exchanges of hospitality and gifts. Though they know that the difference of scale is one of kind as well, Ilongots still hope that a covenant between two groups may prove as binding as an assiduously cultivated formal friendship between two persons. Kugkug, a man from downstream, said, "We call a halt to killing and we hold covenants so that we don't finish one another off." Center stage in the covenant, then, is the attempt of two bērtan to make amends for the past insults that they have suffered at one another's hands.

Though the main event in a covenant is the ceremonial confrontation through which the two major groups make amends a number of more private scenes also take place among people who confer off in the corners of the houses. Bērtan members often air, perhaps settle, or at least mute their internal grievances at the same time that separate bērtan let "stories come out" about unresolved wrongdoings that stand between them.

These low-key talks spring from aspects of feuding that are only peripherally recognized, if at all, in the canonical form of dyadic opposition moving toward union enshrined in the covenant. In the first place, feuds at times implicate, over the course of their lengthy meanderings, more than two bērtan. Those who recruit the victim's avengers, for instance, may call upon certain men of another bērtan because they too, for their own reasons, harbor malice toward the offender or another member of his bērtan. In addition, the people who happen into the raiders' ambush may be a mixed group, thus provoking later retaliation from two or more bērtan. Vengeance killings move, in their chain reaction, both horizontally across groups and vertically through time. Though bērtan settle their feuds in pairs, two by two, their deeds of vengeance tend to spread in an arc that touches three bērtan, then four, then more. Second, any bērtan is rent from within, by its peculiar internal ruptures from the past, and these internal lesions must be patched over in order to present a united fromt for the confrontation with another bērtan. Its existence never lightly assumed, intragroup solidarity is carefully forged by making amends ahead of time and by designating men to go in person and urge the attendance of members of every household in the group. In fact, it is the gradual creation of internal solidarity in preparation for the agonistic assembly that provides a major plot line in my narrative of the covenant in Chapter 3.

Intermarriage or truce, or renewal of feuding. The covenant itself, however solemn its sworn oaths, does little more than wipe clean the slate of misdeeds and create a delicate balance. This balance may teeter on indefinitely, as the two parties to the feud move their homes in the hope that sheer distance will lessen the likelihood of raiding between them. Alternatively, the balance may swing decisively to one side or another, and its swing is as likely to result in a renewal of enmities as it is to lead to a successfully negotiated series of intermarriages serving as ultimate confirmation of the sworn oaths.

At moments during the covenant Ilongots may say "let their children marry," as they voice the hope that the celebration of ceremonial union may be but a prelude to more binding matrimonial union between the two bērtan. In such statements the speakers reify the two collectivities: each bērtan is personified, accorded human character—in fact individuated and spoken of with a singular rather than a plural pronoun. All concerned recognize the element of fiction here, for such unions in marriage are binding only for the husband and wife and their close kin and eventual offspring. Indeed, in one case the son of such a couple attempted to quell incipient enmities by reminding the two parties, "But I am the covenant," the embodiment of the human substance of both bērtan.

Furthermore, nobody is naive enough to regard marriage as a permanent condition of bliss. Ilongot marriages, not surprisingly, have their moments of tension interspersed with those of joy; and even when they endure through time (as most do), shouts of discord between husband and wife may echo more widely, sometimes even violently, as "life-taking threats" are issued between the two bērtan. Yet the dilemma is that marital unions, fraught with explosive risks as they may be, are the only means through which two bērtan can establish a firm alliance. Speaking of any inter-bērtan marriage, Ilongots say that "the 'X' people [bērtan] married the 'Y' people." The limits and potentials inherent in the social construction of alliances constitute the foundation for the conventional fiction that the husband stands for one bērtan and the wife the other, and their marriage, encapsulated in a synecdochic figure of speech, represents the union of one bērtan with the other.

Thus, in the context of the feud, the covenant is a pivotal ceremonial moment in which the form of the enduring two-party enmity is enacted in a repertoire of stories. These stories simultaneously look backward, endowing the past with an intelligible shape, and provide a charter for redress in the present and for possible intermarriages in the future.

THE BUTAGS AND THE RUMYADS

The main protagonists in the feud that I shall consider here were the Butag people and the Rumyad people. Each group is a bērtan; that is a bilaterally claimed category of affiliation that putatively once was or now is residentially concentrated. As social units bērtan become salient in the context of feuding, particularly during a covenant.

The Rumyad population in 1969 numbered 307. They were pitted against the Butag population, which at most numbered 80. Whereas the Butags were located in a single place, the Rumyads inhabited a much wider expanse of territory (see Map 1, p. 34). The Rumyads resided in six local clusters,* listed roughly from north to south with their population figures:

Kakidugen	52	Tauyang	35
Pengegyaben	49	Ringen	91
Kēyat	70	Bēawet	10

The Rumyads had clear advantages over the Butags as they approached their confrontation.

My narrative of the feud will be situated from the perspective of the Rumyads, in particular from the northernmost local cluster of Kakidugen. The house where we lived was located there, and however often we visited and stayed overnight in other places, we were most intimately acquainted with the people of Kakidugen and Pengegyaben. And we knew all the Rumyads incomparably better than we knew any of the Butags. To have visited the Butags (which we never did) in the midst of active hostilities would have required lengthy negotiations through intermediate links in order to find a reliable guide. In fact it was not until early 1969, at the covenant, that we first saw the Butag people in the flesh. By that time we had heard tale after tale of them, as our companions from Kakidugen told stories in anticipation of the dramatic event.

SOURCES OF THE FEUD, 1923-44

The rest of this chapter will summarize the history of the feud between the Butags and the Rumyads. Stories of the feud were told and retold during the process of deciding how much compensation each side should be given as part of the covenant. At once the grounds for its formal celebration and an instrument in the work-

---

*Groups of people may be designated either by their bērtan or their local cluster. Names for local clusters (Kakidugen, Pengegyaben, and so on) are place names; hence these names change every time a group changes its location. Bērtan names (Butag, Rumyad, Peknar, and so on) endure, remaining the same even if their members move, as will be explained at length in Chapter 7.

ings of its negotiations, this repertoire of stories, it is worth noting again, constituted the historical charter for the covenant.

What was most striking as I assembled, compared, and reflected upon different versions of the feuding history was the diversity of courses along which people traced the flow of events back in time to their separate "sources." There simply was no consensus, nothing resembling an official version, about which incident in particular was the "insult" from which subsequent hostile actions emanated.

Through further cross-checking it became clear that it was consistently revealing to inquire into the source of a particular man's motivation for participating in a raid. At the same time, it became apparent that my inquiries into the motivations of the raiding party taken as a totality, though answered, had been tacitly recoded and replied to from a specific personal perspective. In the case of the initial Rumyad raid, for example, in which a Butag man was beheaded in 1952, the party was made up of five men whose respective reasons for participation were as follows:

1. Two of them, Dinwag and Maniling, were related as uncle and nephew (Maniling, the son of Kadēng, had been raised in Dinwag's home), and they held grudges because the Butags had guided the troops that arrested their fathers in 1940.

2. Two of them, one named Luku, were brothers who felt a grievance because the Butags had "threatened the life" of their father in about 1935.

3. The fifth was a man who was courting (unsuccessfully) a woman whose family was temporarily residing with Dinwag and Maniling.

The source of the hostilities, then, was an arrest for two men, a "murderous threat" for two others, and a historical accident, so to speak, for the fifth. Just as when Lakay beheaded the Payupay in 1927, each man followed the peculiar course of his autobiography in reaching back in time to his own reason for participation in the raid.

The divergent motivations for the raid of 1952 indicate how problematic it can be to uncover the historical origins of any particular Ilongot feud. Though the Rumyad people's stories of their enmity with the Butags agreed in that an insult was the point of departure for subsequent enmities, they simply disagreed about which insult was the decisive one. Indeed, the notion of a primary source for later events was more relevant to personal perspectives on certain incidents than to feuding viewed as a collective enterprise conducted over the long run.

It is worth noting that in those societies where there is a consensus about the set of grievances from which a feud has originated, there also tends to be a unified group (a lineage or a government body, for example) from which such action arises. By the same token, the workings of Ilongot society, where raiders are recruited along personal networks of kinship and residence, are reflected in the accepted public relevance of each member's personal reasons for participation.

I should now like to move beyond the viewpoints of the Rumyad actors and attempt to unravel and gauge the diverse strands of events that led to the 1952 beheading of a Butag. The following chronological sequence of insults—all the insults that appeared in the indigenous stories of the Butag-Rumyad hostilities—may help locate and assess the impact of each arrest or murderous threat in the larger, long-term unfolding of the feud.

Lakay's arrest, 1923. Pangpang, from the southern Rumyad local cluster of Ringen, told me that the Butags "have not killed any of us; all they have done is have us arrested." As I inquired further, it turned out that Pangpang had two cases in mind: the arrest of Kadēng in 1940 and the arrest of the old man, Lakay, in 1923. I was surprised to hear the second case cited in this context and immediately replied that, as was well known, I had lived for over two years in Lakay's house and had never heard the old man mention that a Butag was among those who guided the arresting troops in 1923. I added that I had heard Lakay and others tell the story of his arrest over and over, and I had asked every question I could think of, including who guided the troops. Pangpang and a chorus of other Ringen people insisted that the Butag people were indeed there, along with those from Payupay.

On further reflection Pangpang's story became more plausible. At the time of the arrest, after all, he was a neighbor of Lakay and the two men were age-mates, 28 and 29, respectively. Both men, in other words, were adult eyewitnesses to the event. But the difference between their recollections of the arrest, some 50 years after the fact, was that Lakay had at least the three following reasons for omitting the Butag guide from his version of the story: (1) he had directed his retaliation for the arrest toward the Payupay people in 1927, and hence his thirst for vengeance was satiated; (2) after 1923 he and his close kin intermarried with the Tabaku people, who were also intermarried with the Butag people, thereby creating, however tenuously, an indirect alliance between Lakay and the Butags; and (3) he and his close kin had sworn an oath by salt to keep their peace with the Butags in 1952. In short, by the time of the covenant in 1969, Lakay had reason neither to seek indemnity for his arrest nor to urge his successors to seek vengeance against the Butags. During the 1960's and 1970's the detail of the Butag presence among the arresting troops was probably too dangerous in its implications to bear retelling by the old man, and, at least in this case, he, his sons, and his grandsons were willing to let bygones be bygones. The story of the 1923 arrest, then, was not canonized, let alone mentioned, in the context of the Butag-Rumyad covenant.

A murderous threat, circa 1935. It was about 1935 when two Rumyad men went fishing on the Kasiknan River; there they happened upon three Butag men and all of them camped together under a makeshift shelter. After dark that night the Rumyad men overheard the whispered plans of the Butag men to behead them as soon as they fell asleep; naturally enough, the Rumyad men remained vigilant throughout the night. As Insan explained, "Had they not been alert they would have been killed." Insan went on to say that some years later one of the Rumyad men instructed his son Luku by telling him, "When I was in my youth the Butag people threatened our lives by the shelter." Luku, who was five years old when the murderous threat took place, listened to the story and then decided, as Ilongots say, to carry it into adulthood; he said to himself, "These Butag people will feel my hand when I grow up."

Although the Butag action was unambiguously interpreted as a murderous threat, this event alone probably would have led to no more than the payment of indemnities in the post-1945 era when Luku came of age. By 1952 most beheadings were directed outward, toward lowlanders, rather than inward, toward other Ilongot groups. Luku's participation in the raid of 1952 went against the tide, and it probably would have taken (as it in fact did) more than a murderous threat to have channeled the raid toward the Butag people.

Kadēng's arrest, 1940. Guided by men from Butag, among others, lowland troops arrested eight men, including Kadēng, from a Rumyad local cluster that was the nucleus of present-day Pengegyaben. Most Rumyads claimed that there was no motive for the 1940 arrests; however, one Rumyad man who was raised by his aunt near the Butag homeland knew the other side of the story. He said that the arrests stemmed from a Rumyad refusal to sing the song of celebration after a successful Butag headhunting raid; as he put it, the Butags "coaxed and they coaxed us and they said, 'Come and sing the song of celebration with us.' That's why they became angry." In other words, the Rumyads' absence from the celebration was taken by the Butags as a snub—the insult that led four years later to the arrests.

These arrests, I think, were the decisive event in setting the feud in motion. The Rumyad stories of the arrests stressed the brutality of beatings meant to force confessions, the efforts (as repeated as they were futile) to persuade lowlanders to intervene and free the men, and the tears of the bereaved survivors. Their stated grievances were myriad and of undeniable weight.

It was also beyond doubt that the impact of the arrests was a localized demographic disaster for the Rumyad group. Of the seven local men (the eighth was a visitor) who were arrested, three died in prison and four were away for 15 years or more; together, these men were one-fifth of that group of 35 persons. To put the brute facts in other terms, the arrests effectively removed, as if by death, every adult man in the place between the ages of 30 and 55. Aside from three youths who had gone elsewhere to visit at that fateful moment, only four adult men remained in the local group; they had been purposely passed over by the troops because they were so infirm as to be ineffectual, enfeebled by age or tuberculosis or both. All of the able-bodied male adults, then, were in prison, including Kadēng; among the strongest who remained behind was Tukbaw, then 17 and only a novice as a hunter. Throughout the 1940's the surviving women from that local cluster adapted to their situation, suddenly made harsh by the absence of mature men, adding hunting and butchering to their more routine round of home and garden chores. Born of necessity, this shift in the sexual division of labor was so deeply formative for that cohort of Pengegyaben women that they alone among the Ilongots still hunt side by side with their men. In 1974 I participated in hunts in which these women, then over 40 years of age, led barking dogs through the prickly underbrush in flushing out the game. Having endured such fundamental dislocations, it is little wonder that the sons of those arrested, in particular Maniling and his uncle Dinwag, long nursed the hope that someday they might sever a Butag head from its body.

Butag raiders, 1942–44. Unmanned as it was by these arrests, the Rumyad local cluster was left defenseless. The group's very survival hung on the mixture of unmitigated vigilance and good fortune that enabled it to escape the clutches of other Ilongot marauders, particularly during the wartime years of 1942–44, when anarchic internal violence reached epidemic proportions. During those three years, groups of Butag men bent on decapitation were sighted on three different occasions. Once Tukbaw's mother, Baket, spotted raiders by the gardens, and her shouts of alarm frightened the men away. Another time Tukbaw's sister, then 14, absorbed in the tune she was plucking on her bamboo zither, happened to glance out the window and spy the lead man in a raiding party as he wriggled toward her through the underbrush. All silence and speed, she and the others darted from the house and eluded their enemies. On a third occasion the invaders had labored through the night, inching stealthily forward and pulling up bamboo stakes sharpened for defense as they approached; having nearly reached their goal, they evidently lost their nerve and made a furtive retreat. This story was inferred from the stakes found strewn the next morning among numerous footprints surrounding the house. In so raiding, the Butag people were simply attempting to take advantage of the unshielded vulnerability of the Rumyad local cluster. In such Ilongot enmities the guiding idea is to kill without being killed in turn. Whenever possible, the raiders minimized the risk to themselves by seeking victims who could neither defend themselves at that moment nor retaliate in the near future.

An assessment of the sources of the feud. The most crucial event in the formative era of the Butag-Rumyad feud was, I think, the arrests of 1940. The men removed to prison from that local group left the survivors in such a weakened state that they were exposed to further raids by the Butags. Youths and infirm older men nurtured their resentment in silence, while "murderous threats" were heaped upon the earlier arrests; as they saw it, insults had fallen upon insults in a life-threatening deluge of abuses. Yet they had no recourse but to weather the outrages until, their strength of mature men regained, they could seize upon an instant ripe for vengeance. By 1950 the cluster of houses had moved to its present vicinity of Pengegyaben, and the people still harbored their grievances, built up over the previous decade against the Butags.

The murderous threat of 1935 was also a significant step in leading to the raid against the Butags in 1952. Though at least one family, that of Luku and his brother, carefully nurtured its grudge against the Butag people, owing to the murderous threat of 1935, their hopes of eventual vengeance probably would have come to naught had they not been able to join with Maniling and his uncle, Dinwag (who sought to retaliate for the arrests of 1940).

Certainly the arrests of 1923 were of no enduring consequence for Lakay, who bore no particular ill will toward the Butags. By late 1944, however, Lakay and his local group felt at once pushed by their fear of the invading Japanese soldiers and pulled by their longing to live closer to their pre-1923 homeland. Hence they sought haven toward the east, at the relatively interior site of present-day Kakidugen. Since geographical and social distance tend to be congruent for the mobile Ilongots, Lakay and his companions found themselves stretched perilously between their loosening bonds with those close to Butag and their tightening bonds with their kin, Dinwag, Maniling, and the others in Pengegyaben.

Lakay, his father, and his sons correctly assessed their dilemma, and they swore an oath by salt with the Butags. An oath by salt is a serious undertaking. Its violation brings supernatural punishment, for its key ritual phrase states a principle of sympathetic magic: "Just as salt dissolves in water, so shall perish he who breaks this oath." Once sworn, this binding oath is intended to renew social relations through the hope that people will feel secure enough to walk to one another's places and that they will no longer feel frightened when they see one another in the forest. To swear such an oath was clearly no light matter for Lakay and the others who hoped to maintain amicable relations and eventually attain a wider covenant between the Butags and all of the Rumyads.

After 1945, in short, local pockets of Rumyad people had contradictory views of the state of Butag-Rumyad relations. Whereas Lakay and his companions sought to keep the peace, Luku and Maniling, each for his own reasons, awaited the opportune moment to retaliate against the Butags.

AN OATH BROKEN BY A BEHEADING, 1948–56

About six weeks before the Butag-Rumyad covenant of 1969, Disa, Lakay's wife, had the feuding history on her mind when she reminisced about how she feared the Butags on their initial postwar visit to Kakidugen in about 1948. In her words, "Alas, all our men were away, every last one of them. That was when the Butag people came to visit. We pounded rice for their meal. They then spent the night at the house and left in the morning. But why did they come to see us? They gave us all betel chews. Alas, what if they killed us? Oh, how I trembled when I became frightened." No sooner had their Butag visitors left than the Rumyad women fled and hid in the forest out of fear that their treacherous guests might return and behead them. In retrospect this event was interpreted as mere women's fear and not as a more consequential murderous threat. Social intercourse between the two groups had reached such a strained point that amity between them could be restored only through the assiduous cultivation of interpersonal politics.

It was 1950 when, in the words of Lakay's son Insan, the Butag people "emerged before us where we were clearing our gardens and the elders orated together." Later that year they assembled again, and then once again, in preparation for their planned oath by salt. The fragile situation demanded high diplomacy; hence the Kakidugen people were hosts for an oath by salt, then in turn the Butag people agreed to reciprocate.

When the Kakidugens set off for the return oath by salt in Butag territory, it was 1952; unknown to them, deception was in the air. The Rumyad youths, including Insan, then 20, and Luku, then 22, did not participate in the solemn oaths because a man from Tabaku (Insan's mother's people from the northwestern margin) exhorted the assembled elders: "Do not have these children take part in the oath by salt; they should not be made vulnerable to death by supernatural means." The Tabaku man was attempting to protect his "children," for he knew that their "fathers" from Kakidugen could not pretend to speak for the members of other Rumyad local clusters, among whom were such people with known grudges as Maniling and Dinwag. The Butags protested that all present should take the salt in hand in order to allay suspicion. The Rumyad elders protested that their intentions were pure, for who but they stood to suffer the consequences should the oath by salt be broken. In the end the exhortation proved persuasive, and the solemn ceremony concluded on a note of shared hope for the future celebration of a covenant that would encompass all the Rumyad people.

As they returned on that trip from Butag, the Kakidugens did not realize that Luku, silently harboring his father's grudge, had gone with them because he wanted to study the lay of the land in anticipation of a raid he would initiate. What was in Luku's heart became evident three months later when five men set off on a raid against the Butags without saying a word to the people of Kakidugen. One of the raiders, Luku's older brother, was courting a woman who lived adjacent to Maniling and Dinwag; these three, plus Luku and another man who was also courting nearby, retaliated for past insults (the arrests of 1940 and the murderous threat of 1935) and found a Butag victim upon whom Luku might vent his anger.

By Ilongot standards, Luku had bolted beyond the pale and was regarded more as a public menace than as a man admirable in his capacity to fuse "knowledge" and "anger." Thus the impetus of his companions to raid was in part self-protective, designed to mollify the incorrigible Luku, whose boundless anger had led him to chop the carrying baskets of his sister into shreds; to fire his weapon in wild bursts into the air; to refuse the year before, because it was beneath him, to sever the head of a lowland victim from the Hukbalahap movement; and to insist that unless he beheaded, not a lowlander, but another Ilongot he would seek his victim among his closest kin.

Once in Butag territory, the raiders heard the barking of hunting dogs, and they lay down in ambush. As Insan told it, it was not long before a man and the dogs "came near and then arrived. They immediately shot the man along with three of his dogs. They threw his head in the air. They then returned."

Word immediately reached the people of Kakidugen that their Rumyad companions from Pengegyaben and what would later become Ringen had just beheaded one of the men with whom they had sworn the oath by salt. The news was phrased, "They have killed your fellow oath by salt." Lakay from Kakidugen despaired as he replied, "Luku allowed us to go ahead and swear the oath by salt without telling us anything and now the words we spoke in that assembly have been snapped in two." That day Lakay and his father sent a man bearing the message that the two groups should gather together whenever and wherever the Butags wished, so that they could explain precisely who it was that had beheaded the man with the dogs.

Out of concern for their safety, the Kakidugen people denied the unity of Rumyad, a residentially concentrated bērtan, by distinguishing among the following dispersed bērtan: Tabaku, Peknar, Bēsilid, Yamu, Pasigiyan, and "true" Rumyad. Lakay and the others affirmed their Tabaku identity and thus, verbally at any rate, brought themselves closer to the Butags and further from the raiders, whom they identified as "true" Rumyads and Peknars. Pangpang from Ringen, a "true" Rumyad, told a version of the story, that differed only in its emphasis. He told me that the 1952 oath by salt was never intended to encompass all Rumyads (as everybody involved would agree), and that it was strictly a Bēsilid-Butag affair. Hence, he said, the "true" Rumyads broke no oaths when they beheaded the Butag huntsman in the forest.

The man sent by Lakay and his father returned to Kakidugen with a string knotted in indication of the number of days that were to pass before the two groups would meet at the fork of the Reayan River. On the appointed day Lakay, his father, his younger brother, his son Insan, and certain other youths, including an Aymuyu man who had married into their group, all began to walk toward the meeting place with the Butags. While the sun was high they set up camp for the evening, and the youths went to hunt in the forest. When the youths returned a number of them carried game on their backs. As he arrived, one young man tossed his wild pig toward the very spot on the ground where a gun was lying. The loaded gun discharged, and Lakay's father, standing in the line of fire, was hit in the chest and died instantly. The dead man had reached that venerable age for Ilongots when, as his local group's eldest living member, he was regarded as the "source" and the "grandparent" of its members. The cruelly orphaned "sons" and "grandsons" sat stunned for some time; then, abandoning their mission of restoring the broken oaths, they turned back to bury their elder above the banks of the Kakidugen River.

The Kakidugens perceived that fatal gunshot as bristling with significance beyond a mere accident (which at the same time they perceived it was). After all, the moment they learned of Luku's violent misdeed they had hurried to make amends, impelled by the fear that the curse unleashed by the oath's violation might ferret out a man who held the salt and deliver him a mortal affliction. Memories of the terrible force set loose by violations of oaths by salt had been vividly impressed upon Ilongot minds a scant seven years before, in 1945. Then the widespread decimation of local clusters was viewed as, among other things, retribution for the previous ruptures of other such oaths. Especially during that historical period, the oath by salt was not to be sworn lightly, for people knew they possessed no shield against mystical forces. The otherwise arbitrary snuffing of Lakay's father's life only served to confirm people's view of the ominous consequences of breaking the sworn oath. Seventeen years later, in 1969, the Kakidugens requested compensation because their elder's death was due to supernatural retaliation for Luku's taking a head; thus the death was counted as if it were at the hands of the Butags.

Yet, for Ilongots, such inexplicable events often are said to ema-
nate from multiple sources. When for instance, I told Insan my
firm opinion that ultimately Luku was more at the "source" of his
grandfather's death than were the Butags, I was surprised that he
readily assented, adding that by his act Luku had as much as killed
his own "body" (betrang), that is, his own kinsman. Insan explained that had Luku been "another person" (not related or of
another bērtan), they simply would have killed him. Nonetheless,
he rationalized that Luku, because he was not at the scene of the
gunshot, did not stand precisely at the source of that momentous
death. With visible relief Insan identified the owner of the lethal
weapon, the Aymuyu man who had married in, as the source of his
elder's death. Indeed, in 1952 he and the others schemed to wait
until the Aymuyu man's vigilance was diffused by allowing time
for the then 6-year-old son of Lakay's younger brother to come of
age and avenge the death. In the meantime, Lakay's youngest son
took a vow to kill as a means of "lightening" his grief, and later
that year he beheaded a lowlander.

Four years later, in 1956, a Rumyad raiding party from Ringen
and Abēka, a place on the southwestern margin, beheaded the second Butag victim. Commenting on this raid in his most matter-of-
fact manner, Insan simply said that "because they [the Rumyads]
already had acquired a taste for killing them [the Butags] they did
so once all over again." By all accounts the 1956 raid was a matter
less of vengeance than of plain opportunism. Throughout the
1950's the Butags raided repeatedly against the Rumyads, particularly those in Kēyat and those from Kakidugen who had moved
into Pengegyaben. During this period the Rumyad targets of these
raids protected themselves every evening by implanting sharpened
bamboo stakes around their houses. They also set up ingenious devices that, if one of the stakes were pulled up, would spring a trigger, thereby releasing a cord and dropping a stone on the floor to
warn those inside the house. The men said that they arose well before dawn, weapons in hand and alert in case of possible attack.

Once, in broad daylight, three Rumyad women at work in their
gardens spotted a group of Butag raiders. They began to shriek
and wail, evidently so frightening their enemies that they fled at
once. The Butags, Insan said, tried and tried again but failed to

retaliate because of their "incompetence," pure and simple. Such remarks, imagined or overheard, were doubtless at the root of the Butags' apparently persistent efforts to take a head before celebrating the covenant of 1969.

When assembled, the stories about the sources of the Butag-Rumyad feud show certain of the complexities involved in the celebration of the 1969 covenant. Through their silences and emphases, recollections of the past entered political arguments about compensation owed one party or the other. Moreover, the tales that were told pointed to enduring enmities within Rumyad that would have to be patched over in order to present a united front before the Butags. In particular, the people of Kakidugen occupied a contradictory position in the whole affair. During the period of their residence on the northwestern margin (1923–45), they intermarried with the Tabakus and thereby indirectly became closer to the Butags. When they moved toward their former homeland in 1945, however, they became closer, both socially and geographically, to their fellow Rumyads, to whom they were linked by ties of kinship and marriage. The outbreak of overt hostilities in 1952 caught them between loosening ties to the Butags and tightening ties to the Rumyads. Both relations were still vital.

CHAPTER THREE. THE CELEBRATION OF THE COVENANT, 1969

Ilongot covenants are social dramas in which virtually all the members of a bērtan gather together and make visible their social unity by confronting another similar group. Solidarity within the bērtan must be artfully negotiated well ahead of time: a few members are delegated to extend personal invitations to the other households, and all possible grievances within the group are mended for at least long enough to present a united front to the opposing group. The social construction of Rumyad solidarity and its transformation during the covenant is the central topic of this chapter.

What follows examines, first, the increasing Rumyad consciousness of Butag anger during 1967–68, then the events designed to create Rumyad unity on the eve of the covenant; the chapter closes with a narrative analysis of the covenant.

HOW THE BUTAG REPUTATION BECAME ESTABLISHED, 1967–68

Long before the celebration of the covenant, the Rumyads had come to believe that the Butags were brimming with "anger" (*liget*; see M. Rosaldo 1980 for an extended analysis of this key Ilongot term). No sooner had we arrived for our first lengthy stay among the Rumyads in Kakidugen than we learned the name of their infamous enemies, the Butags.

At the end of October 1967 we arranged to reside with three Ilongot families in a Kakidugen household. On December 2 we set off from a local cluster on the northwestern margin of Ilongot territory toward our new home, a long day's hike to the east. We were guided by schoolchildren whose parents or relatives resided in Kakidugen; the children helped carry the packs of supplies we had purchased in Manila following an earlier month-long survey of the Ilongot region. After an inauspicious beginning, when a cloud of bees swarmed over us, we stopped to rest at the trail's midpoint. There, fully armed and combing their long hair, were the half-dozen men who were to accompany us the rest of the way. Dusk was approaching, so we quickly set off.

As Michelle noted in her journal, we "never really understood the walk from there." Our companions darted here and there, stalking unseen prey with their loaded weapons cocked; they alternately shouted to the hills and whispered to us. Eventually it became clear that we were being told not to be "frightened," and that the shouting was a warning for the Butag people to stay away. Members of this escort explained what was happening as best they could, but our feeble grasp of the language screened out all but that two men had been killed, perhaps recently, and a covenant either had just been broken or was soon to be held.

Almost two months later, on January 29, 1968, a Butag raiding party was rumored to be in the hills surrounding our new home of Kakidugen. The rumor spread, as Ilongots say, like a grass fire, and it created local panic. This time there was no armed guard, for the men had all left on a several-day hunt in the forest. The women from across the river fled their house to hide in their field shelter; I could hear an old man from there as he shouted magical spells to his dogs so that they would bark and defend him from the raiders. The women in "our" house were relatively calm because, they said, nobody would dare attack a place so centrally located. But by nightfall their daytime bravado had been clouded over by fear, and Lakay's wife, Disa, handed me a pistol with two bullets, explaining that I should wait to shoot until the enemy had climbed inside the house and I could see their eyes shining white. I lay awake that night, tossing and turning and trembling every time the pig, tethered beneath the raised floor, grunted or snorted in its sleep. Once again, I failed to catch a glimpse of the Butags.

As I attempted in writing this to reconstruct further the character of the Butag presence, both in our own awareness and in that of the people of Kakidugen, I scanned our 1968 field journals in search of less traumatic but illustrative incidents that might have lapsed from memory. On June 3 a group of siblings from five to ten years of age were hiding in ambush on opposite sides of the fence by the sweet potato patch. They howled and whooped as they bolted up and hurled their toy spears, made of *Miscanthus* reeds, at one another. The littlest brother, "wounded," sobbed that it took more than a glancing blow to kill a Rumyad man; his big sister, hands on her hips and lower lip forward, screeched back that Butag people never miss their mark, and he'd better lie down on the ground because he was dead. Even children played the game of Butags and Rumyads.

Later, on June 16, a man who was to be the armed escort of two women on their hike to visit a sick relative in Tauyang decided that he had no time to go because he was too busy burning and cleaning his garden. When a relative who is "lying down in illness" sends word for his or her close kin to visit, for Ilongots the call has the morally binding force of a grave family emergency—as indeed it often is. The two women decided to hike, not on the main trail, but on a little-known detour to the east; they said they did so out of fear of the Butags. By then it was clear to me that the Butag people were (believed to be) raiding in an attempt to even the score of deaths on each side before holding the covenant. The Butags had inflicted punishment both by guiding arresting soldiers and through "threats on lives." But their rumored further action to even the balance was understandable because two of them and none of the Rumyads had been beheaded.

On July 12 rumors of Butag anger reached their heights, breaking well beyond usual interpretations of the law of the talion. That day we were walking downstream during a six-week stay on the northeastern margin of Ilongot country when we heard more rumors of Butag raiding parties. Whether inspired by actual Butag actions or by the sheer elaboration of repetition, the news this time was that the raiders, ever more ferocious, were scouring that furthest corner from their homeland in search of any human being—lowland Ilokano, Agta, Ifugao, Chinese, Ilongot—to cross their path. The Butags, as the tale was told, would stop at nothing before venting their anger. Once they had taken a victim, and only then, would they settle into the more conciliatory mode of conduct that the covenant entailed. This rumor was taken so seriously that an Ilongot man whose neighbors were lowland Ilokanos declined an invitation to go upstream and attend a bridewealth assembly. He feared that the Butags might behead one of his neighbors in his absence, and blame for the homicide would surely be cast upon him. Our companions on the walk were warning lowlanders of the Butag menace because they did not want to be arrested, perhaps pistol-whipped, and probably imprisoned, as so often had happened in the past, for other people's misdeeds.

It was, as it turned out, while we were away on this six-week stay that the Butags and Rumyads held their first preliminary meeting. The meeting had been arranged by two men from Tenga who had married into the Butag neighborhood but were also close kin to certain Rumyads. Since the two men from Tenga had chosen not to ally with one side against the other (as they might have), it was in their interest to mediate between the two groups and promote the covenant.

That initial confrontation of the two bērtan was by all accounts as brief as it was tense. The meeting was held near the Butag homeland, and it took the Rumyad party three days to arrive there. The party, all men, moved with slow caution because, they said, they were frightened of treachery; along the way they stopped overnight at two different houses, where they orated and assured themselves that they were all of a "single heart" in the face of their enemies. When the actual confrontation arrived they maintained their watchfulness and solidarity; afterwards they repeatedly recounted how each man had decided ahead of time which one of the enemy he would kill and which window he would leap from, should violence shatter the assembly.

Both sides dispensed with oaths sworn by salt, proposed in order to guarantee their safety during the meeting; they were eager to jump immediately to the covenant. The speakers came straight to the point and quickly agreed that first the Rumyad people would host and pay compensation for the two Butag victims, then the Butags would host and make amends to the Rumyads. The date was set: the first covenant would be celebrated after the rice harvest, in late 1968 or early 1969. According to a young man with a watch, the assembly, however protracted in the retelling, took only half an hour by the clock.

After July the rumors of Butag raiding parties subsided nearly as abruptly as they had come to our attention the previous December. The reason for the slackening off was probably the agreement to hold the covenant toward the end of that year. Or perhaps rumors and raiders alike had lost their earlier zeal for travel as the weather became wetter and cooler and the trails slipperier and more overgrown from July to November. It may be because raiders were never actually sighted that the short step was taken from viewing such rumors as a charitable warning to dismissing them as a hoax. Whatever the reason, we heard no further news about the Butag threat from July until the celebration of the covenant.

THE SOCIAL CONSTRUCTION OF RUMYAD SOLIDARITY, 1968–69

While Michelle and I were spending the year's end holidays of 1968 in Manila and in Ifugao country, Lakay and his son-in-law, the orator Tukbaw, walked from Kakidugen in an attempt to mend their grievances with certain people in Ringen. In his initial remarks on arrival, Lakay established his good intentions as he affirmed that he and his listeners were related as "brothers" who had come from a single "source." In so setting a tone of solidarity, Lakay felt free to demand compensation on behalf of his Aymuyu "son" (MZDS),* whose son had been beheaded in 1963 by a Ringen-based raiding party. But the father of a Ringen man parried this thrust by demanding payment for his Aymuyu "brother" (FBS), beheaded in 1943 by a raiding party of which Lakay had been a member.† Tukbaw told me later that he felt chagrined to

---

*Genealogical linkages among persons are indicated by the following conventional abbreviations: M, mother; F, father; D, daughter; S, son; Z, sister; B, brother; W, wife; H, husband. Thus, MZDS should be read as mother's sister's daughter's son, and FBS as father's brother's son. In addition, I specify the Ilongot kin category by using a term in quotes or by indicating that the person in question is classificatory kin of a certain category.

†The incidents reported here are elaborated later in the chapter. Throughout, I attempt to provide the context needed to understand particular incidents. Readers who desire deeper context should consult the Chronological Index to events (p. 299). It should be kept in mind that different historical epochs were distinctive in character: the beheadings of 1943, for example, took place at a time of rampant internal violence brought about by the pressures of Japanese occupation of the Philippines.

walk so far, only to reach a stalemate from which there was no exit, not even for the most quick-witted of orators. As Tukbaw and Lakay prepared to return homeward, the Ringen people beseeched them to stay for two more days because the New Tribes missionary in residence there had especially invited them to take part in their New Year's celebration. Lakay and Tukbaw agreed to stay.

The following day both parties exchanged bolos accompanied by the ritual "rubbing" (touching metal, to fortify oneself and remove mutual threats) that suffices to make amends between relatives. Through this ceremonial exchange they saluted their mutual recognition of their relationship and further cleared the path toward Rumyad solidarity. The next day they celebrated the New Year of 1969.

The following morning, Pangpang's younger brother asked to speak with Lakay and Tukbaw because Luku had just arrived with news about the coming covenant with the Butags. Coy in his response, Lakay declared that he was delighted to learn of the forthcoming Butag-Ringen covenant, an event he had eargerly awaited ever since the day Luku had broke the Butag-Kakidugen oath by salt. Much as he lauded the act of redress, however, Lakay intended to stay at home because the people involved were not from Kakidugen, but Ringen. Ever impetuous, Luku blurted out that he, their "younger brother," wanted Lakay and Tukbaw to sit beside him at the covenant; and in order to "cheer their hearts" he presented them with a bolo and a firearm. In an act that was a pledge to attend, Lakay received the firearm at the same time that he ritually affirmed, as he returned Luku's bolo to him, that Luku was indeed his "son."

Pangpang and Tukbaw then agreed to meet in three days at the house of Luku's older brother in Tauyang and there make their final arrangements and set a firm date for the covenant. When they met in Tauyang, Pangpang made his formal request of Tukbaw: "You should speak together among yourselves in your own place. All of you should attend, especially the uncle of Kadēng's son Maniling [Dinwag, one of the 1952 raiders]; all of the people from Kakidugen should come." In other words, Tukbaw's charge was to take word of the covenant to Pengegyaben and to ensure that everybody from Kakidugen attended on the date, February 2, 1969, indicated by the knotted string.

On his return to Kakidugen on January 10 Tukbaw requested the other members of his local cluster to meet at his house so he could tell them about his news from Ringen. Tukbaw reviewed for them the details of the trip. He stressed how surprised he and Lakay were when the Ringen people announced that the covenant was about to happen. He recounted how he and Lakay tried to excuse themselves from attending the covenant. Two men, as Tukbaw had anticipated, sat through the meeting in stony silence because they were miffed that no Ringen man had had the grace to come in person and request their presence. As dusk neared, Tukbaw slowly counted aloud so that everybody could record the number of days until the covenant. He concluded by exhorting all present to attend, and to pound rice and hunt game in preparation for the feast.

Though Tukbaw's influence emerged to its fullest in the context of such excursions into the outside world, his invitations were persuasive more because of their tact in bending wills than because they were backed by coercive force. For several days after the meeting, the orator walked to every house and in relative privacy explored people's dispositions toward the coming event. With Lakay's younger brother, agreement was quickly reached that they were of a single heart, and their conversation soon drifted toward tentative arrangements for the hunt and the more jovial banter that tacitly confirmed their pledge to participate in the common enterprise.

Two men, however, remained recalcitrant. Despite his taste of vengeance in 1952, Dinwag was adamant in his insistence on receiving compensation for his father's death in prison after the 1940 arrests. He relented only after coaxing and repeated assurances that the Butags had agreed to host a return covenant. Radu, another man from Kakidugen, proved more intractable. Tukbaw pleaded with Radu to "let his heart emerge" and not keep it hidden from view. As it emerged, his grudge was against Pangpang and other Ringen men who in 1921 had massacred about a dozen of their houseguests as they slept. Among the beheaded guests was Radu's uncle, and he still held the slender yet firm hope that someday his ten-year-old son might avenge that heinous deed. Reasoning, cajoling, teasing—nothing swayed the steadfast Radu, who became as unbending in his purpose as he was deliberate in his slow, unadorned speech. In the end he did not budge and the covenant was celebrated without him.

Everybody else in Kakidugen agreed to attend and to bring rice and meat to the covenant. As Rumyads they were requested to pool and later redistribute a supply of food: this practice of collecting ('upug) and then sharing (beret) was customary procedure for any Ilongot large gathering, where in consenting to attend, a person simultaneously agreed to contribute food. As the knotted string grew shorter, the women began to pound rice and to load their carrying baskets with it and the men set off to hunt in the forest where they would butcher and smoke chunks of meat.

THE ENACTMENT OF COLLECTIVE IDENTITY, 1969

Through gatherings and collective feasts the Rumyad people expressed their otherwise geographically scattered and socially diffused sense of group identity. The covenant was a social drama through which their collective identity would come into focus. The ceremonial covenant was designed to persuade themselves, as well as the Butags, of the reality of the social relations and historical experiences behind their self-designation by the name Rumyad.

On the trail, January 31 to February 2, 1969. We departed for the covenant on January 31 and that day reached Pengegyaben, where some of the 21 of us slept at Baket's house and others at Kadēng's house. As dusk approached, Tepeg confirmed the rumor that he had refused to contribute food for the coming event: he was angry because his wife, Midalya, had been "murderously threatened" in 1958 by Pangpang's youngest brother, Bangkiwa. As everybody there knew, Bangkiwa had courted Midalya until their relation was severed by her mother, Baket, who still bore a grudge against Pangpang because in 1921 his raiding party had beheaded her classificatory brother (who was also Radu's uncle).

After nightfall a man from Kēyat called on Tukbaw, saying that he wanted to talk about the 1958 incident when Bangkiwa, still smoldering with rage, had in turn threatened his life while they were on a fishing expedition. Feigning reluctance, Tukbaw muttered that he had been trapped, hunted, and ambushed, and then went on to discuss the heated issue. In their conversation the two men let their hearts emerge, and as they warmed up for the covenant they fell into the rhythmic cadences, the ornate rhetorical flourishes, and the taut upright postures, that together marked the style of oratorical speech in public assemblies. Both of them went on to attend the covenant.

Our numbers swollen by people from Pengegyaben, the next morning we slowly walked the short distance down the steep hill to Kēyat. From there we could see southward across the Kanuwap River to the grassland near Ringen, our destination. Our pace became more leisurely as we literally "collected" people at their houses in order to reach the site of the covenant as a unified mass.

We spent the midday hours in a Kēyat house while Tukbaw and others engaged in an oratorical debate that had arisen from an event of that morning. A young man had cut a deep wedge in a log footbridge so it would break under the weight of the next person to cross. It so happened that the next to approach the footbridge was his maternal aunt (MFZD), his classificatory mother, who had spied the treachery before she stepped on the log. As we arrived, she was screaming and scolding her "son" for his lethal prank: how could a man know no better than to murder his "mother"? In the advent of the covenant the quarrel was amplified, elaborated through the protracted rhetorical devices of oratory, expanding the implications of the near mishap to such higher considerations as motherhood and the nature of filial respect. More foolish than vicious, the young man was regarded as still a "child" who lacked full "knowledge" of human relations, and he was finally instructed in the proper way to behave toward his relatives. By then it had become clear that the airing of such disputes in formal discourse was designed as much to rehearse for the high oratory of the coming celebration as to mend wounds that still divided the group.

We walked a short distance farther, then spent that night in Tauyang. About noon of the following day we reached the Kanuwap River. There we washed; people helped one another, sensu-

A group of Rumyads, some resting and others combing their hair, on the banks of the Kanuwap, February 2, 1969.

ously combing, posing, preening. They decorated their hair with gay red kerchiefs adorned with white horsehair and tufted wool, and their throats with tight necklaces of tiny, delicately etched mother-of-pearl droplets. Women delighted in the occasion to wear their skirts of bright new store-bought cloth; men prided themselves on their flashing, dangling earrings made from the red beak of the hornbill. Well groomed and in full dress, "beautiful" as they had become in their eyes and mine, they lolled and lounged in the shade amid the boulders on the banks of the river and awaited Tukbaw. He had stopped off to meet and escort Kugkug, among others, who had walked there from the distant down-stream region of Ilongot country. In time Tukbaw arrived with a surprisingly small group from downstream; the others, it was ex-plained, had remained behind in fear and for self-defense because for the first time in over a decade they had recently sighted an armed band of lowland guerrillas. (It became clear in 1974 that this was the New People's Army.)

Arrival, February 2, 1969. It was nearly three that afternoon before we walked up the treeless hill toward Ringen. Our stately, silent, single-file procession through the two kilometers of grassland was visible from the nucleated 15-household mission settlement above. When we reached the airstrip (for the New Tribes' Piper Cub) we were formally greeted by a Kēyat man, who soon was joined by Pangpang and Bangkiwa. Because people had become excited by their oratorical rehearsals and splendid dress, they were in no mood to hear the news that each local cluster was assigned to eat and sleep in a separate Ringen household and that the rule for the duration of the covenant was no firearms in public. Tukbaw protested that this was not the Ilongot way to conduct a covenant, and that those who had walked together along the trail cared deeply for one another and did not wish to be housed in separate places. It was decided to retreat from the airstrip and discuss this delicate matter at Luku's house.

Plans, February 2–3. That evening the people of Kakidugen and Pengegyaben ate and slept apart from the others in the house of Pangpang. Tukbaw had decided to comply with the wishes of the Ringen people, who, after all, were providing the houses. They also decided to disarm themselves and more generally follow what they saw as lowland ways. Thus two men named aloud the "captains" for each local cluster (on the model of barrio captains in the surrounding valleys). In the absence of the captain appointed for Kakidugen by the local mayor in 1968, Tukbaw was named to stand in his stead. In following lowland usage, men from the margins spoke with special authority because they had been to school and had interacted more with people of the surrounding valleys. Hence they announced that all captains should speak straight, rather than answer back and forth in the dated oratorical manner; captains spoke in a sequence as their names were read aloud from a written list, so that they never interrupted one another in the outmoded fashion of Ilongot public assemblies.

Kugkug suggested that people follow the precedent of last year's

covenant, celebrated downstream, by greeting the Butags at a lav-
ishly decorated archway and feeding them there from their cupped
hands. But he was talked down by the advocates of law and order,
who were reiterating that all firearms should be stashed away in a
public show of amicable intentions and in order to avoid an accidental gunshot. In a discordant rhetorical finale, one captain exhorted the others to enforce the compliance (which they could not
do) of their "soldiers" (which their young men emphatically were
not) in the preservation of peace during the covenant.

By the next morning one of the Tenga mediators had arrived in
advance of the Butag party. He brought word that the Butags had
withdrawn the demand that they enter Ringen with safe-conduct
guaranteed by a Rumyad hostage, held by the tail of his G-string
and with a knife at his throat. The Rumyads then discussed what
they planned to give to the Butags as indemnity payments. As compensation for the two victims, two valuable wide-mouthed metal
cooking pans were proposed. One would be given after the initial
greeting as part of the ceremonial rubbing, designed to wipe away,
as the ritual phrase had it, the mystically sanctioned prohibition
against eating with those who had killed one's "body" or one's
"kind" (bērtan). The other would be given later, after the Butags
had entered the Rumyad houses. Similarly, two bolos would be
given because the two beheaded victims had also been stabbed. It
required more subtle argumentation to reach the consensus that
because the "old people had never returned the belongings of their
victims from distant places," the Rumyads should not yield before
Butag pressure to replace the two firearms they had picked up
after the beheadings. Since the two Butag victims had been
"stolen" (their beheadings had gone unavenged), the Rumyads decided that it would be tactless and probably pointless to discuss
the return covenant until after they had actually handed over the
indemnity payments. People planned but were not able to introduce a further ritual representation of order through the trinary
seating arrangement of Rumyads on one side, Butags on the other,
and Tengas in between.

As afternoon wore on, the people assembled grew more anxious, for the supposedly approaching Butags had not yet been
sighted. Talk then turned to the moment of initial greeting. The

The Rumyads, dressed in their finest
and walking in single file to greet the
Butags, February 3, 1969.

A Rumyad man, fully adorned, facing
the Butags, February 3, 1969.

Tenga mediator reported that the Butags, aware of their lesser
numbers, planned to carry weapons, but they would be unloaded.
Bangkiwa burst out that in that case he felt compelled to carry his
firearm as well; but he was soon swayed by the prevailing sentiment, grumbling that, unschooled as he was, he could only remain
silent and go along with this lowland law. Keyed up and tense,
people one by one abandoned the debate and retired to their separate lodgings. It was about 3:30 that afternoon before word of the
Butags' arrival reached us. As Tukbaw wryly commented a week
later, "It is not our Ilongot custom to arrive so late; those people
are like cats [who see in the dark]."

The Butags arrive, February 3. After the Butags' arrival, a Rumyad man (the hostage of earlier plans) carried a flurry of messages
back and forth between us and the Butags. Rather than enter Ringen, the Butags demanded to receive their initial greeting on the
outside, where they then stood. Unarmed, and with women along

to demonstrate good intentions, the Rumyad people walked in silent, orderly single file through the high grass of former swiddens
to greet the Butags. Dressed in their finest and fully armed, the Butags were squatting on a hill as they awaited our arrival; several of
their men with firearms were placed in strategic positions, should
there be deceit. Speaking in a stage whisper, Bangkiwa from Ringen urged people to sit still, to avoid confusion and trouble, "because we are all mixed with one another."

A census made for us by one of the participants indicated only
47 Butags faced 92 Rumyads and 98 Abēkas from the southwestern margin (who also took part in the 1956 raid against the
Butags). The possible mediators from near the Butag homeland
numbered 115, but most of them avoided the initial greeting and
remained in Ringen households. Also back at the houses were
118 people from the eastern perimeter, who had been invited to
the covenant by the Rumyads. Normally 92 in number, Ringen
was swollen during the covenant to some 470 persons.

A Tenga mediator embellished his speech with oratorical tropes
as he called for the relaxation of vigilance, especially on the part of
the Butags. He said that he felt assured because Insan, his
"brother" from Rumyad, was among those assembled there. Two
men from the margins followed lowland usage, in contrast, as they
spoke on behalf of the Rumyads: one, from the southwest, introduced himself, "My name is Lindeb," while the other, from the
southeast, made the rounds, shaking hands with his fellow captains as he went along. Once the initial greeting was concluded,
those assembled moved on, in short stops and starts, until they had
passed the first Ringen house. With dusk upon them they drew to
a halt by a pea patch.

Butag demands, February 3–4. The halt was called by a Butag
man named Kama, who pronounced an end to pointless walking,
then sitting and sitting, then walking. A Tenga mediator burst in,
as he put it, to fill the air with words and to keep negotiations
alive; the Tenga man expounded on the worth of what they were
to receive, a wide-mouthed metal cooking pan, its value enhanced
because it dated from peacetime. Another Butag man, denying any
flair for oratorical gyrations, announced bluntly that he had

Butags standing firm before the Rumyads. Kama with machine gun, February 3, 1969.

Men orating: true Rumyad in front, his Butag counterpart in shirt and red hornbill earrings, February 3, 1969.

walked the arduous trail, not to receive mere redress, but to satisfy his unbending demand that the Rumyads replace the firearms that had belonged to the two victims. Correctly assessing the crisis, Bangkiwa from Ringen chanted as he spat his red betel juice on a brass ring and presented a metal pan to the Butags as wergeld for one of their victims. Night had fallen by the time this ritual rubbing was completed. With the mystical prohibition on so doing thus wiped away, members of the two groups ate their initial meal in the pea patch.

While he ate, Kama from Butag grumbled that he was forcing his food down his throat, implying that his anger would not be dissipated without compensation. In a quavering voice of optimism, a Rumyad man invited everybody assembled in the pea patch, once they had finished their meal, to come in from the cold and retire to the houses. A Tenga mediator interjected a more somber note when he announced that, before they moved another step, the Butags demanded to be shown the firearms that were to replace those picked up from the victims; they meant what they said, right there on the ground and not inside the house. Kama from Butag theatrically proclaimed himself "I who live upstream on the Kasiknan River" as he dramatized his demand, rising taut to his full height, his vintage 1945 machine gun, as whispered rumor had it, fully loaded and aimed at the weaponless crowd. The other Butag men likewise arose, their firearms poised. The Butags justified their uncompromising stance on the grounds that they "had not yet killed" the Rumyads; furthermore, their relatively small numbers made them especially vulnerable to deception, and they sought to protect themselves.

A Rumyad spokesman from the southeastern margin arose, as noble in his purpose as he was patronizing in his tone, and instructed the unschooled Kama from Butag that he should conform to the rule and accept the wergeld payments for both victims before even discussing the replacement of belongings picked up after the beheadings. Kama's response was simply, "No." When the Rumyad spokesman repeated himself as if he had been misunderstood, it was the blunt Butag man who this time said, "No."

People then debated the issue at length. As evening wore on and its biting chill grew more severe, the Ringen people, many of them dressed in overalls and shirts yet visibly shaking with cold, urged Kama, clad as he was in only a G-string, to sit down and put on a blanket. He refused. Then an old Butag man took a stick and drew a line on the ground between himself and the nearby house, saying that unless he saw the demanded firearms he would never cross to the other side. At long last the Rumyads brought out the firearms. Four in all, they were inspected one by one until two of them were found that met the Butags' satisfaction. The Butags then pressed for two bolos and five bullets to accompany each of the firearms. Clearly their reputation for unyielding anger, which had developed over the past year, enabled the outnumbered Butags to succeed in driving a hard bargain during the covenant.

It was 11:00 P.M. by the time the gifts had been presented, and everybody left the pea patch and entered the house. Inside the house, Bangkiwa distributed betel nut chews to the Butags; Tukbaw, with even greater solemnity, presented a betel quid to Kama from Butag, and he recalled with regret the oath by salt that was broken in 1952. Talk then became less punctuated by the yea and nay of demand and denial, and rather more unbroken as people narrated the stories of the two beheadings. As agreed outside, the Rumyads delivered the ten bullets to accompany the firearms. With the gift thus given, the Butags relaxed their vigilance and put down their firearms. Group sentiment shifted from icy hostility to warmer overtures of friendship. Caught up by the mood, a Tenga mediator somewhat disingenuously proclaimed that the Rumyads had accepted the Butag demands out of their deep desire for social harmony; as he put it, they "truly wanted all of us to eat from a single leaf." Another Tenga man added that those assembled should speak frankly about what they wished to receive and what they were able to give; for they were to follow the Ilongot oratorical way and discuss these matters, if need be, through the night and into the next day. At 3:00 A.M. all those assembled ate a meal together.

After the meal, Tukbaw urged that the issue of compensation be raised once again. Kama from Butag returned to his earlier tough stance, saying that he had been called there so that he could be given whatever he requested; he concluded, "Hurry up now and do speak loudly, because I've grown deaf from the buzzing of the sawmill at my home place." Kugkug from downstream countered by attempting to shame the Butags into lessening their demands; he remarked that the proposed payments were so enormous that gossip would call them bridewealth and not a covenant. The blunt man from Butag retorted that, just as he had expected, once inside the house the Rumyads would try to renege on their earlier pledge; but he refused to bend, saying, "I have not avenged either deed, and hence my demand for the other victim's wergeld is not a matter for debate." During the discussion, which continued through the night without pause, a second wide-mouthed pan and two more bolos were given as indemnity for the second victim. It was not until after dawn that these agreements on compensation for the beheadings were concluded and the main speakers paused for a nap.

It should be noted that, while food and drink was provided by the Rumyads as a collectivity, the participants in the beheadings assumed responsibility for indemnity payments, either paying directly themselves or requesting aid from their close kin. The sociocentric liability of their potential victimship defined the collectivity of Rumyad as the group of food-givers; the egocentric network that was activated in the recruitment of raiders defined the membership of the group of indemnity-payers.

Solemn oaths, February 4. By 9:00 A.M. the dozing speakers had been awakened because the meeting was to resume. Those assembled announced that they would follow a written agenda prepared in lowland fashion. After his name had been read from the list, each captain spoke in turn, with no interruption between speakers. In their speeches one and all pleaded for law and order; a number of the advocates paced up and down and gesticulated spasmodically in what I could only perceive as a rude parody of lowland political speechmaking. The Butags were then reprimanded and asked to pay ten bullets in compensation for having held their trigger fingers on loaded weapons pointed at the Rumyads. Cheerfully compliant this time, the Butags delivered the ten bullets as asked. Another meal was served about noon that day.

That afternoon a domesticated pig was to be sacrificed, in order for men from both groups to swear by salt not to kill in the future, for the 1952 oath needed renewal. The initial issue was who would and who would not participate in the solemn oath. They first proposed to recruit one person from each of the following bērtan: Bēsilid, Yamu, Peknar, Pasigiyan, "true" Rumyad. As debate wore on, people glossed over the internal differences by reaching the consensus that the summation of those bērtan was Rumyad, all one people. Hence a few men, indeed even one man, might take the salt in hand in the name of the collectivity.

While this discussion took place outside the house, Tukbaw from Kakidugen was inside. In low tones he reminded the Butags there of the Peknar loss suffered when Lakay's father died in 1952 after the earlier oath was broken. Rather than await the return covenant, Kama from Butag insisted that, because the old man's death was a separate matter, he himself would walk to Kakidugen in the near future and make amends there.

About a dozen men from Rumyad and Butag gathered on the ground in a circle around a squealing and squirming pig, which one of them stabbed in the throat with a sharpened bamboo stake. The men rubbed salt in the blood of the sacrificial animal as they swore to keep the covenant and never kill one another in the future. Ritual phrases, some standard and some coined for the occasion, explicitly stated the conditions of the oath. Those who kept their word as sworn should expect to live a "long life like a plant that extended in its growth to its leafy tip." Those who, on the other hand, violated their solemn oaths would become vulnerable to mystical forces that might make them "dissolve like salt in water" or "vanish from sight like a tiny bead dropping between the slats in the floor" or "topple over like a shelter felled beneath the blows of a bolo." The image of the collapsing shelter, alluded to the "murderous threat" of 1935. To dissolve, to drop from sight, to be smashed—people heaped together feared images of obliteration as they chanted. When the men had completed their oath, they placed the pig in a pot of boiling water.

Formal conversation was set aside as the men rested from the strenuous night before and sat in anticipation of the meal; it was a time for gossip and casual conversation, a chance for members of the opposing parties to get to know one another. In this setting Kama from Butag abruptly became amicable; he looked, as Michelle wrote in her field journal, "like a rich man" who sat visibly pleased with himself as he bestowed upon those assembled the gift of his beaming presence. He urged Rumyad parents to send their children to a school near his home; he went further and asked Rumyad families to move to his place and help prevent the incursions of settlers into Butag territory. The Rumyad people responded in kind, with a spokesman from the margin offering his aid in disputes over land titles and with other men warmly inviting Kama and his companions to hunt in their territory and saying they would shout "brother" on seeing their tracks in the forest—they no longer had reason to fear one another. Moved by the drift and tone of the conversation, the blunt Butag man asked the names of his Rumyad companions, and he addressed each one as "brother" as he repeated each name with chuckles and friendly merriment.

About dusk Kama from Butag raised his final demand: in addition to the two men, three dogs had been killed in the 1952 raid, and compensation was imperative. His speech was firm, yet more playful and sentimental than it had been the evening before. After all, he began, dogs are valuable companions in the hunt; evidently inspired by vivid hunting memories, he called the three dogs in turn by their names. He then invoked his listeners' sympathies by recalling the women's arduous labor in feeding the dogs: mounds of sweet potatoes, the women ever planting, digging, boiling. Coyly, he demanded cloth by requesting a certain something checkered like the skin of a lizard. Carried along by this winning plea and by the jovial mood, the Rumyad people hastened to make their payments: pieces of cloth were given for the women's labor in raising two of the dogs; a roll of thin brass wire was delivered by Luku as indemnity for his having beheaded the third dog. This episode was an almost comic recapitulation of the high seriousness of the earlier payments.

The blunt man from Butag then insisted that the Rumyads sacrifice a chicken and swear a second and confirming oath by salt. Before assenting to the demand, Bangkiwa from Ringen lamely excused himself because he could not locate a child who was willing to yield his or her chicken. Both Tukbaw (who by then was carrying his firearm) and Lakay stepped out of the house and refused to "hold the salt," because of their bitter experience with the oath of 1952. Those who remained inside to join hands and swear the oath were Kama and his blunt companion from Butag along with "those who had chopped together"—the Rumyad men who had actually been on the two raids.

The live chicken was wrapped in a bead necklace, and in its sacrificial death blow the ritual phrase was made visible as the tiny beads scattered and fell between the rattan strips of the floor and vanished without a trace into the earth below. The previous images of obliteration were repeated, and one man added that any violator of the oath should become brittle "like dried-out bamboo" and shatter into smithereens. In an allusion to the arrests of 1940, the oath's violation was extended beyond decapitation to include "also turning us in to be arrested by the lowlanders." Kama from Butag shouted out, "Let our children all marry." Another echoed his sentiments, yelling, "May nothing other than a woman [in marriage] follow upon this oath." A third called out, "May she have many children." In this mood of festive relief and hopeful anticipation, the assembled people ate together and retired shortly afterward at about midnight.

Final day, February 5. The compensation and oaths completed, the key events of the following morning took place simultaneously in different houses. A small number of people gathered at the house where Kama from Butag was staying and agreed that the return covenant should take place later that year during the dry season (March–May). At another house, a man from a distant place who had married Insan's Aymuyu "sister" (FMZDD) helped Tukbaw's chronic back ailment by sucking out the intrusive object that (he said) he had found lodged there. In the meantime, Lakay and his Aymuyu "son" (MZDS) spoke with Bangkiwa from Ringen about indemnity payments for the incident of 1963. It was 11:00 A.M. when the morning meal was served to those assembled.

About noon the captains from both groups filed off to the home of the New Tribes missionary, where they had been invited for lunch. Meanwhile, a group of unmarried youths, Rumyad and Butag men and women, inside one of the houses started to eat collectively from a woven tray; like the Tenga mediator's image of harmonious union, they were eating from a "single leaf." Repeating the joke he had made over and over since the initial oath, the blunt man from Butag shouted that he had come in search of a fair Rumyad maiden. Paying little heed to this elder's antics, the youths were more intent on the high excitement of their shy, giggling, blushing, yet exuberant flirtation, as they touched and fed one another with their cupped hands, saying as they did so, "may we stick together like glutinous rice" or "like resinous glue." This shift from the feared images of obliteration of the day before to more hopeful invocations of solidarity suggested the desired (though far from certain) happy ending represented by the possibility of marital union between the two groups.

As the celebration progressed, the relational terms for participants increasingly moved beyond the opening day's confrontational idiom of Butag versus Rumyad and came to encompass kin terms and personal names. People initially had used their collective bērtan names and had spoken of "we" from Rumyad as opposed (explicitly or implicitly) to "they" from Butag; this was a rhetoric of internal group unity, excluding and opposed to other like units.

Gradually people addressed one another by name or kin term, verbally invoking interpersonal role relations that transcended without denying the social reality of the closed circles of "Butag" and "Rumyad." Personal names were learned by asking and repeating. Appropriate kin terms were selected by sex and estimates of relative age: approximate age-mates were "siblings" and relatively older people were "fathers" or "mothers" to their "children." People thus reached past the limits of their collective Butag and Rumyad identities and conversed with their named "siblings" from the other side, as the mood of the covenant developed from initial fierce confrontation through later relative relaxation to the flirtatious finale.

By 2:00 P.M. the Butags began to compose themselves for the sequence of deliberate movements of leave-taking from their hosts. As they bid farewell to the Rumyads about an hour later, they called people by name and shook hands all around. They paused to say that nobody held bad feelings, then they waved their grand farewells and turned and walked westward in slow and stately single-file procession. Bangkiwa and four young women from Ringen carried the packs of the Butags until they disappeared from sight over the first hill, heightening the solemnity of the exit.

Once the procession had gone beyond hearing distance, Luku and Tukbaw remarked that an old man from Butag had walked off with all the melted fat collected from wild pigs. The two Rumyad men agreed that their sense of shame would have inhibited them from carrying out such a deed; Luku, however, said that when the Butags hosted the return covenant, he intended ("because I am a man") to take their fat and eat it the moment he left their place.

Later that afternoon the Rumyads and their allies once again assembled to discuss certain intragroup matters. Before nightfall their assembly had dispatched these three items: (a) Bangkiwa from Ringen supervised the roll call, through which he solicited contributions to pay for the sacrificial pig; (b) his older brother, Pangpang, redistributed the ten bullets from the Butags and aroused bad feelings by skipping over the captains from north of the Kanuwap River; and (c) Bangkiwa explained that the Butags had pledged to deliver, 27 days from then, the knotted string setting the date for the return covenant. Discussion then turned to the more vexed issues of compensation for other beheadings. An Aymuyu man demanded wergeld because a man from Kēyat had deceived his "mother" (FZ) and beheaded her while they walked together on a trail in 1940. Before the 10:00 P.M. meal, it was decided that the Aymuyu man should visit Kēyat later that year during the dry season and receive his compensation. Two further issues were raised and their resolution postponed until morning, because the assembly broke up at about midnight.

Departure, February 6. In the morning the assembly reconvened to discuss further the demand of the previous night that the Rumyads perform the ritual rubbing and pay indemnity for the five Aymuyus that were beheaded in 1943. Debate on this matter, Tukbaw explained to me, was brief and only playful as compared with the more protracted, painful, and weighty manner of "true speech" (oratory). In effect the grievance had already been settled in 1963, when a Ringen woman was married by an Aymuyu man whose father and paternal grandfather had been among the victims of the raid. Though viewed by everybody as a form of compensation, the marriage was regarded by certain people as a cove-

nant in redress for the earlier misdeed. In raising the issue of the
1943 beheadings, the Aymuyus sought rather more to consecrate
than to inaugurate their settlement. After the ritual rubbing,
people agreed that members of each bērtan that had participated
in the raiding party (Rumyad, Pasigiyan, Peknar, Bēsilid) should
contribute at least one bullet toward the total of 15 paid as indemnity. Thus the matter was brought to a quick conclusion.

The other issue remaining from the night before was that, as an
indirect consequence of the 1963 marriage, the Ringen people had
been led by the Aymuyu groom in a raid against other members of
his own group. It was in this raid that the child of Lakay's Aymuyu
"son" (MZDS) had been beheaded. Late into the day Lakay and
his son, Insan, stayed and spoke in support of their Aymuyu relatives who sought redress for the 1963 beheadings; their efforts,
though arduously pursued, were inconclusive. Tukbaw said he felt
fed up with the whole Aymuyu issue. In late December, after all,
he lent his tongue to speak on Lakay's behalf, and his efforts had
resulted only in feelings of chagrin. In any case, the Aymuyu situation was snarled beyond unraveling until tempers had cooled with
the further passage of time. Some people still remained locked in
debate at about noon, when we set off following Tukbaw and
others on the return walk to Kakidugen.

Kama's visit, February 17–18. Less than two weeks after the
covenant, Kama from Butag visited Kakidugen in order to discuss
the death of Lakay's father in 1952. His guide and constant companion during the visit was a youth who, in the roving manner
characteristic of his stage in life, spent 1967 in Lakay's house and
from the following year lived with Kama in anticipation of his
marriage to a neighboring Butag woman. The young man's family
of origin was from the northwestern margin; hence his marriage,
though timely, would not constitute a union between Butags and
Rumyads.

In the early afternoon of February 17, Kama and his companion
entered the house in silence and sat down. Without a word Tukbaw prepared a betel quid and, as he placed it in my hand, whispered that I should enhance the formality of the occasion. Following my "brother's" wishes, I walked in measured steps across the

room and with my left arm bent horizontally before me I squatted and, moving in slow motion, handed Kama the quid with my right hand.

During the afternoon, Kama told about the news from his place in a series of exciting stories that reflected local tensions with settlers there. A bold Butag man had repeatedly dared in broad daylight to rob the stores of the Chinese merchants engaged in serving the loggers who were gradually intruding into the valley. Once, as he fled from a store with his booty in hand, the audacious man was shot in the back of his neck by a .22 bullet, but without breaking stride he made his escape as if unaware of his bleeding wound. The lowland Christian eyewitnesses were reportedly left in terrified awe of his apparent invulnerability. Kama also told about how his favorite hunting dog had run away, only to be found by Kallahan and Ifugao squatters, who killed and ate it. More painful for Kama than the loss of his valuable animal was the repulsive act (from the Ilongot viewpoint) of eating the dog; thus the story provided a negative commentary on the character and customs of the squatters.

After dark the discussion became more formal, as it turned to the business at hand. Kama wished to postpone the return covenant until his people's supply of rice became more plentiful after the next harvest, unless there was an objection to the delay. Nobody present objected. Nonetheless, Kama went on, he still wanted, before the return covenant took place, to pay the Kakidugen people in compensation for the death of Lakay's father as a consequence of the oath violated in 1952. Insan, Lakay, and Tukbaw agreed that they should avoid bad feelings with Luku by making their separate amends. All of them decided to assemble again when Kama made another visit in the near future.

The following morning Kama packed his belongings and then sat patiently in readiness while Insan addressed a farewell speech to his young companion who was about to marry, counseling him not to drink too much store-bought liquor and urging him to earn money by working as a guard at the sawmill. Kama and his companion said farewell and left for their home.

The Kakidugens commented on the admirable elegance of Kama's dress: he wore a beautiful bolo and scabbard on his hip;

bands of thin brass wire and cowrie shells adorned his calves; a large clasp made from a boar's fangs and white horsehair stood above his metal armband; a long comb, a bright red sweatband, and a tall black feather decorated his head. Tukbaw remarked how surprised he was that Kama had dared to visit so soon after the covenant; indeed, he added, if he were in a comparable situation he would never make such a visit before the return celebration. Disa, Lakay's wife, smiled as Tukbaw spoke, for she had realized that Kama was more apprehensive than he appeared. Throughout the night, she explained, Kama had only feigned sleep; he had remained vigilant against possible treachery by his hosts.

Whatever its risks, Kama's visit was a significant confirmation of the covenant, coming as it had before the mood of solidarity between the groups had dissipated. Only through such personal visits could people cultivate their social relations with a view toward possible intermarriage and toward inhibiting further enmity.

In April 1969 Kama from Butag was killed on his way from the lowlands back to Ilongot country by a logging truck that ran off the road and overturned. Up to the time of his accidental death the date of the return covenant had remained uncertain. The Ringen people had pressed for its celebration as early as April 30, but the people from Butag and Kakidugen favored a delay until after the rice harvest, perhaps early in 1970. As a consequence of Kama's death, the Butags did not host their covenant until after our departure from the Philippines.

In retrospect, 1974. On our return in 1974, we heard nothing in conversation about the Butags. When I asked for news of them I was told that Wagat, her husband Tukbaw, and her brother Insan once stopped off on their way to the lowlands and got drunk with some Butag people. Otherwise, they said, there was no news to tell. The Butags—in contrast with their having been the topic of endless talk in 1967–69—had become virtually invisible to the people of Kakidugen. It certainly was clear that, without further cultivation, covenants do not necessarily lead to ever-increasing amity. Neither intermarriages nor further enmity had punctuated the years from 1969 to 1974, and the Butags and Rumyads might well continue their uneasy truce into the indefinite future.

When I asked further, I learned that the Ringen people played the major role in arranging the return covenant because they had made up the core of the raiding parties against the Butags. Tukbaw told me that the Ringens had been lazy and had never really invited the Kakidugens and Pengegyabens to attend the return covenant, so he and all but one of the others had stayed home. Only Maniling attended the 1970 covenant, and he went to receive 300 pesos (about $75) as compensation for the imprisonment of his father, Kadēng. No one else from Kakidugen or Pengegyaben was present.

The laziness of the Ringen people probably resulted from the unresolved tensions concerning the beheadings of 1921 and 1963 that had surfaced during the 1969 covenant. The tensions between the northern and southern Rumyad local clusters had worsened by 1974, exacerbated by the emerging pattern of conversion to missionary religion. During 1969–74, ever-increasing numbers of people in Kēyat, Tauyang, and Bēawet followed the religious path that Ringen had taken. Immediately after our departure in 1969 a New Tribes missionary couple spent a brief period of residence in Kakidugen, then moved for a slightly longer period to the Butag homeland. Kakidugen and Pengegyaben stood out as an enclave where the majority of the people were not followers of the New Tribes Mission. Like the Butag presence, the reality of Rumyad solidarity had receded into the background of people's consciousness. In retrospect it was evident that the covenant had created a strong sense of both the Butag menace and the unity of Rumyad.

PART II. SOCIAL STRUCTURE SET IN MOTION

CHAPTER FOUR. THE SOURCE OF
COLLECTIVE MEMORIES, 1941-1945

Bronislaw Malinowski's (1929) popularization of the so-called biographical approach, his technique of presenting a schematic version of the life cycle, represented a great step forward for ethnography, a genre too often quaint, flat, and timeless. Inflated with Malinowski's ethnographic flair and personal charisma, the biographical approach appeared to overcome the problem of the short span of anthropological fieldwork; it promised to show how the life cycle intersects with other institutional forms and thus increases the time depth and plausibility of studies of social systems. Yet in retrospect it is clear that Malinowski's method for the study of lives was not the great final stride, but simply a step along the way toward an ethnography rounded and deepened by a fuller sense of the passage of time. To begin, the very notion of constructing a typical life—if taken as literal realism, a statement of how certain people always have lived, live, and will live—creates the illusion of a static and homogeneous primitive society. It presupposes the answer to the question that should have been asked: how have people experienced and represented the passage of time? Moreover, composite biographies say nothing about the issue of whether people's characters and life experiences are the product solely of their phase of life, or of their life phase in combination with the historical moment.

Given the present state of the art, the problem is to show the articulation of structure and event in human cultures. The task of ethnography today, in other words, is to move beyond former versions of social structures, many of them as static as they were reified, and show the intersection of personal history, general history, and the changing structures of developmental processes. In what follows I attempt to use a number of central concepts, including the life cycle, age and sex roles, intergenerational bonds, and the domestic cycle, as a set of structural reference points for the study of individual biographies. I hope at the very least, as George Homans once said in another context, to put the people back into ethnographic studies.

THE CONCEPT OF COHORT ANALYSIS

The notion of cohort analysis is the master concept used in this and the next two chapters for transforming the composite biography into a collection of individual biographies in their historical, cultural, and social structural contexts. Although the concept of cohort analysis has hardly entered anthropological discourse, apposite though it may be, it has been widely discussed in other disciplines. The technique was initially developed in demography and was later applied in sociology and social history, where it is now as canonical a method of investigation as the domestic cycle is in ethnography. In its demographic origins, the notion referred to longitudinal quantitative studies of birth cohorts, that is, large numbers of people who were born near the same time. In its subsequent development in sociology and social history, the concept was fused with the earlier idea of historical generations, referring especially to such artistic and literary movements as the "Generation of '98" in Spain. In this crucial conceptual shift, what remained the same was the idea of following a number of lives as they unfold through time. What changed was the mechanical centrality of birth dates; instead the subjects of study were defined, first, by that formative historical moment when their shared collective identity was forged and, second, by their enduring character as a self-conscious group in society. Such groups are composed of people who came of age together, then later grew old together.*

---

*Initially I explored this problem area through the theory of historical generations in the works of the Spanish philosophers José Ortega y Gasset (1923) and Julián Marías (1970). Their ideas have been applied to the Spanish peasantry by the anthropologist Carmelo Lisón-Tolosana (1966). I am indebted to Hildred Geertz and Clifford Geertz, who first

When a number of individuals reorient their lives in relation to certain historical events that impinge upon them over a particular span of time—for example, as many young Americans did during the Vietnam war—they emerge to a greater or lesser degree as an identifiable group within their larger society. Thus a likely consequence of marked discontinuities in the lives of members of adjacent generations is the genesis of relatively well-defined groups of peers. Such groups emerge, not with the birth of their members, but during those youthful years when the often irreversible life choices are made about such matters as occupation, marriage, and place of residence. In such cases impressionable youths find themselves confronted by vexing situations that were unknown in the world their parents inhabited. Indeed, it is usually during the transition from childhood to adulthood that groups of people become especially receptive to what Karl Mannheim has called fresh contact, that is, the capacity (also evident in immigration and social mobility) to transform one's character and culture in response to novel, even threatening conditions.

The point of entry in cohort analysis is an inquiry into the extent to which a number of individuals have become self-conscious about their identity as a group in the face of life chances terribly different in appearance from those of their elders and their juniors. The formation of such a group, indeed, the very shape of its collective identity, is based initially on a shared sense of life possibilities and later on the shared knowledge of and reflection about life outcomes. The character of its members is molded by living through the concatenation of events peculiar to the historical slice in time framed by the dates of their births and deaths. To say that the members of successive generations pass through critical periods during which their collective identity is (or is not) formed is not, however, to deny matters of degree, for the impact of formative historical events can vary both in scope (the number of people influenced) and intensity (how deep the influence runs), resulting in

called my attention to the literature on cohort analysis, including unpublished lecture notes by C. Geertz, after they heard me read a draft of Chapter 1 at the Institute for Advanced Study in Princeton, New Jersey, on January 28, 1976. The most useful articles synthesizing cohort analysis are by Karl Mannheim (1952), Norman Ryder (1965), and Alan Spitzer (1973). These three papers provide a basic orientation to the concept and to the literature about it.

groups of differing size and salience. Such groups also have their own internal makeup: perhaps they have clearly defined centers and margins, or people who drop out or join over time, or members who are markedly older or younger than the rest. And each such group has a distinctive cultural idiom through which it conceives, at once actively shaping and reflecting upon, its collective identity.

Cohort analysis directs inquiry toward the various developmental processes through which groups reproduce themselves, perpetuating, modifying, or abruptly changing their social structures. This analytical method of following the universal process in which a group of predecessors are falling from their structural positions at the same time that their sucessors are rising to replace them calls attention to the mechanisms that produce both intergenerational continuities and the distinctive character of each generation. What this method points to as a problem is the complex orchestration of the culturally defined phases of the life cycle, the personal histories of individual lives, the formative impact of historical events over a certain span of time, and the social metabolism through which one generation takes the place of its predecessor.

AN APPLICATION OF COHORT ANALYSIS

Ilongots have had ample historical basis for the perception that social order is forever improvised anew. Their sense, as described in Chapter 1, is that each successive generation follows its own path by moving back and forth between the opportunities provided by the historical moment and the desires lodged in the hearts of its members. Cohort analysis, therefore, is especially applicable to Ilongot society.

To summarize briefly, from the beginning of this century the Ilongot population has experienced such shifting historical conditions that a sense has emerged that each generation grows up into a world unlike that of its predecessors. During peacetime the world political economy spiraled from boom through bust to war, and its local reverberations were manifested in alternations between the concentration and dispersal of population, as well as between the flourishing and cessation of headhunting. In 1945, "the time of the Japanese" was, for the adults I knew more than two decades later, a watershed in the remembered past, when a massive influx of retreating Japanese troops resulted in the traumatic loss by disease, starvation, or bullets of about one-third of the local population. In the postwar epoch of 1946–74, younger generations of Ilongots have continued to find their world transformed through the Hukbalahap guerrilla movement of the early 1950's, the increasing number of missionaries and settlers from the late 1950's, and the declaration of martial law in 1972.

Although applicable in principle to the Ilongot population as a whole, cohort analysis gains in depth as it narrows its scope to small groups whose members lead interconnected lives. Biographies then are so intertwined that an individual history becomes more intelligible in relation to the whole, and the collective history can largely be reconstructed through the aggregation of multiple personal histories. Indeed, in his seminal paper on cohort anlysis the sociologist Norman Ryder (1965) spoke of such histories as macrobiographies. More than a collection of autonomous life histories, such longitudinal studies explore the many-stranded connections that join individuals as they participate in their unfolding collective destinies.

I have chosen to follow the lives of 20 people from Kakidugen and Pengegyaben who acquired a self-conscious, though loosely bound, sense of their collective identity through a series of intermarriages in 1955–58. In the language of demography, the 20 people are a marital cohort. My purpose, however, is to achieve a broader historical understanding; I wish not simply to document a final outcome in a series of intermarriages, but rather to show the concatenation of historical events, developmental processes, and cultural patterns that operated together as the biographies of the 20 grew so intertwined as to be analytically inseparable.

The ten young men who entered the marital alliance were related in the manner shown in Fig. 1. Their characters, briefly sketched as I knew them in 1967–69 and 1974, were as follows:

Insan (b. 1932) was Lakay's second oldest son. His reputation for "anger" was enhanced in 1950, when he became the first Rumyad man to take a head after the cessation of raiding in 1945. Because of the Kakidugen people's residence in and near the low-

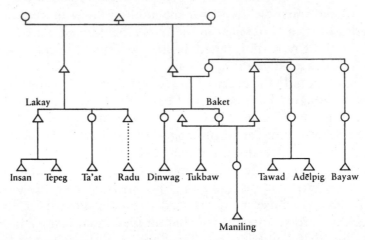

FIGURE 1. Genealogical relations of the ten young men of the 1955–58 marriages. (Dotted line indicates tie by adoption.)

lands, he became a fluent speaker of Ilokano and was adept at dealing with outsiders. Not given to reflections on the meaning of life, he was straightforward, outgoing, and astute in discussing the politics of marriage, schools, land, and settlers.

Tepeg (b. 1934) was Lakay's son and Insan's younger brother. He suffered by contrast with Insan, who was "thinner at the waist," as Ilongots say, and lighter in complexion than he; indeed, Lakay often criticized him, bluntly saying that he was lazier about hunting and fishing than his older brother. Quick-witted and able to engage noted orators in verbal horseplay, Tepeg was too painfully shy to speak in public assemblies. Intelligent and of fine sensibilities, he was something of a loner, deeply skeptical about his culture's beliefs.

Ta'at (b. 1931) was the son of Lakay's sister. He was orphaned in 1945, when both his parents died, and was then raised in the home of Lakay's younger brother. His movements were quick, and he was thin at the waist and not a little vain. Unlike others of his age, he cultivated intense friendships with younger men, with whom he hunted and hung out as if still a youth himself. Ta'at was adept at playing the violin and bamboo zither, and he was skilled as a craftsman in making delicate jewelry.

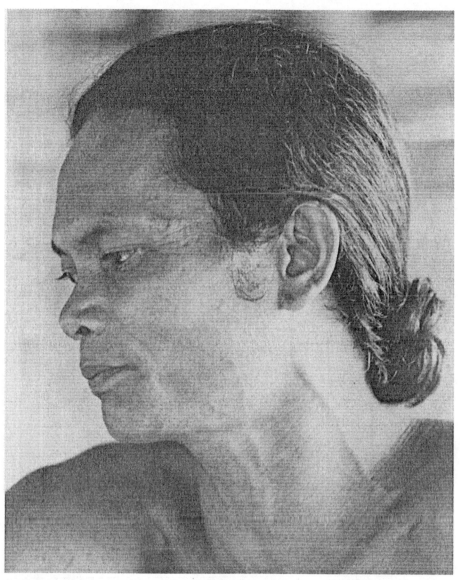
An Ilongot man.

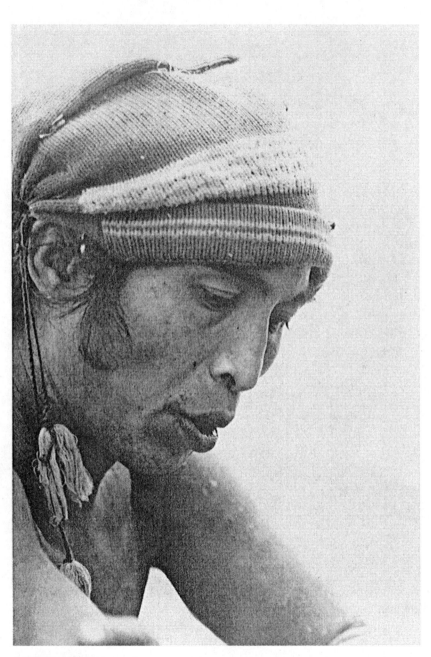

An Ilongot man.

An Ilongot man at rest from spearfishing.

Radu (b. 1931) was the half-brother of the wife of Lakay's younger brother, in whose home he was raised (along with Ta'at after he, too, was orphaned). He was quiet, kind, and accommodating. He was outstanding at spearfishing and was known as the finest violin player in the vicinity. As an informant, Radu most enjoyed reflecting on the meanings of "deep" words.

Dinwag (b. 1918) was the son of Baket's sister. Imaginative and erratic, he was as lazy about work as he was gifted in the performance of magical spells for curing, hunting, and fishing. His "anger" as a youth was still remarked, for he had beheaded two Japanese in 1945 and a lowlander in 1955. He died of illness in 1971.

Tukbaw (b. 1923) was Baket's only son by her second marriage. Self-reflective and a forceful personality, he was gifted in speech and widely known as a fine orator. On the other hand, his slight Tagalog and lesser Ilokano led him to allow younger men to deal with lowlanders. He was deep, at times moody, always delicate and indirect in his sense of the fragile fabric of human relations. (For a biographical portrait of Tukbaw, see R. Rosaldo 1976.)

Maniling (b. 1935) was the son of Baket's daughter by her first marriage. After his father, Kadēng, was arrested in 1940 by the soldiers that the Butags had guided, he was raised alongside his "uncle," Dinwag, by Baket's sister. Raised under the same roof, Maniling and Dinwag were two of the four men who went with Luku in 1952 when he beheaded the lone Butag man and triggered the Butag-Rumyad feud. Like his father, he had an exceptional memory; in addition he was articulate about the meanings of words and the ways of his culture. He was reliable, energetic at work, a man to be counted on.

Tawad (b. 1925) was the classificatory son of Baket, for his maternal grandfather and her father were half-brothers. His father was among those arrested in 1940 by the soldiers that the Butags guided; his sister, mother, and maternal grandmother were shot and killed by a Japanese soldier in 1945, leaving him at the age of 20 to care for his three younger siblings. He was lean, withdrawn, and good at playing the violin.

Adēlpig (b. 1928) was Tawad's younger brother, also the classificatory son of Baket. Less quick-witted than others, he still enjoyed the men's joking and horseplay. He was skilled with medicinal herbs and magical spells and, like Tawad, was good at playing the violin.

Bayaw (b. 1929) was the classificatory son of Baket, for his maternal grandmother and her mother were sisters. He was devoted more to the pleasures of fathering his children than to the rewards of speech in public assemblies. Bayaw killed more game in 1967–69 than any other man in the vicinity. Both his prowess as a hunter and other people's stomachaches were attributed to the potency of his hunting magic.

All of these men were born between 1918 and 1935; Insan, Radu, Ta'at, and Tepeg grew up in Kakidugen, and the other six in Pengegyaben. When the ten men were children, the people of Kakidugen and Pengegyaben resided far apart, because after the 1923 raid by soldiers they had fled in separate directions from their former homeland in central Rumyad. Lakay and the others were initially held under house arrest on the northwestern margin, where the others from Kakidugen eventually settled after spending four years in hiding near the 1974 location of their local cluster. Meanwhile, Baket and the Pengegyaben people fled due west and settled on the Kasiknan River, still within the Ilongot heartland.

More than a decade later the two groups made major moves to the east, returning, through gradual steps, closer to their former homeland. The Kakidugen people moved in 1935, followed by the Pengegyaben people in 1936. During the years of 1936–41 the people of Kakidugen and Pengegyaben began to rediscover one another as relatives, and Lakay and Baket renewed the "knowledge" that they were "siblings."

The ten young men were the actual or classificatory children of Lakay from Kakidugen and Baket from Pengegyaben. And Lakay and Baket themselves were classificatory siblings, for, as they reckoned it, Lakay's father (who died of the gunshot wound in 1952) and Baket's father (who died in a Bayombong jail in 1909) were born of a single father and two mothers (see Fig. 1). But kin ties between the children of Lakay and Baket were growing tenuous because of the short span of Ilongot genealogical memory. Due to their reticence about the names of the dead, plus their reluctance to repeat stories about predecessors whose lives did not overlap their own, Ilongots whose parents or grandparents are not siblings are unlikely to be able to specify the genealogical links through which they are related. Thus the children of Lakay and Baket knew they were related because their grandfathers were half-brothers, but they knew that their children would no longer know the exact nature of their connections, and they felt themselves to be drifting apart as kin. Had they not renewed their kinship through intermarriages (as would have been almost certain had the Kakidugens remained on the northwestern margin), the bonds of diffuse enduring solidarity between them would have loosened considerably.

During the years of 1936–45 the Pengegyaben people visited their kin in Kakidugen more frequently than the reverse. The two groups often hunted together in the forest midway between the two local clusters, camping where the Kakidugens sought refuge in 1945 and later settled. From there the hunters used to walk to the northwestern margin, where they traded with lowlanders, giving dried meat and rattan in exchange for cloth and metal pots. In the course of cultivating their lapsed ties, one of Tukbaw's older half-brothers from Pengegyaben began to court a Kakidugen woman. Thus, on the eve of the Japanese invasion of the Philippines, the bonds among those 20 people were still in the earliest phases of reactivation through the efforts of Lakay and Baket.

In this chapter, I shall delineate the source of the collective consciousness of the group in their interlaced memories of the catastrophic events of 1942–45.* Chapter 5 will show how the ten young men came to take heads. Three of them took heads in 1945 and another in 1950. Shortly after Luku beheaded the Butag huntsman in 1952, five more of the group took heads. The young men recollected that they were mutually energized by the rivalry among peers, and hence they followed one another by taking heads in quick succession (much as their historical consciousness, as discussed earlier, would dictate). The last member of the group to take a head did so in 1954. In Chapter 6 I describe how the youths, already connected through mutual visits and collective raids, "wove their hearts together" in a marital alliance that took place over the brief span of 1955–58. The intermarriages endured, at least until after we had left in 1974, as the 20 people "followed" and "held one another's hands" through coordinated residential moves. The people who had come of age together grew old together.

THE YEARS OF WAR, 1941–45

The Japanese invaded the Philippines on December 8, 1941. Immediately thereafter, news of the alien soldiers reached the Ilongot hills. During the following years of war, news of Japanese troop movements made its way to even the most interior reaches of Ilongot country. "We hear about them (the Japanese)," Tukbaw said in his life history, "all the time throughout the year: some news comes from Tegē, near Kasibur; some news comes from the other

---

*This chapter suggests a number of parallels with Fussell (1975). In particular, I would stress that a catastrophic event may have enduring consequences for the remembered past at the same time that it is recollected through conventional storytelling forms. In the Ilongot case, memories of the harrowing days of June 1945 were a crucial ingredient in making the 20 people a well-defined historical generation.

side toward Carranglan" (see Map I, p. 34). The Kakidugens (then living in Tegē, on the northwestern margin) relayed the news from Kasibur, while the Pasigiyans (then living in Abēka, on the south-western margin) brought the news from Carranglan.

Most of the Rumyads, having experienced only the worst from soldiers, responded to what they perceived as a threatening incursion of troops by completing their return to their pre-1923 homeland in the most central sector of Rumyad land. In so doing they sought a place of refuge that was at once deeply familiar and as far as possible from the lowlands. During this period only the Kakidugens did not reside with their brethren in the center of Rumyad-lands, for they still felt the contrary pull of their eight intermarriages of 1923–41 with Ilongots from the northwestern margin, where Lakay and the others had been held under house arrest.

Meanwhile, in the center of Rumyad country the number of absent Kakidugen people (then 57) was in the end made up for, more than twice over, by the arrival of increasing numbers of apprehensive families from the western margin of Ilongot country. Those who moved inward followed the particular Rumyad people who "beckoned" them because they were kin and because they had been neighbors on the western margin in 1929–35. During the wartime years the Rumyads and their kin from the western margin lived within shouting distance of one another, gardening up the same slopes and hunting together in the forest; together they "held one another's hands" in mutual support as they confronted their common fate. Through their strategic retreat this heterogeneous group of Ilongots gathered together, so that their increased strength of numbers would fortify them from the perils they faced.

Throughout their early attempts to fend off the Japanese threat, Ilongot actions, as will be seen, repeatedly followed their deep cultural pattern of gathering forces in the center and protecting themselves along the perimeter. The notion enacted in this instance is that of confronting external threats and unexpected afflictions by "concentrating, focusing, gathering together" ('upug) in one place and surrounding that place by a "protective ring, barrier, barricade" (keren). Though this conception orders social action in many areas of Ilongot life, it is perhaps most strikingly objectified in miniature during rice magic, a ceremony of harvest increase, when tiny structures are erected in the center and on the edge of the garden, the former representing a concentration of force and the latter a protective shield. A similar notion, less fully elaborated though more complexly ritualized, guided people's conduct through the 1969 covenant, when they gathered their numbers in order to increase their strength for the confrontation. Unlike its performance on such formalized occasions as magic or the celebration of a covenant, the relatively spontaneous repeated enactment of this conception in the face of the Japanese danger provided an indication of how pervasive and deep this cultural form, an integral part of their sense of history, actually was.

Through the wartime years, the Rumyads and their companions lived in ever-increasing danger of violence, both from the alien soldiers and from other Ilongots. Like the period of 1923–28, this epoch was characterized by the presence of soldiers, who were a major factor in producing a sharply increasing spiral of internal beheadings among Ilongots. Kadēng said that during this time "there was no more government," and thus "young men rushed to take heads." And indeed they did. In 1943, for instance, Tukbaw (then 20) participated in the second of two Rumyad vendettas, one on the heels of the other, against the Bēduk people. The Rumyads were taking advantage of that moment of general violence and retaliating for the role of the Bēduks (along with the Butags) in the arrests of 1940, as well as for their having egged on the soldiers who in 1942 murdered Bayaw's brother. Tukbaw and the others from central Rumyad mounted their attack during the first light of dawn, killing the inhabitants of two households of Bēduks who had sought refuge near Carranglan (on the southwestern margin) earlier that year after six of their companions had been beheaded by the first Rumyad raiding party. But just as the raiders were about to climb into the two houses and behead the corpses strewn there, a band of Japanese soldiers arrived on the scene and began to open fire, following after them through the forest in hot, if brief, pursuit. That was the first time Tukbaw had seen a Japanese soldier.

His aroused hopes frustrated, Tukbaw pleaded with his father over the course of the next year, saying, "Father, why am I still the same? Why have I not yet taken a head?" His father urged him to be patient.

The year of 1944 was a precarious time for the Pengegyaben people, with whom Tukbaw's fate had been cast. Infirm men, hapless women, and orphaned children, these were the 28 who remained after the Butag-instigated arrests of eight able-bodied men from their midst only four years before. At this time Tukbaw was the only able-bodied man in his household, but at 21 years of age he had not yet acquired the skills and stamina of adulthood. The only other men in the house, his father (aged 64) and his older half-brother (30), were both enfeebled by tuberculosis; the seven women residing there were his mother (62), two older half-sisters (42 and 40), whose husbands had been among those arrested, two younger unmarried sisters (19 and 15), and two nieces (14 and 13). Pengegyaben was clearly vulnerable, inviting the three attacks by Butags that occurred during those years of war.

Although the removal of its healthy adult men doubtless diminished its supply of meat, Tukbaw's household enjoyed an extraordinary harvest of rice. Finding themselves unencumbered by newborn infants as an indirect result of the arrests, the women were free to labor with such intensity that in that year they yielded the still-discussed harvest of 150 "units" of 10 "bundles" of rice. (One hundred units of 10 bundles is considered a bumper crop.) Following a pattern dating from the incursions of soldiers in the 1920's, the men of the household built two granaries in hidden recesses of the forest and there stored a portion of the rice. Rumors circulating in the hills that year made them uneasy, and they feared that once again, as so often in the past, soldiers might raid and burn their homes and crops.

In about March 1945, when Ilongot men were clearing the forest for new swiddens and women were cleaning their gardens from the year before, a group of Pasigiyan people, as Tukbaw told it, arrived from their homes in Abēka on the southwestern margin with the following news: "The Japanese have burst upon us; they drove us from our homes and we have taken flight. We must kill them at our place; we must repay those who drove us from our homes and made us feel hunger." Though the Ilongots seem not to have made this connection, the arrival of the Japanese in Abēka was surely a preparation for defense against the returning American troops. It was clear that the main line of Japanese defense would extend along Highway 5 on the western margin in an effort to close every approach to the Balete Pass area near the southwestern corner of Ilongot territory (see Smith 1963: 491–531; see also Map 1).

As the older men orated about this calamitous turn of events, Tukbaw had his father ask the Pasigiyans to escort him on their raid against the Japanese in Abēka. The older men quickly agreed that Tukbaw (then 22) and none other would take the head of their first victim. They lost no time, immediately starting to walk westward.

Once near Abēka, Tukbaw and the Pasigiyans spent the day spying on the Japanese troops as they went through their daily activities. That evening they decided to wait in ambush for the lone unlucky soldier whose chore it was to come to the stream at dawn and fetch water. The next morning, Tukbaw said, "In an instant I grabbed that head with the short hair." He then tossed away the head and fled into the forest.

After the raiders had returned to central Rumyad, they went off on a hunt in which they collected meat from ten animals, while the women stayed home and pounded an extra store of rice from their abundant harvest of the year before. The people from the immediate vicinity then gathered at Tukbaw's house, where they killed a chicken and a pig in sacrifice. After they had feasted on the game and rice, they danced with their arms outstretched, their legs flexed, and their bodies taut. A chorus of women squatting in the center sang in resonant antiphony with a chorus of men swaying in rhythmic anger and circling around the outer edge, in yet another enactment of the idea of collecting force in the center that radiates out toward the perimeter of the social field.

As soon as the celebration had ended, Tukbaw carried a share of the meat and rice to the Pasigiyans who had just arrived in central Rumyad with the intention of setting up new homes alongside the Pengegyabens. The Pasigiyans were to be the last group of refugees to migrate into the heart of Rumyad territory before the massive influx of Japanese.

Meanwhile, out of fear of the Japanese, the Kakidugen people had moved east in the first month of 1945 to what would be their post-1945 location. Late in May, a man from Buwa on the northwestern margin arrived with the unsettling news that his people had been driven from their homes by ten armed Japanese soldiers. Like the Pasigiyans and the Pengegyabens before them, the Buwas and Kakidugens banded together in a relatively interior place, increasing their numerical strength in order to retaliate against the enemy on the periphery.

Lakay and his father rushed from Kakidugen back to Buwa with the displaced people. After sizing up the situation, they decided that the best course would be to offer their services to the ten Japanese soldiers. Because the soldiers were all armed with modern weapons, the Ilongots' only hope was to deceive them through shows of cooperation until an opportune moment arrived. When the Japanese major asked them to search for an escaped carabao they did so, and when he told them to carry a machine gun to Kasibur they did so. One night all ten soldiers fell asleep—the awaited moment. Caught off guard, every Japanese in the house was beheaded. Their belongings were taken and their bodies were burned, for Lakay and the others, fearing retaliation from another band of soldiers, wanted to leave no traces of their deed.

The Japanese threat was thus eliminated for the time being. Unlike the Pasigiyans, the Buwa people remained in their former homes and continued to plant their gardens. Lakay and his father returned to their homes, where they continued planting in the company of a few newly arrived lowlanders, in hiding because they had just escaped from Japanese prisons.

In the meantime the Japanese forced yet a third group to abandon their homes and flee east, this time to the Reayan River, where the Bēawet people lived. This refugee group included Butags and Tengas (the mediators in the 1969 Butag-Rumyad covenant), and they were received as relatives and given a portion of freshly cleared garden plots to plant and harvest as their own. Together the refugees and their hosts made every approach to the Reayan homesteads bristle with sharpened bamboo stakes and lethal devices that would fire an arrow into the heart of an unwary passerby.

It did not occur to the Rumyads at that moment to retaliate for the Butag-instigated arrests of 1940. The violent tenor of Ilongot feuding over the previous three years had abruptly become a thing of the past as all Ilongots united in the face of the Japanese, who spread homelessness and fear before them.

But about noon one day in early June 1945, Ilongot dogs on the Reayan River suddenly began to bark at unseen quarry. In an instant the Japanese arrived on the scene and the people bolted into the forest. Once they had set up shelters, the Ilongot men went hunting, and then returned to share the catch. Food and shelter taken care of for the moment, the men, thirsting for vengeance, set up an ambush near their former homes and beheaded two of the Japanese. One of the heads was taken by Bayaw (then only 16), who almost 30 years later recalled the Japanese pursuing him, firing all the way, and he in turn cursing them: "Fuck yourselves, you who brought us hunger."

These beheadings, however, were more a beginning than an ending, for massive numbers of defeated and starving Japanese troops were about to fan out, suddenly and unexpectedly, over the Ilongot landscape. This moment and its aftermath was called the time of the Japanese, an episode of such impact that it became the conceptual dividing line separating the past from an era that merges into the present.

At the time, American troops were pushing north as fast as possible, because they feared that their campaign against the Japanese might become bogged down by the monsoon, which they expected to begin in late May (Smith 1963: 503). In early June of 1945 the American Thirty-seventh Infantry Division spearheaded a lightning drive down the valley along the western edge of Ilongot territory. They followed Highway 5 over Balete Pass and then swept, in a single continuous motion, north down the Magat Valley, moving from the southernmost town (Aritao, June 4) to the northernmost town (Bagabag, June 9) in less than a week. The successful American plan of battle was to take the towns and hold a narrow strip of land on either side of the highway, forcing the Japanese into what a military report called the "uninhabited" hills to the east, where the enemy soldiers would either starve to death or eventually return to the lowlands and surrender. The historian of the Thirty-seventh Infantry reported that as early as June 5 "the remnants [of the Japanese troops] had fled eastward into the foothills of the Sierra Madre Mountains" (Frankel 1948: 353).

The hills where the "remnants had fled," as harsh fortune had it, were the homeland of the Ilongots, who willy-nilly became victims of World War II and suffered epidemics, starvation, and death side by side with the Japanese. For the Ilongots, the timing of this influx of Japanese troops could not have been less opportune, because they were caught in their planting season when the new rice had barely sprouted and the rice from the previous harvest was nearing depletion. Favorable as it was for the movement of troops, the end of the dry season was a time when the Ilongots were at their most vulnerable.

As he began, in 1974, his tape-recorded story of the time of the Japanese, Lakay pointed out the window of his house in Kakidugen and said, "We were in the middle of planting over there, right over there." Dilya, the wife of Lakay's younger brother, in another text described that moment, saying, "I saw two of them and I thought, 'They're soldiers.' They almost caught me, but as soon as I saw them I grabbed Latun [her daughter, then 3] and we fled up the Kakidugen River." Lakay's son Insan recalled his first sight of the Japanese as follows: "About sunrise one morning, as we warmed ourselves by the fire and cut rattan into strips [for carrying fish], our older brother said, 'Soldiers are here. Oh no, they're Japanese.' " Lakay also cited that moment: "My son said to me, 'Father, they're Japanese. They're Japanese, father.' "

While the others fled, Lakay stayed and hid his share of the canteens, tools, and clothing that had belonged to the ten Japanese beheaded at Buwa; he feared retaliation by their companions. But he was captured, and the Japanese captain used emphatic gestures to demand food from him. In Lakay's words, "I gave them corn and they ate it raw; they were starving." The soldiers grabbed every knife and pot in sight before motioning insistently toward the forest, where Lakay fled wthout any implements to get or cook his food. Dilya heard echoing volleys of gunfire which, in Ilongot fashion, she took for a sign of Japanese "anger" at her escape. Lakay knew better, for from a forested hill he saw the soldiers shooting every chicken, pig, and dog that had been left behind. Dilya, carrying her daughter on her back, came upon Insan (then 13) followed by his younger brother, Tepeg (then 11), who was stumbling up a slope with a puppy in his arms. By dusk Lakay, his father, and his younger brother had found their families. That night they ate nothing and slept on the ground.

During the following weeks of flight they went hungry, as Insan described: "Alas, they took our rice and we had nothing to eat. Alas, we went hungry and had to live on hearts of rattan fruit and nuts." Sleeping in 16 different places—one night here, two there, at most four nights in one place—over the next 25 days, the Kakidugens scrambled through the forest as fugitives.

In their stories of wandering in terror, people uniformly listed the names of every foraged item of food and where it was found; every brook crossed and every hill scaled; every spot where they stopped to rest or eat or sleep. Piling place name upon place name, people's sagas of 1945, as noted earlier, appeared initially to be as irrelevant for Ilongot ethnography as they were impossible to suppress. The main virtue of the tales seemed to be their veracity, for no matter how great their detail they showed a high degree of consistency. Misled by the long string of place names, I was slow to realize that what seemed to be at least a year of nothing but hapless wandering actually took only 25 days.

Eventually I came to understand that my mistaken impression was based on a half-truth. The recitation of place names in Ilongot stories is designed to invoke the culturally valued notion of movement through space. Beyond their sheer beauty, such lists indicate that a story is true because the teller has actually seen the named places, which thus lend significance to narratives as disparate as headhunting, hunting, fishing, and the changes in residence and garden sites over the course of a person's life. This is an especially clear instance of the difference between calendar and human time. The events of 1945 as they were told and retold were protracted by naming one place after another, hence the cultural perception of one's passage through an expansive reach of human time in June 1945.

The morning after the Japanese arrived in Kakidugen, Lakay's eldest daughter and his younger brother walked south toward central Rumyad, where they told Tukbaw and the others from Pengegyaben that the Japanese had driven them from their homes. Tukbaw says the response was "Yes, we'll leave [for Kakidugen] tomorrow morning because Tubbē [who was to be a Tenga mediator at the 1969 covenant] has not yet taken a head. We'll go there and kill them [the Japanese]."

The following afternoon the people from central Rumyad reached those who had remained in Kakidugen, and together they decided that by the light of the moon that night they would stalk the two Japanese soldiers who had taken over Lakay's house. Two Pasigiyan refugees from Abēka stepped forward, saying, "Leave it to us, we'll strike the first blow by throwing this hand grenade at them. We known how to do it." It turned out that they did not know how to do it, for the grenade thudded against the house without exploding. Thus warned, one of the soldiers ran through the underbrush and escaped the arrows of his pursuers. The other soldier was caught and beheaded, as planned, by Tubbē. No sooner was the head tossed away than the raiders vanished into the forest, beyond reach of their victim's companions.

Later that night, Tukbaw said, the older people spoke together, saying, "Now what should we do about our companions from Kakidugen? The thing to do is to take them with us to our homes in Keradingan [central Rumyad]." In so "beckoning" their companions from Kakidugen to central Rumyad, the people of Pengegyaben intended to follow a common Ilongot pattern for constructing alliances—whether marital or residential or both—between local clusters. This pattern of alliance formation begins when the prospective host is escorted by the prospective guests on a headhunting expedition that if successful, constitutes at once a gift to the hosts and a statement of mutual allegiance between guests and hosts against the common foe. Sooner or later thereafter the hosts invite the others to live at their place as guests. Social action patterned in this manner shaped events, not only when the Pengegyaben people received their Kakidugen brethren, but also in the three episodes of movement toward the interior described earlier: (1) when the Pasigiyans fled to central Rumyad, (2) when the people from Buwa temporarily retreated to Kakidugen, and (3) when the Bēawets hosted the Butags and Tengas. It was in this context that two of the ten young men listed earlier, Tukbaw and Bayaw, found the opportune moment to take heads.

Escorted by the raiders, the remaining Kakidugen people walked slowly south toward central Rumyad. His companions planned to camp overnight at the trail's midpoint, but Tukbaw felt hungry and decided to go on ahead and reach his home before nightfall. He had passed the trail's highest point and begun to walk downhill toward home when he came upon his brother-in-law sitting motionless on the trail. Startled, fearing the worst, not bothering with the decent silence and betel chews of Ilongot greeting, Tukbaw blurted out, "Why have you come here?" His brother-in-law replied, "We'll never survive. We've been overrun by the Japanese." Tukbaw says that he sobbed and his eyes turned red as he heard that all their crops, even much of the rice from the granaries hidden in the forest, had been devoured by the Japanese.

The rest of the Pengegyaben people gradually arrived. Stunned and in tears, they realized that neither kin nor friends, neither food nor shelter remained as a refuge farther to the interior. They had no place left to go, because the Japanese hordes had penetrated to the very center of Ilongot territory. They began hiking uphill to the midpoint of the trail, where they joined the Kakidugen people.

During the next ten days the two groups traveled together, ever on the move, hoping to discover a haven and finding only that the alien soldiers were ubiquitous. While some of the troops had scattered over the hillsides, most of them at that moment were marching north by northeast along the major rivers in columns so multitudinous that Tukbaw, whimsical in retrospect, likened the sight to that of cockroaches, numerous beyond count, as they crawled along the rattan strips of his floor.

Though on two occasions the refugees stole and shared small portions of food from the soldiers' supplies, what little rice and sweet potatoes were retrieved from central Rumyad granaries and gardens were shared only rarely and never widely. Because they had been forced from their homes so abruptly the Kakidugen people were carrying no rice of their own, and hence they suffered disproportionate hunger. Dilya, for instance, said that even the wife of her uncle (her mother's brother) from Tauyang "turned them away" and told them to leave "because in her flight she was carrying a little bit of rice," and she refused to share with them. Impelled by their relative deprivation, Lakay and his family left the others and hiked north to Kakidugen in the hope that their second-year swidden, nestled away in the forest, might have been overlooked by the Japanese. Fortunately, their hunch proved correct, and for two days Lakay stood guard while one of his daughters and two of his sons, working as hard as they could, dug up sweet potatoes, chopped down sugar cane, and carried load upon load of each into the forest. Then, as Insan said, they "joyfully" began to eat.

On the third day Lakay's worst fears were realized. He arrived only to find that two Japanese soldiers were busily digging sweet potatoes in his garden. While his sons looked on from the safety of a nearby treetop, Lakay (to make a long and oft-told story short) sneaked up on one soldier as he slept that afternoon and, in three swift death blows with a bolo, slashed his victim's face down the middle, then cut a deep gash into his shoulder, and finally severed his hand from his arm. The dead soldier's companion was there in an instant, and he hurled his bayonet at the same time that Lakay released the long-tipped arrow from his bow. Both missiles flew wide of their marks. Brandishing his by then blunt bolo, Lakay chased the soldier, caught him by the seat of his pants as he climbed a fence, and hacked him about the shoulders until he dropped to the ground on the other side. Moving swiftly on his hands and knees, the wounded soldier reached his rifle and began to fire wildly until Lakay withdrew; the soldier than staggered from sight and made his successful escape upstream. Lakay returned at once to the dead soldier, and his eldest son cut off the head and threw it away; his second son, Insan then threw it; and Lakay threw it a third time.

The next morning, Lakay's younger brother and the others arrived from central Rumyad. Lakay immediately asked their help in tracking down the wounded soldier, for he hoped that Insan might take a head. But Lakay's brother refused, saying "Alas, my child is dying. Let's just walk on downhill [to the lowlands]." According to Insan, his father's brother reported the rumor that the Americans were about to bomb the Ilongot hills. The idea that they faced imminent bombardment was simply too much for them: they were already weakened by starvation, plus constant hiking, and they had suffered four deaths from illness on the trail over the past 16 days. They quickly reached their decision and began to flee toward the lowlands.

Tukbaw from Pengegyaben complained that his people were abandoned by the Kakidugens, who "sneaked off" to the lowlands without telling him a word of their plans. Dilya from Kakidugen told me that the situation was more complex, because through their years of house arrest on the northwestern margin she and her companions, in contrast to the Pengegyabens, had come to know the westward trails and had lost their fear of lowlanders. Furthermore, she added, they had no food, and the Pengegyaben people had not only salvaged small stores of rice from their hidden granaries, but they had also brought their hunting dogs with them as they escaped. The people of Kakidugen, as they saw it, had been robbed of the means to survive in the forest and had no choice but to take advantage of their long-term familiarity with the route of escape toward the lowlands.

Lakay and the others spent nine days on their westward trek to the lowlands. On the first day of walking they listened in fear to the heavy cannon fire coming from Buwa, the place where they had earlier beheaded ten Japanese. On the third day they slept in an abandoned lowland village, where they so gorged themselves on fresh corn that their fluid feces burst from their bowels, as Lakay said, "like arrows from a bow." From there they moved slowly for almost another week until, waving white flags above their heads, they entered the first populated village on their path. The next day Lakay bought a chicken, which he sacrificed during a celebration for his eldest son, who some ten days before had "arrived" and taken a head. For the next six months the Kakidugens continued their nomadic existence, moving along Highway 5 from one lowland town to another. They subsisted as best they could on a combination of rations they received from American soldiers and wages they earned, both from agricultural labor for lowlanders and from road construction for soldiers. In January or February 1946 the lowlanders, according to Dilya, turned away the Ilongots, telling them, "Go on and leave now for your homes. There are no more Japanese." Lakay and the others, sensibly enough, took the advice to heart and returned to their homes in the hills, where they renewed their annual horticultural cycle of clearing, burning, planting, weeding, and harvesting.

The Kakidugen survivors who returned to the hills were reduced by 35 percent of what their number had been on that fateful June morning in 1945 when the first Japanese soldiers came down-stream and displaced them from their homes. During that trau-matic historical moment the lives of 20 (out of 57) Kakidugen people were claimed by starvation and by a mysterious ailment that was attributed, probably falsely, to their having inhaled poi-son. The symptoms of the so-called poisoning were a rash of ooz-ing red blisters that erupted on people's legs in the morning and by evening had "climbed" to their "hearts" and inflicted death. For the people of Kakidugen, the events of the time of the Japanese were cataclysmic beyond hyperbole.

In the meantime, the Pengegyabens never walked down to the lowlands. Instead, from June through early August 1945 they re-mained hidden in the depths of the forest, where their salvaged and stolen rice supply was soon depleted. They were compelled to subsist exclusively by foraging, by hunting game, and by gathering wild plants, fruits, and nuts. Fortunately, they had escaped with their hunting dogs; and both men and women participated in bag-ging deer and wild pig. In this crisis, marked as it was by inventive adaptation for survival, the Pengegyaben women exploited their more than four years of experience in the hunt, acquired as an in-direct consequence of the arrests of 1940. In other respects, people from that local cluster simply revived practices of their grandpar-ents, reverting to sparking tinder by striking steel against a flint-stone rather than using matches and pounding the bark from trees into a pliable fabric rather than wearing store-bought cloth. How-ever great their hardships, none of the Pengegyaben people died during their initial period of hiding in the forest.

Not until silence had succeeded the sound of gunfire did they venture out of the forest, in August 1945. Tukbaw said, "We went to our houses and found that gunfire was nowhere to be heard." All was quiet.

Tukbaw's father, still uneasy, explored central Rumyad. In time he came upon a house where he found abundant stores of rice, and pots and pans and canteens and shovels. He surmised that Japanese soldiers were living there and that they had gone to bathe at the river; he immediately gathered his children, and together they car-ried off all the rice and as much of the rest as they could manage. As they fled they heard gunfire behind them; then all was silence once again, and their "hearts lengthened with joy" while they ate the rice.

A few days later they cautiously approached their gardens, where they hoped they might find, still growing and nearly ripe, what little rice they had managed to plant some two months before. On the near end of the garden they saw the stalks bending beneath their full heads of ripened grain, and they listened to the calls of ricebirds as they flew in to feed there. The women could not contain themselves and insisted on caring for their valued food, saying, "Even if I die doing it, I'm going to shoo the ricebirds from the garden." While a young girl (the sister of Tawad and Adēlpig) and her maternal grandmother remained behind to shoo the birds from the rice, the others set off to forage in the forest.

Meanwhile, a lone Japanese soldier was spying on the two women at work in their garden. Later that afternoon he crept closer and closer and then fired two quick shots, killing both women instantly. Despite the danger, the Pengegyaben people could not bear to leave the corpses to rot there in the garden; they were, after all, of the same "body." In fact, Tawad's mother (whose husband had been among those arrested in 1940) in that instant had lost both her mother and her daughter. When a small group from the local cluster returned to bury their dead in the garden, the soldier once again shot and killed a woman, Tawad's mother—completing by grotesque coincidence his slaying of three generations within a family line.

About a week later, the Pengegyabens explored their territory with care and found that only three Japanese soldiers, living in one house, remained. They decided that they would neither flee nor abandon their homes. By the first light of dawn the next morning, they attacked the house where the soldiers were lodged and killed all three of them before they awakened. Heads were taken on that raid by Dinwag (then 27) and two other men. The three decapitations drew the curtain upon the threat from alien soldiers, and so ended the time of the Japanese for the people of Pengegyaben.

Wandering terror, desperate hunger, and gruesome death made the collective memories of 1945 a watershed for the 20 people I first met more than two decades later. Before the Japanese soldiers arrived, they were children who knew nothing because they had experienced nothing. For them the catastrophe became a shared beginning point—a deep trauma later recollected in compelling stories—that extended without a break into their adult years.

CHAPTER FIVE. THE POLITICS OF HEADHUNTING, 1945-1954

Social life, as projected through time, is attuned to the processes of biological reproduction and the phases and duration of human lives. In this sense the life cycle is key among concepts for the study of social reproduction, such as rites of passage, age and sex roles, intergenerational bonds, and the developmental cycle of domestic groups. The human life cycle—linked as it is to the biological processes of birth, growth, maturation, aging, and death—follows a curve from one's initial dependency on those older, through the possibility of one's assuming adult social standing, to one's final dependency on those younger in age. The trajectories of human lives are thus as constant in their broad outlines as they are variable in their myriad and divergent cultural formulations.

It is in their cultural typifications, rather than their concrete particulars, that the course of the life cycle, labor in a garden, and the affairs of domestic life can become embodied in narrative form. The generalized cycles of personal, domestic, and horticultural life are described by Ilongots, not as a formless scatter of points, but in the pattern of a meandering line. Such a synoptic view of the resting points of a lifetime, for instance, informed Tukbaw's transformation of his discrete series of residential moves into a playful winding continuum along which he flew downhill and, descending like a bird, landed at the bottom. Similarly, Ilongots describe the life cycle as continuous movement along a line—initially highly differentiated, then becoming less so (following the pattern of the domestic cycle and indigenous stories, as seen in Chapter 6), as it makes its progression from birth to death.

But cultural typifications do not govern conduct. Ilongot lives are guided less by the automatic application of rules than through political struggles where the stakes are constrained by structural factors and understood in cultural terms. Thus cultural views of the life cycle provide both an idiom for debate during the unfolding of events and the terms for retrospective interpretations of particular outcomes. In what follows I begin rather than conclude with cultural typifications, because only they can render intelligible the politics of headhunting.

THE ILONGOT MALE LIFE CYCLE

My outline of the Ilongot male life cycle—a composite rather than a particular biography—is based on my knowledge of a number of Ilongots at various phases of their lives. Through a synthesis of interviews and observations over 30 months of research, I have pieced together a generic version of an Ilongot man's life. Though Ilongots did not, in the day-to-day course of things, recite the phases of the life cycle, they immediately understood and readily described a generic life cycle, one for men and another for women. The idea was clearly close to the surface of Ilongot conceptions of life. Culturally, the schema of the life cycle represents a set of expectations in terms of which people live their lives, and without which their lives would remain relatively opaque, both to them and to me. Like all conventions that shape and inform human life, the typification of the male life cycle provides an idiom for interpreting individual life experiences, whether unique or universal, surprising or humdrum, rebellious or conformist.

Ilongots construct the life cycle more as a continuous process of movement than as a series of neatly compartmentalized stages. In their approach to the middle years, as Ilongots view it, people move through three successive stages: (1) the infantile development of motor skills; (2) the youthful learning of subsistence tasks; and (3) the adult knowledge of effective speech in delicate social situations. This movement goes outward in space from home and parents into the more distant domains of subsistence labor and public assemblies; its rate is slow, as it unfolds gradually in the cumulative mastery of a series of discrete skills. By the middle span of life the incremental movement nearly ceases altogether, as adults draw close to their apex of cultural mastery. It is not until the onset of the infirmities of old age that the direction of movement shifts, as people "return to their childhood" in what Ilongots regard not as a second childhood on the far end of life's arc, but as a return to one's former state (much as a traveler returns home after a long journey). In Ilongot terms, life's departing trek from childhood is slower, more differentiated in its steps, than the return to childhood brought by senility.

Though stressing continuities over the discontinuities of movement through a lifetime, Ilongots still divide the life cycle into the four phases of childhood, youth, adulthood, and old age. I shall restrict my discussion to men, rather than women, as they move through these phases (see R. Rosaldo 1976).

Childhood. Childhood is conceived of as the progressive mastery of a series of adult forms of competence, beginning with motor skills and moving on to subsistence tasks. Infants become toddlers through the following culturally recognized series of steps: (1) he smiled; (2) he lifted his head; (3) he sat up; (4) he crawled; (5) he tried to stand; (6) he walked; (7) he spoke. Before he speaks, the infant is said to be without "thought" (except, some allow, when he cries for his mother); once he speaks, he is said to have acquired the capacity for "thought" and "knowledge." Sawad, for instance, said of toddlers, who from their second year are "told to fetch" (*tuydek*) things inside the house, that "the source of their knowledge is our telling them to fetch things." When a toddler is "told," she explained, "Go and fetch water," and actually does so, the adult says, "There, he now knows it; there, he found that word." Knowledge, for a child at any rate, is a matter of knowing how to respond to instructions.

In later years the child is told to fetch things away from the house, perhaps some sugar cane from the garden or a container of water from the stream. Still later, boys begin to "follow" their fathers and girls their mothers as they learn an increasingly gender-specific series of skills based on the sexual division of labor. Initially boys play among themselves, shooting toy arrows and later pollarding small trees and bushes; then they hoe in the gardens with the women, and eventually they follow after the men as they clear trees and brush for the gardens and hunt in the forest. In these years the progressive acquisition of cultural competence is more loosely ordered than before, because the child is mastering not only kinds but also degrees of skill. For instance, the child who knows how to pollard a tree still has to acquire the strength, stamina, and further skills to climb higher and do a full day's work.

Childhood gradually shades off into youth, more as a pair of overlapping phases than as two discrete stages of life. While this transition is protracted and elastic, it is marked in part by the physical changes of puberty and in part by increasing autonomy in work, that is, the increasing capacity to do chores without being told what to do. As boys look forward to the rest of their lives they see beyond their youths to their adult years as the culmination of their progressive mastery of cultural competence.

It was when Ilongot men reflected on their past that they most clearly distinguished youth from childhood. They recalled their childhood years without a word about carefree play or lost innocence; instead, they spoke of the frustrations of ever learning yet another adult skill as they struggled to realize in themselves their culture's design for adult manhood. Youth, at least looking backward, was an entirely different matter; it was idealized by an old man as the high point of his life, a time of beauty charged with strength, energy, and anger. Older Ilongots often sighed with nostalgia, as they remembered events from those irretrievable years when they were graceful, vital, agile, and thin at the waist.

Youth. Youth is a time of beauty, ordeals, and stress. Paragons of beauty, as vain as they are uneasy about their ever-changing bodies, young men adorn themselves with bright red kerchiefs, tight metal armbands, and delicately crafted calflets, belts, necklaces, and earrings. They are called the "quick ones," for they are energetic, light of step, and free to travel widely and often. Those years, for Ilongots, are the prime of life.

I often saw unmarried young men clustered away from the rest, where they would wrap their arms and legs around one another as they whispered secrets, giggling and blushing now and again. If at those moments they seemed bent on nothing more than the cultivation of their own vanity and silliness, at other moments they

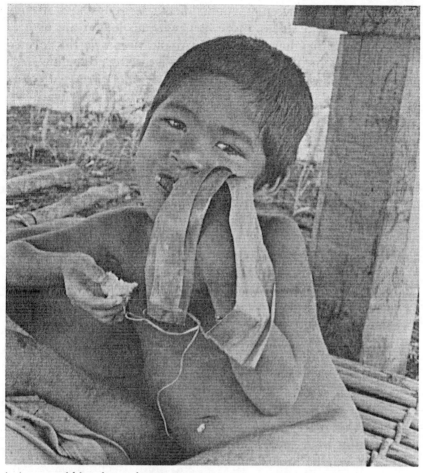

A six-year-old boy beneath a rice granary.

lived lives of intense emotional involvement. As a group they would go through a series of ordeals—their *rites de passage*—from teeth-filing (out of fashion from about 1960) through head-taking to marriage. Subject as they are to such severe tests of manhood, it is little wonder that youths are regarded as volatile. Indeed, their moods and passions are subject to dramatic ups and downs; and many youths describe themselves in song and story alike as weeping in their fierce, as yet frustrated, desire to "arrive" and take a head.

The source of the weeping youths' fierce desire is above all envy of their peers and elders, those men who no longer are novices (*siap*) because they have taken a head and thus won the coveted right to wear finely curved red hornbill earrings dangling from their upper lobes. During a raid it is the older men, with their greater stamina and knowledge, who "care for" and "lead" the youths through their critical life passage. In fact, an older man is usually the first to reach the victim, and it is often he who severs the head so it can be thrown away by the youth, who thus ceases to be a novice. The point in Ilongot headhunting is not for one man to take more heads than others, but for all men who are peers to take at least one head and thereby lose once and for all their status as novices. To take a head is, in Ilongot terms, not to capture a trophy, but to "throw away" a body part, which by a principle of sympathetic magic represents the cathartic throwing away of certain burdens of life—the grudge an insult has created, or the grief over a death in the family, or the increasing "weight" of remaining a novice when one's peers have left that status.

Regarded as a ritual, headhunting resembles a piacular sacrifice: it involves the taking of a human life with a view toward cleansing the participants of the contaminating burdens of their own lives. Taking a head is a symbolic process designed less to acquire anything (whether so-called soul stuff or fertility) than to remove something. What is ritually removed, Ilongots say, is the weight that grows on one's life like vines on a tree. Once cleansed through participation in a successful raid, the men are said to become "light" in weight, "quick" of step, and "red" in complexion. Thus youths accentuate and older men recover—if only for a relatively short and gradually fading span of time—their characteristic youthful vigor as "quick ones." In other words, the raiders regress through this ritual process to a culturally idealized phase of life.

When a victim is beheaded, older men discard the weight of age and recover the energy of their youth, whereas youths advance from novice status and adorn themselves with red hornbill earrings. To wear such earrings, they say, is to gain the admiration of young women and to be able to answer back when other men taunt. And taunt they do. Novices who marry, for instance, must somehow withstand the culturally stereotyped "insult" that they

A young man uprooting clumps of runo grass to clear a garden site.

have designs on beheading their wives. Maniling put the matter more broadly: "Others will scorn you if you marry without taking a head." While at certain historical moments they have married without doing so, it is little wonder that young men have usually hoped to take a head as a prelude to marriage. In effect, by taking a head the young man has cleared his path toward marriage: he has become at once more attractive to women and better able to defend himself by "answering back" throughout the ordeals imposed on him by his girlfriend's father and brothers.

Lest there be confusion, let me emphasize that it is not obligatory for Ilongot men to take a head before marriage. The view that the former is a necessary precondition for the latter is as mistaken as it is widespread in Philippine ethnography and popular culture. After a brief visit to the region, Albert Jenks reported that, among the Ilongots, "no man may marry who has not first taken a head" (1905: 174); thus this mistaken view made its appearance in the modern ethnographic literature. Jenks's version, however, was little more than a sober rendition of the lurid tale that has circulated in the valleys surrounding Ilongot territory from at least the late nineteenth century (see Campa 1891: 568–69; Savage 1904: 329).

When the firetree blossoms, the tale has it, the Ilongot mating season arrives and lustful unmarried young men go on the warpath in search of Christian heads. Those who find victims present the severed heads (or other body parts) to their prospective brides as a gift. On June 8, 1963, for example, the *Chronicle* of Manila reported: "It is during the summer months when Ilongots observe their mating season. It is part of the Ilongot's marriage ritual to present a Christian head to his prospective bride." Like other stereotypes of supposedly alien peoples, this tale endows Ilongots with a bestial character (their mating season) and barbaric folkways (their wedding gift; see R. Rosaldo 1978a). Suffice it to add that the victim's head is presented neither to the bride nor to anyone else; it is, as I said, simply thrown away.

It is through taking a head (if he does so) that the young man takes the first major step from his childhood and youth, centered in his family of origin, toward his adult and elderly life, centered in his family of marriage. Headhunting and marriage are the two critical moments in a period conceived of as the only significant rupture in the otherwise continuous course of the life cycle. Unlike the gradual transition from childhood to youth, the young man who marries ceases definitively to be a youth and becomes a man. Celebrated in ritual, story, song, and oratory, this change in social status is culturally elaborated to a greater extent than any other throughout the Ilongot lifetime.

Adulthood. Adulthood begins with marriage. At that time the couple is described with phrases that suggest at once sexual union and the cessation of more youthful movement; they are said to have "had intercourse" or "sat down" or "stopped." To marry is to come to rest for a moment.

Initial postmarital residence is uxorilocal by household: the husband moves into the home of his wife's parents. There he is marked as an outsider: he calls his in-laws by coined personal names or the appropriate kin term because he is forbidden to use their true personal names, while they are free to use his. In time, especially if the wife has younger sisters who later marry, the married couple may move out of the house, yet continue to live nearby and thus still "follow" the wife's parents in moving from one place to another. As time passes and the wife's parents become feeble with age, they in return begin to follow a younger married couple, usually their youngest daughter and her husband. In the end the husband ceases to be a stranger to his own home, for the married couple begins to "lead," while their daughters and sons-in-law follow over the course of their various residential moves. In that manner the developmental cycle of the domestic group returns once again to its beginning point.

When they reach adulthood, men have mastered the cultural "knowledge" available to them. Certainly by the time they marry, they have already become competent in the routine subsistence tasks of hunting, foraging, and horticulture. Adult men are said to be the "same"; none stands out above the others, and no man commands or flatly tells another what to do. In hunting, for instance, people insisted that all men were equally competent, or else they singled out a "quick one" for his ability to track game or hunt alone at night. Yet when I tabulated the number of animals killed by 32 men of Kakidugen, Pengegyaben, and Kēyat during September–November 1968 (the season when game is fat from feeding on acorns), I found clear variation both within and between age groups, as follows:

Age of men	15–24	25–34	35–44	45–54	55–64	65–74
Number of men	6	7	6	7	3	3
Mean number of animals killed per man	7	8	13	10	5	0

To my surprise, I discovered that men were at the height of their abilities in the middle years of 35–44, rather than in their youth. The least able in the hunt, it turned out, were men under 25 and over 55. Hunting ability was best represented in graphic form

An adult man dressed in a red hornbill head-dress and wearing a headhunting bolo. He holds a shield as he duels.

neither as a horizontal straight line nor as a line declining steadily downward from youth through adulthood to old age; instead, it more nearly resembled a classic bell-shaped curve, with its apex in adulthood and its two outward-sloping lower edges in youth and old age.

Adults both refused to boast about how much game they had bagged, and persisted in maintaining their doctrine that no man was a more gifted huntsman than another. When I told Tukbaw what he already knew full well—who had killed which animals and when—he admitted that some men had more "energy for work," or more effective hunt magic than others. But I should tell nobody, he said, especially himself, about the rank order I had

An adult man resting from the hunt. His bow and arrows, betel pouch, and bolo in its scabbard are next to him.

constructed. As others said much the same thing, it became clear that they held a long-run view and saw that they too would age and those younger would in turn take their places. The gifted huntsman of today would become the incompetent old man of to-morrow. Moreover, the idea of a hierarchy based on hunting ability or anything else was culturally alien, indeed suppressed, in large measure because Ilongots coordinated their movements in social activities—whether in raiding, making a covenant, arranging a marriage, or organizing a hunt or fishing expedition—through the conventional idiom that all men were the same, equally men. Men who found themselves again and again compelled to cooperate on short-term projects felt they could not enlist the aid of men who stood above or below them on any imagined ladder. Only equals, as they saw it, could work together in improvised and coordinated harmony.

Though youth is celebrated for its freedom of movement and physical beauty, it is during adulthood that a man reaches his prime of productivity and influence. What a man has lost in quickness he has more than gained in stamina, and the edge of his youthful "anger" has been tempered by wider experience and deeper knowledge. His knowledge during adulthood increases less through the already mastered chores of subsistence than through the refined accomplishments that different men cultivate to various degrees. For instance, some sing, or play the flute or violin or bamboo zither; others practice such crafts as jewelry making or wood carving or tying elegant knots to adorn and support houses; still others develop their verbal abilities and become orators. A noted orator whose speech is forceful in its persuasive power and subtle in its elaborate tropes may come to achieve influence and reputation beyond his local cluster. Talikaw described a generic man's coming to orate:

He fully knew how to seek everything for himself. He now learned how to answer back and forth in speech; he learned how to answer back even when people said bad things to him. He now truly orated. For a long time it is he, the one who orates, who is called to every single public assembly where people orate because he has learned; he has come now to know everything. When he was a child he always got things just right and that's why he knows so much so well.

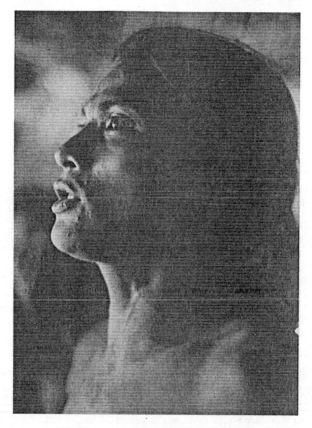

An adult man orating.

Indeed, in general Ilongots view oratory as a man's ultimate achievement, his most significant way to gain a social confirmation of worth.

Culturally less glorified than a youth, an adult man is clearly in his prime as a hunter, an orator, a craftsman, or a musician, for he still has enough strength to bring to bear the knowledge of his years. But as a man reaches his fifties, his body becomes undeniably heavier; his eyesight grows dimmer; his legs begin to ache more sharply than before. These changes, like the gradual change from childhood to youth, take place piecemeal, and no clear line of demarcation separates adulthood from old age. In time, nonetheless, a man and those around him agree that he has grown old, and he begins to be called *lakay*.

Na'mung as an adult man in the prime of life, 1908. Photograph by William Jones. (*Courtesy Field Museum Natural History, Chicago.*)

Old age. Old age is a time of decline from the prowess of adulthood and the idealized energy of youth. Their tendons too aged to climb trees, old men chop the underbrush in clearing gardens; their eyes too dim to hit the mark, they tend the dogs in collective hunts; their wits too dull to muster the sharp retort, they retire to the margins in oratorical confrontations. Respectfully cared for because they once cared for those who followed after them, the elderly have lost too much of their strength and their "anger" to be highly venerated for their wisdom.

In their local groups, old men are related to everybody younger except their own children as '*apu*, "parent's parent/spouse's parent." They are regarded, at times even revered, as the "source" of all those in succeeding generations.

But this reverence is more a passive acclamation of sentiment than an active entitlement to privilege. If elders are idealized, it is less in their own eyes than in the memories of those younger than themselves. The most extreme case I came upon of a venerated elder was that of Na'mung, a man who as a vigorous adult had hosted William Jones in 1908. When, 60 years later, I showed copies of Jones's photographs of Na'mung to a man of about 40, he began to weep and thump his chest, saying he had never seen this old man in his prime. He then reminisced about how devoted he was to his hunchbacked 'apu, whom he had known over a quarter of a century before as an enfeebled old man near death. He remembered Na'mung as follows:

We learned from him and from no other person. He taught us everything, all that we know of the forest. He showed us how to prepare the trap for wild pigs; he told us how to do everything. Whenever he asked anything of us we followed his wishes because he was our 'apu. He used to ask us to give him our belongings, and we could not refuse for we feared and respected him.

If old men retain any active influence, it is no longer based on their prowess in productive labor or their forceful persuasiveness in oratory. Instead, their influence is more restricted in scope, residing either in their memories of past events or, perhaps, in their pivotal position in a locally dominant sibling set. In the latter case, siblings achieve a dominant local position, if ever, during a late phase of the domestic cycle; they do so through private maneuvers designed to bring an entire set of brothers and sisters together in one place, where they can constitute the "trunk" of their local group. Such fortunate siblings are assured, not that they can boss their neighbors, but that in their old age they will be able to count on the support of nearby relatives.

In the former case, the remembered past becomes critical in moments when knowledge of the early phases of a feud, or of the distant genealogical links between people, might affect the negotiation of payments during a covenant or a marriage. Ilongots accept as veridical not what a man has heard secondhand, but what he has witnessed. Kadēng, for instance, nicely illustrated this cultural tenet when he began his life history by saying, "When I opened my eyes and first knew who other people were, I saw our grandfather while he was still alive." Kadēng's point of departure was not hearsay about his grandfather's deeds, but his certain remembered knowledge of what he had seen. Seemingly secure at the very least as repositories of the remembered past, the very old, however, are caught in a dilemma as poignant as it is inexorable: those who have seen the most in their lifetimes are the most likely to be afflicted initially by lapses of memory and later by the chronic forgetfulness of senility.

Lakay's situation is representative of the predicaments of Ilongot old age. When I last saw the old man in 1974 he was 80 years old. At the time he was the only living member of the sibling set whose fading shadow still dominated Kakidugen. He often told me stories of what he had seen during his youth—of his arrest in 1923, of his raid against the Payupays in 1927, and more. If anything he was more approachable than five years before, when he was less accustomed to his condition and more acutely ashamed to forget a name or garble an incident. That year of 1974 he had worked, as people said, with the energy of a youth in clearing the underbrush from his garden. Proud as he was in his accomplishment, his fear was clear to all: next year, the following year, or perhaps the year after that, he would probably become too feeble even to clear underbrush. Lakay's daughter-in-law Midalya told me in private that eventually, as with others she had seen age, his eyes would grow dimmer, his hearing fainter, his memory more confused, and his back more hunched, until he became a dependent invalid.

Lakay said to me that, grateful as he was to be surrounded by his grandchildren, he nonetheless became lonely every time he thought about how few of his age-mates remained alive—they, after all, had been "quick ones" together. Even as we were preparing to leave Kakidugen in late November 1974, an old man from far downstream, Lakay's classificatory brother and peer, sent a youth with the message that he had fallen ill and that he wished to see Lakay, his "brother," one last time before he died. Lakay was too ill with flu at the time to meet the request. The day before we left,

Lakay as an old man, feeding his hunting dogs, 1968.

the old man gave me his bow and arrow: perhaps, he said, we would not see one another again.

In depicting more generally the debilities of old age, Talikaw concluded his narrative of the generic life cycle with the following speech, that of a younger man silencing the ramblings of his aged father:

He [the aged father] has now returned to his childhood. We [his children] now say to him, "Why do you, old as you are, go right ahead and speak. Try now to remain silent, because things no longer are the way they were when you were a quick one; things no longer are the way they were when your body was unbent and your tendons were taut for, alas, you now have grown old. It no longer is the way it was when we entrusted ourselves to you, our father. Do not misunderstand and take offense because we, your children, tell you to be quiet because you have now become old.

If only you were still quick, we would not then come and say anything to you, and you would do things however you were doing them because you already had knowledge. But the reason we come and silence you is because it no longer is the way it was when you could answer back to those who were the same, equally human."

Indeed, as I saw a number of times, youths sometimes sharply tell their failing elders to shut up when they speak out of turn; at other times they silence them with Talikaw's equally insistent blend of anxious concern and delicate tact. What is at issue in both cases is that the aging man who has lost his more youthful strength and anger must retire to the margins of social life, where he can expect, Ilongots say, to be cared for with respect by the younger men who have come to replace him. A man may idealize his lost youth but never his old age, for the final years are not easy.

A TIME OF REGENERATION, 1945–1949

My use of cohort analysis as a conceptual tool for viewing society in historical perspective has certain consequences for the study of developmental processes, including the life cycle and the domestic cycle, that should be made explicit at this juncture. Like other facets of social structure, the regularities of developmental cycles have all too often been reified as if they were immutable structures that generate events, yet somehow remain invulnerable to the vicissitudes of historical change. The alternative view I would propose is that developmental processes be seen, not as the automatic application of structural rules, but, in a statistical manner, as one or more central tendencies in a scatter of possibilities.*

Reconceiving social regularities as a number of probabilities, rather than as the mechanical outcome of structural rules that govern conduct, has at least two consequences for doing ethnographic history. First, the observed outcomes of social processes must be understood in political terms. Because things might have turned out other than they did, the problem is to reconstruct events as

---

*The distinction I have drawn here is similar to that made by Claude Lévi-Strauss (1966) between mechanical and statistical models. In these terms, Ilongot society requires the use of statistical models for its elucidation. It is worth noting that Clyde Kluckhohn (1941) advocated a probabilistic model for the study of cultural patterns.

they unfold in order to determine what the actors thought was at stake. How did they attempt to realize their ambitions? And what in the end were the intended and unintended results of their actions? Second, social regularities should be conceived of as cultural typifications, that is, a loosely organized body of constructs that serve less to regulate conduct than to provide the terms within which action becomes intelligible. In retrospect, people use cultural typifications to see the pattern in past events, and perceptions of the past can in turn guide people's conduct as they attempt to shape their futures.

The aftermath of 1945 was a four-year period during which the dominant concerns of the stunned Ilongots were regeneration, recovery, and restoration. Tukbaw, for instance, concluded his story of the time of the Japanese by invoking the intertwined themes of production, growth, and reproduction. He spoke of the renewal of the horticultural cycle, from an initial lean year to increasingly fat years; he recalled the year-by-year growth of his younger sisters and nieces, saying, "These children had nearly become young women who could be entrusted to do tasks on their own"; he remembered his own coming of age, his gradual entrance into courtship, and his first marriage—in 1948 when he was 25. Like Tukbaw, the other four men who married into or out of Kakidugen and Pengegyaben in 1947–48 had taken Japanese heads. These marriages provide another index of the immediate postwar stress on generativity, in that they were the only five that took place in those two local clusters during the decade of 1945–54.

The Kakidugens at this time were still intermarrying with the Bēnabēs of the northwestern margin, where Lakay had been confined after 1923.* In 1948, for instance, Lakay's oldest daughter, Wagat (then 23), married a Bēnabē in the ninth marriage between the two peoples over the quarter-century 1923–48 (during which

*In Chapter 2 I called the people on the northwestern margin Tabakus rather than Bēnabēs, because I was referring to the intermarriages with the Kakidugens. Both bērtan names—Bēnabēs and Tabakus—apply to people who live in the same area, but the Bēnabēs are all the people in the area, whereas the Tabakus are but a part of the larger group. All Tabakus are Bēnabēs, but not all Bēnabēs are Tabakus. The relationship between Bēnabēs and Tabakus is like that between Rumyads and Peknars. Insan, for instance, could, depending on context, say he is Peknar (through his father) and Tabaku (through his mother), or Rumyad (through his father) and Bēnabē (through his mother). I shall consider these issues at some length in Chapter 7.

there were only 17 Kakidugen marriages; thus over half were with the Bēnabēs). This marriage, then, was also a political union—at least in its consequences, if not in the designs of the two lovers. Wagat said that she and her Bēnabē lover had "wrapped our legs around one another like vines" and talked together, affirming their true mutual affection, with her father's full, if tacit, knowledge. Much later Lakay exploded in "anger" because he said, his daughter's marriage was a surprise to him. Wagat insisted, when I asked further, that Lakay's only reason for this conduct was the general practice of Ilongot fathers (and brothers, if they are of age) to display their "anger" by challenging the young men, who must show their mettle as part of the slow process of marriage.

Lakay had a different version of the same episode to tell. He insisted that it was not until one day in 1948 that he suddenly discovered that his daughter had been sleeping with a Bēnabē man all along. That day, Lakay said, he had just arrived from central Rumyad, where he had gone to bury his oldest son, who had died of illness in the prime of his youth only three years after beheading the Japanese soldier in the garden. When Lakay discovered Wagat's lover he was already in a foul mood, and he immediately began to fire his weapon into the air, hoping to frighten his daughter's lover or at any rate to test his courage. The sources of Lakay's anger were two. First, he felt his opinion had been ignored, for he had wanted Wagat to marry Tukbaw from Pengegyaben. Second, he thought the marriage was a political mistake because too great a proportion of the Bēnabē men had taken Kakidugen women (seven of the nine intermarriages).

In the end the Bēnabē suitor remained unbending in the face of such threatening gestures, and Lakay consented to the marriage of his by then pregnant daughter, saying (according to Wagat), "What can be done once they've gone so far? We can't take her back because she's become an old woman." Shortly thereafter, the Bēnabē man moved into Lakay's house with Wagat, and his relatives came and presented Lakay with a large blanket and a small metal pot. At that point the marriage was public and completed. Wagat's first child, a boy, was born in 1949; he died shortly after he sat but before he crawled, later that year. Their second child, a girl, was born in 1950, and she lived long enough to walk. Wagat had no more children after that, and her first marriage ended in divorce.

Ilongots describe the initial postwar years as the time when they became "still, stopped, motionless" (*pedeg*). The term pedeg in this usage refers at once to the preoccupation with marriage, the cessation of headhunting, and the lack of residential moves. With respect to headhunting, Ilongots claimed that their population losses had been so drastic (about one-third) that they reached the tacit understanding that both internal feuding and external raiding should cease for an indefinite period, lest they literally finish one another off. With respect to residence, the Rumyads simply remained wherever they happen to have found themselves in June 1945, and those who had sought refuge in central Rumyad quietly returned to the margins. After they returned home, for instance, the Butags and Tengas effectively closed their territory to movement from the outside; they warned the lowlanders to the west that they were certain to be decapitated if they ventured into Ilongot country. In the wake of their catastrophe, the Ilongots struggled to settle down and remake their domestic lives.

THE RENEWAL OF RAIDING, 1950–52

In the rest of this chapter, the process by which the ten young men took heads is viewed against the background of the male life cycle. The reader should notice that details of the following narratives are designed to show the sense of politics and history embodied in headhunting. When, in 1952, five of the young men took heads in quick succession, their conduct was seen, looking backward, as one realization of the Ilongot historical sense that peers move in the same direction at the same time. At the same time, participation in raiding parties and the unfolding of the Butag-Rumyad feud were major determinants of shifting political alignments, manifested in residential moves and broken marriages.

While all of the ten young men were old enough to remember the events of 1945, only two of them were over 21 at the time, and the average age for the group was 17. Nonetheless, three of the ten succeeded in taking Japanese heads in 1945: Tukbaw (then 22) beheaded the hapless Japanese who had come to fetch water at dawn; Bayaw (16) decapitated one of the troops who had driven his people, along with those from Tenga and Butag, from their place of refuge; and Dinwag (27) was among those who beheaded the last three soldiers who remained in central Rumyad. Dinwag, as it turned out, was the last Rumyad man to take a head for five years, until Insan did so in 1950.

How Insan took a head, 1950. Insan had good reason to be especially eager to "arrive" and take a head. His "fierce" desire dated from 1945, when his father, Lakay, had slashed the Japanese soldier to death by the sweet potato patch. At the time Insan (then only 13) had begged his father to let him take the head and throw it away; but instead the first throw had gone, as was only proper, to his older brother, who had thereby gained the much envied right to adorn himself with red hornbill earrings. Not until 1950 could Insan persuade his father to organize a raid on his behalf.

Insan in the end was able to persuade his father that they should no longer remain "still," because the tenor of the times in the surrounding lowlands had in fact changed. By early 1950 what had started some eight years before as the Anti-Japanese People's Army (popularly known as the Hukbalahap, or Huks) had re-emerged in central Luzon and the Sierra Madre Mountains just south of Ilongot territory as a powerful people's guerrilla movement. It was in January 1950 that "all units of the people's army were ordered to make simultaneous attacks on provincial capitals, cities and enemy camps on March 29, August 26 and November 7, 1950" (Guerrero 1970: 70). During April and May of that year, towns in Nueva Ecija near the southwestern margin of Ilongot country were successfully attacked by the Huks. In the aftermath of these raids, news of an imminent Huk takeover of Manila was given credence in the Ilongot hills. Ilongots heard other news as well: late in 1949 they learned that companions of the Huks had been victorious in the homeland of the Chinese (whom they knew as well-to-do shopkeepers in lowland barrios and towns); and by late June 1950 word was spreading about the outbreak of the Korean War. It was evident in retrospect that "mid-1950 marked the flood tide of the Huk rebellion" (Lachica 1971: 131). Lakay and the others could no longer deny that yet another epoch of lowland violence was upon them. These years of 1950–54 were later known as *ka'ukbu,* "the time of Huks."

By July or August 1950, Lakay and his younger brother from Kakidugen had organized a raiding party, as Insan had asked. In doing so they recruited their brethern from Pengegyaben. When he asked the Pengegyaben people to join him on the raid, Lakay made a public statement confirming that Baket was his "sister" and that her son, Tukbaw, was his "son" as well. In thus consecrating their kinship, Lakay and Baket were setting the stage for what surely was their unspoken hope that their children might intermarry, as happened some five years later.

Those of the ten young men who participated in that raid of 1950 follow: from Pengegyaben, Tukbaw (then 27), who had taken a head in 1945, along with the novices Tawad (25) and his younger brother, Adēlpig (22); from Kakidugen, Bayaw (then 21), who had taken a head in 1945 and whose family had just joined that local cluster, along with the novices Ta'at (19), Radu (19), and Insan (18). The three youths who did not take part in the raid were Dinwag (32), who had taken a head in 1945 and was ill at the time, and the two youngest members of the group, Tepeg (17) and Maniling (15), who were regarded as "still children" and hence unable to withstand the hunger and deprivation that a long-distance raid would entail. In all, the raiding party was 18 strong. Five men were from Pengegyaben and the rest from Kakidugen; there were six married men, of whom only one was a novice, plus 12 unmarried men of whom seven were novices. Lakay was planning to "lead" his son Insan in taking a head, and Tukbaw was hoping to do the same for his classificatory brother Tawad.

The customary agreement about the sequence in which victims would be "shared" was more critical than usual. In the first place, all the men were pent up with "anger" as a result of the grief they had not yet "thrown away" over deaths suffered in their families in 1945. And Lakay was still mourning the sudden death of his eldest son only two years before. Second, the presence of so many eager novices who had been restrained from acting out their "envy" of older brothers who had earned red hornbill earrings in 1945 meant that the older men present had to keep the youths from cutting one another up in attempting to realize their desires to take a head.

After discussion of their plans, the men reached a consensus about the order in which the youths would "follow" one another in taking heads. The first victim was to be for Insan from Kakidugen, because his father had initiated the raid. The second victim (had there been one) was to be for Tawad for the following reasons: he was from Pengegyaben, and one of the guests should be "next in line"; he was the oldest novice among the group, and it was felt that he had remained an "unmarried young man" (*buintaw*) for too long; he had to throw away the grief from having been orphaned by his father's arrest in 1940 and by the killing of his mother, his grandmother, and his sister in 1945. The third victim was for the married novice from Kakidugen, because he was long past due to "arrive" and because the pattern of sharing should alternate between the Kakidugen hosts and their Pengegyaben guests. Regarding the victims, Tukbaw said: "Should they be many, it seems that there is no other kind (bērtan) among us, so if we get more we will give them to the other novices among us." Rumyads all, they would not fight over victims the way they might if their raiding party were mixed with other bērtan.

The plan was set. They were to head downstream on unfamiliar paths as far from Kakidugen as possible, in order to avoid reprisals for this, the first Rumyad raid of the post-1945 era. After their decimation in 1945, the raiders were more than ever determined to kill without being killed. They held no notion of the valor of death in open combat, for they could not conceive of asking a brother, a son, or a father to lay down his life—"to sell his body," as they said of soldiers, less in contempt than out of sheer moral incomprehension.

The day before the raiders left Kakidugen, all the signs they sought out were auspicious for their departure. At high noon that day, the man gathered on the cleared yard of Lakay's house and there implanted a woven bamboo basket in which they had placed betel nut, sugar cane, and sweet potato as a food offering for the spirit they called "from the forest." As the offering was made, an Aymuyu man (whose gun two years later accidentally killed Lakay's father) chanted the invocation in a loud voice: "Now, you, eye of the sun; there now, you are on high." Abruptly, "tightening" his voice to its highest pitch, he tweeted, he clucked, he warbled—'*uu kudēkudek*—and lured the "heart" of the victim, which was likened to a bird. Finally, his voice loosened and became deep in pitch because the hearts of the victims had come; they hovered for a time near their beheaders-to-be and then perched on the upper lobes of their ears (the very spot where, if he succeeded, the headhunter would place his red earrings). The "person of knowledge" drew near and grabbed the hearts where he found them perched, the first on Insan, the second on Tawad, and the third on the married novice from Kakidugen. All was as it should be, and the hearts were then placed in the bamboo basket; drawing their bolos, the men encircled the hearts in the basket. The person of knowledge looked to see whether any of the men was destined to be wounded on that raid. Their fates appeared favorable. That night in the forest, the men softly played their stringed instruments, the violin and the bamboo zither, and listened for the calls of omen birds. All signs were propitious, and they decided to leave the next day.

Moving toward their victim slowly and with deliberation, as was done in hunting and fishing as well, the men waded downstream along stretches of shallow water, peering downward through their homemade goggles as they went. Though the first of the seasonal sporadic rains had come, the waters were still low enough for fishing. Ever searching for small river fish, tiny crabs, or frogs, the men repeatedly stretched their elastic strips (cut from automobile inner tubes) and released the attached sharpened umbrella rods toward their targets. At the still, deep pools they stopped and dove with longer spears, peering into crevices and holes where mudfish and eels might have hidden for the day.

Along with the men were ten women. They had come to sing farewell, inspiring the men and lending beauty to their departure. Though two were married, none of the women had children to care for and they all were regarded, in this loose sense, as "quick ones"; six of them later married six of the young men. The women carried the supply of rice for the raiders in rattan baskets held by tumplines, freeing the men to wade, to dive, to leap from rock to rock, to run in short bursts, spurred on to display their prowess by the competitive ethos of foraging and by the very presence of the women.

More or less in coordination with the men, walking steadily along the banks or crossing the river here and there, the women went downstream along the Kakidugen to the fork of the Tubu River, and there they stopped to cook the rice. Most of the cooked rice was stuffed inside bamboo tubes for future consumption, so the raiders could avoid having their presence known by the smoke from their fires. What rice remained was eaten along with the fish in a tender feast of farewell. After the meal, each woman handed her "brother" or husband or lover a neatly tied betel quid to save and chew in the moment before attacking the victim. The women said, "Take this now, it is my betel quid," and the men answered with this ritual incantation: "May you [the betal offering] make me light of foot. Let all the reeds blossom [an allusion to the feather headdress worn only after taking a head]." Then the head-hunters departed downstream while the women stood singing, one after the other, their melodious farewells.

The men walked slowly, in single file and in silence. On this long-distance raid, walking in a direction where they had neither hunted nor raided before, they knew neither where to walk nor how far it would be—only that they were certain to suffer hunger and fatigue before they reached their lowland victims. Often moving on hands and knees, their progress was painfully slow as they sought out the most forbidding thickets along the highest ridges, hoping to avoid attention.

The first day out they found a rifle with still usable parts dating from 1945; clearly, no Ilongot had walked by that spot for at least five years, probably longer. But the next day they discovered that the game trails farther downstream were riddled with pits filled with sharpened bamboo stakes, and everywhere there were rattan triggers set to release arrows pulled taut for the kill. The raiders saw that these traps were freshly erected and deduced (correctly, as Kugkug and others later confirmed) that a hunting party of Tamsi people from far downstream was in the vicinity. They re-doubled their caution, for as Insan said, "We were afraid of the Tamsi people." Tukbaw explained that they had heard the "story" of how certain Rumyads and Tamsis had long ago lived together in Ulawi, a place on the Tubu, but "we thought it [the story] was a lie because it didn't make sense to us; we thought it was just a story, a mere story." In those days there was no social intercourse between Rumyads and Tamsis, for they had not yet even "walked back and forth" and "seen one another." Five years were still to pass before the two peoples became neighbors and began a process of union through joint raiding and four intermarriages.

Once they had safely skirted the Tamsis, the men walked on downstream for about ten days more. Aside from a fawn that Tukbaw shoved off a cliff, they ate only the rice from the bamboo tubes and whatever fruits and nuts they happened to find on their path. So short did their tempers become as they walked that they began to fight among themselves. In that crisis (by no means unique for long-distance raids) it was the tubercular older half-brother of Tukbaw—by then himself so thin that, Insan said, "he looked like a monkey"—who calmed the men's "thumping hearts" as he played his soothing flute and thus dissipated their twin feelings of hunger and anger. At last they spied the weeks-old footprints of lowland hunters, and soon after, as it started to rain, they reached the grasslands at the edge of the forest nearly 25 miles from Kakidugen.

That day they spent hiding in the brush at the top of a hill above a swidden, while two of their members went to scout and determine where to set up the ambush. Before sunrise the next morning the men thought of their "sisters" or wives or lovers as they chewed their parting gifts of betel nut; with their manhood thus inspired, their hearts were further moved by anger. The older men then advised the youths to be cautious, saying, "Do not cut one another; do not let yourselves be seen by the people [lowlanders]." Certain men agreed to keep track of one another during the attack. The Ilongots purposely distinguished themselves from the lowlanders (who would be dressed in pants and shirts) by wearing only G-strings and white kerchiefs tied for easy visibility in the buns of their long hair. Those who had already taken heads adorned themselves with their feather headdresses, thereby stirring the hearts of the novices by exciting their envy. It was shortly after dawn when the men fanned out and took their positions in the ambush.

While the sun rose higher and higher they waited and waited, neither speaking nor moving. It must have been noon or a little after when they saw a man come riding along on a carabao. He was a lowlander, all alone and whistling a cheerful tune to himself. As the raiders watched from above, he tied his carabao by the bank of the river, then took off his pants, waded into the water, and began to fish with a net. Lakay's younger brother took careful aim at the fisherman. It had been agreed tht he would fire the first shot because, after his infant daughter's death earlier that year, he had vowed never to use his weapon until he shot a victim with it, thereby, in Ilongot terms, dissipating and tossing away the weight of his grief. When the shot rang out the victim fell over on his face and the raiders, 18 strong, charged forward at a full run with their vision "focused" ('upug) solely on the victim. Tukbaw said, "There is no other than that they [the raiders] see, except for the victim." In a taped story of the raid told to Maniling, Insan recalled the confusion of the moment he reached the victim:

Father said to me, "Baah, hold on to it [the head]." Then father said, "Cut it off. Uh, let me do it. I'll cut it off."

Then our uncle said, "Leave it to me. I'll cut it off." Then the two of us, father and son, held on to it while our uncle cut it off. . . .

Then the old man [Insan's father, Lakay] said to me, "Throw it away," and I threw it away. I just threw it out there where there were no people.

Then I just said, "Booh, male victim I beheaded, I snatch away your life."

The men vented their pent-up anger on the cadaver and chopped it up until "it had no body and you couldn't see its bones," until "it was like ashes."

Tukbaw then spotted a 20-year-old member of their party who had become so sick, as sometimes happens, from the chaos and the smell of gore that he was wandering vaguely away from the scene. As he staggered along, dizzy and dazed, his wide eyes rolling in circles, the more experienced Tukbaw ran and grabbed him brusquely and cut a lock of his hair. Then together the two shouted 'a 'ee 'u 'u until the youth recovered his senses. In the meantime, Tawad had climbed to the top of a tall tree nearby and began shouting to his companions that he had spied houses just a short way downstream. The men bolted off and vanished into the forest.

The raiders fled without stopping. From the moment of decapitation they paused only now and again to shout and to sing the song of celebration. In so doing, they said, they lifted the weight from their bodies and made themselves light of foot; through their celebratory song they sought to acquire the speed and grace that epitomized Ilongot versions of health and well-being. Close to where they stopped that first night, they collected the leaves from a sweet-smelling fern and tucked them into their metal armbands in order to modify and preserve the smell of the victim.

The following morning on the Tubu River the men tried to dive for fish, but gave up because they were too weak from hunger. They had eaten the last of the rice before the attack, and as Insan said, "Alas, our ribs stood out like so many sticks placed side by side for sitting in the forest." That afternoon they shot a doe by a salt lick, and then Tukbaw's older half-brother killed a large male wild pig. As they ate the game, their bodies, by then pale ("white") from the rain and deprivation, once again took on color ("red"). Indeed, in other such narratives men claimed that taking a head, pure and simple, gave their bodies color as a visible sign of health.

As the raiders neared Kakidugen shortly before sunset on the second day of their return trip, they shouted out 'a 'ee 'u 'u just once to indicate that they had taken only one head. An old woman met the raiders, and she asked them and they in turn asked her whether everybody was alive and well: "Are you all there? Are all of you alive?" They were all in good health. No sooner had they entered Lakay's house than the women, in chorus, began to sing the song of celebration; the men replied in unison to their verses. The women took up the gongs (stringed instruments were forbidden at that moment); and one at a time the men and women took turns dancing, their bodies arched and arms spread wide. Their "hearts lengthened with joy" as they sang and danced and played the gongs through the night and into the early morning. Even a few people from Butag who happened to be visiting at the time joined in and sang and danced in celebration for Insan.

After resting for a day, the raiders walked to Adiw, where the Pengegyaben people lived. They and the women there "answered one another" in song, and they all danced and played the gongs far into the night. The clanging gongs were audible through central

Rumyad, and word spread quickly that Insan had taken a head. It was not until the next day that the raiders dispersed to their separate homes.

How Luku set off the Butag-Rumyad feud, 1951–52. The following year, 1951, Luku dramatized his outrageous demand to behead a fellow Ilongot rather than a lowlander by refusing to behead a Huk guerrilla. The victim spurned by Luku was a lone straggler who probably had been separated from his unit during Operation Sabre, part of the systematic anti-Huk campaign being waged by Secretary of National Defense Ramon Magsaysay in collaboration with the U.S. Military Advisory Group. The tide of Huk victories had been turned late the previous year by Magsaysay and his advisors, after the capture of a major portion of the Huk leadership in Manila on October 18, 1950.

As he told me this story, Insan recalled that the turn of events from Huk ascendancy to decline was marked by the sudden appearance of distinctively uniformed troops called *bisitis*. I finally realized that he was speaking of the acronym BCTs, and eventually it became clear to me that these were the 1,200-man Battalion Combat Teams especially trained by American advisors for counterinsurgency warfare in what proved but a prelude to action in Vietnam. Quite casually by later standards, the BCTs sought to make the Ilongots their allies by giving them weapons and legally licensing the firearms they had picked up from dead Japanese soldiers, in the hope that they would be used (as they sometimes were) against the Huks. The BCTs also promised to defend the Ilongots should other lowlanders attempt to arrest them for their headhunting forays. Thus armed with new legal weapons and promises of safe conduct, the people of Kakidugen and Pengegyaben came to feel that they could raid without fear of reprisal. This feeling of security was further increased by their knowledge that the party guilty of decapitation was difficult to detect, in the confusion of widespread violence and crisscrossing attributions of gruesome acts of terrorism now to Huks, then to BCTs, and again to Ilongots.

It must be stressed, nonetheless, that Luku's unyielding demand to behead an Ilongot violated the tenor of his times. The stress on recovery from the catastrophe of 1945 remained in evidence despite Insan's raid. Indeed, the Ilongots still attempted to avoid internal feuding by raiding only against lowlanders. This new direction in raiding was due not only to the widespread apprehension that their own self-inflicted extinction was the most likely result of further feuding, but also to their conviction that the groups that had suffered severe depopulation in 1945 had been the targets of supernatural retribution for their prior violations of oaths by salt; and hence renewal of the feuding process would risk repetition of the massive consequences of such violations.

Why, then, was Luku so disruptive as to run head-on against the wishes of his elders and the practice of raiding only against lowlanders already set in motion by Insan in 1950? The brief answer is that Luku was simply more disturbed and volatile—even granting the extra leeway culturally allowed for the storm and stress of youth—than was tolerable for his companions. Luku also occupied a position in the social structure from which, given his evident susceptibility to the afflictions generated by pressure, he could not help but be seized by "envy" of his brethren and therefore feel goaded into a state of seething and uncontrollable "anger." Worse off than Insan, Luku had seen not one but two of his older brothers as they took heads in 1945, and he wept because he could not yet wear those dangling red ornaments "perched" upon his ears. To make matters more unbearable, Insan, who "arrived" before him and became the first Rumyad man to take a head after 1945, was two years his junior.

So it was that in 1952 Luku beheaded a Butag man who was out hunting with his dogs. Through that act, the long-smoldering Butag-Rumyad feud burst into its definitive and irrevocable "beheading" phase.

Raiders "follow" one another, 1952. In a curious chain reaction, fed by the Huk presence, Luku's raid had an impact that went well beyond the triggering of a feud. To begin, it resulted indirectly in the death of Lakay's father, killed by an accidental gunshot on his way to attempt to mend relations with the Butags. One consequence of that death was that Tepeg, Lakay's youngest son, vowed that he would kill in order to "throw away" the weight of his grief over his grandfather's death.

In the meantime, a large raiding party of 28 men was mounted from all the Rumyad local clusters except Kakidugen: it included certain Abēkas and Bēduks from the southwestern margin who during the war had resided in central Rumyad, plus those two of the ten young men, Maniling and Dinwag, who had accompanied Luku in his raid against the Butags. The raid was conceived as a reply in part to Insan's success (hence his absence from it) and in part to Luku's brazen transgression (hence Maniling's presence).

On this raid, if ever, haste made waste. Against their explicit designs, the raiders were spotted on their downstream trek by other Ilongots. They were thus obliged to behead three Payupay men who attacked them.

It was immediately thereafter, still in 1952, when Lakay's younger brother—coping with his father's death as well as the uncontainable urges of the young novices—organized a raiding party of 16 men: six from Kakidugen, seven from Pengegyaben, two from Kēyat, and one Abēka from the southwestern margin. Their first victim would be for Radu (21 years old) because Lakay's younger brother had adopted and raised him. The others were ordered by place and relative age: second was Tawad (27) from Pengegyaben; third Maniling (17) from Pengegyaben; fourth Ta'at (21) from Kakidugen. Thus four of the ten young men were designated to take heads if there were victims enough. Three of the ten, Dinwag (34), Tukbaw (29), and Insan (20), had already taken heads. After consulting the omens, the headhunters set off on their arduous trek downstream, following the path of 1950.

Certain men felt too ill, too old, or too young to undergo the debilitating deprivations of the raid and decided to stay at home; among them were Lakay, his son Tepeg, and Tawad's younger brother, Adēlpig. The raiders had gone but a short way downstream when Insan fell ill and returned to Kakidugen along with his classificatory brother-in-law from the northwestern margin.

The next day a man from the northwestern margin reached Kakidugen, only to discover that he had been left behind by the raiders. In his "anger" he spoke with Lakay and the others who had remained behind in "fear" of the gruelling trek downstream. Maniling said that they talked about how "they felt envious when they thought about our arrival and about how we might sing the song of celebration."

That settled matters. The men decided to risk the greater danger of detection in walking upstream the shorter distance to the lowlands. They were nine in all: three from Kakidugen, one from Pengegyaben, and five Bēnabēs from the northwestern margin, of whom two had married Kakidugen women. They decided to share their victims, alternating between Rumyads and Bēnabēs, as follows: (1) Tepeg (19) because he vowed to kill after his grandfather's death; (2) a Bēnabē man; (3) Adēlpig (24); (4) a Bēnabē man; (5) Lakay because of his age (58) and his father's death earlier that year.

At first the omen birds (sent by the spirit from the forest) called out from behind, a sign of illness at home and no luck on the raid. But so determined were the raiders that they ritually prepared and listened once again, until the bird calls beckoned them onward from up ahead. The next morning they departed upstream.

On a morning about 20 days after the first raiding party had left, Lakay and the others returned to Kakidugen. They shouted out four times because Tepeg, Adēlpig, and two of the others had taken heads. That very afternoon the other raiders arrived from downstream and shouted 'a 'ee 'u 'u twice, because two more of the ten young men, Radu and Tawad, had taken heads. Lakay's younger brother, Radu, and the others did not learn until they reached the houses that four of their companions had taken heads in their absence.

Upon his arrival from downstream Maniling recalled, "I became angry when I met the others [Lakay, Insan, and the rest] because they had sneaked off that way, and because I had not yet taken a head and I could have beheaded the one that Radu beheaded." In 1952, after all, Maniling had already gone on three raids with his uncle, Dinwag; on the first and last of those raids Maniling was so designated that, had there been but one more victim, he would have taken the head. No wonder he was beside himself with anger. Not able to bear hearing the song of celebration (truncated because Radu's "sister" died the next day as a result of stepping on one of the sharpened bamboo stakes freshly set up for protection against Butag marauders), Maniling immediately left for home. Five days later he, Dinwag, Bayaw (23), and four others from Pengegyaben sneaked away and headed upstream. On the raid, at last, Maniling and another man took heads.

Thus over a 30-day period in 1952 five of the ten young men (plus six others) "arrived" and by taking heads threw away their status as novices. Pushed on by their mutual envy and their common desire to be the "same" as their peers, the youths "followed" one upon the other in a manner that epitomizes the Ilongot sense of historical process as a quick succession of individual acts conceived as if they were people moving in single file along a path. At this point Ta'at remained the only one of the ten who had not taken a head.

SHIFTING POLITICAL ALIGNMENTS, 1952–54

During the two years after Luku had beheaded the Butag huntsman, the Kakidugens became at once more distant from their longtime marital allies, the Bēnabēs from the northwestern margin, and closer to their Rumyad kin, especially the people of Pengegyaben. The composition of raiding parties was an index of the political realignments that were taking place. The waxing Kakidugen-Pengegyaben alliance was signaled in the joint raid during which Insan took a head, in 1950, and in all but one of the subsequent raids of 1952. The waning Kakidugen-Bēnabē alliance was indicated in 1952 when the first of the two inter-bērtan marriages that ended in divorce was terminated.

In fact, Rumyad marital unions have generally been monogamous and enduring except during periods of abrupt realignment among groups. In 1967–69 there were 42 men and 47 women who were or had been married in the Rumyad local clusters of Kakidugen, Pengegyaben, Kēyat, and Tauyang. Of the 42 men, 34 had been married once, 6 twice, 1 three times, and 1 four times; of the 47 women, 39 had been married once, 7 twice, and 1 three times. In other words, only ten, or 9 percent, of the 109 marriages ended by divorce. In my doctoral dissertation, I interpreted these figures to mean simply that Ilongot marriages tend to last a lifetime. What I did not perceive until I began to view Ilongot society from a more historical perspective was that all but one of the divorce cases happened during two transitional periods in the readjustments of intergroup allegiances: the first was in 1952–54, when the Butag-Rumyad feud indirectly resulted in weakening ties between the people of Kakidugen and Bēnabē; and the second was in 1960–62, when relations grew tense between the people of Kakidugen-Pengegyaben and those of Ringen, as will be seen in the next chapter. The rupture of divorce, then, can usually be viewed as a symptom of broader schisms between groups.

Indeed, of the five 1947–48 marriages, four had terminated by 1954. One of them ended in the wife's death and the following three in divorce: (1) in 1952 a Bēnabē husband and a Rumyad wife were divorced by mutual consent after five years of childless marriage; (2) in 1953 Tukbaw ended his childless marriage of five years by divorcing his wife, Yennaw, because of her affair with Tawad; (3) in 1954 Wagat (whose two children had already died) divorced her Bēnabē husband of six years because he refused to follow her when the Kakidugen people moved to central Rumyad.

In the first case, the Bēnabē man had impregnated his wife's younger sister (both women were sisters of Bayaw), whose child died at birth. The Bēnabē man justified his act as a form of retaliation against the Aymuyu man whose firearm had accidentally killed Lakay's father earlier that year (1952). The Aymuyu man was doubly related to Bayaw and his two sisters, because his wife was another sister from that family and he was their classificatory brother (MZS). When the Bēnabē man pressed his demand to take both sisters in marriage (against the monogamous norm), his father-in-law objected vehemently, and in the end all parties concerned agreed amicably to the divorce. The relative ease of this separation was a sign of the continuing strength of the Kakidugen-Bēnabē alliance. At the same time, the fact that the divorce took place at all pointed to the beginnings of a growing distance between the Bēnabēs and the people of Kakidugen.

In the second case, the divorce of Tukbaw from Yennaw was precipitated in 1953. That year a number of Pengegyabens joined with the Kakidugens near the present location of the latter local cluster. The two groups gardened and hunted in cooperation with one another that year. The Pengegyaben people had left their former location so suddenly that they simply moved into the homes of their kin. Tukbaw and his younger sister Midalya, for instance, temporarily moved into Lakay's home. The reason for this abrupt major move was that the Pengegyaben people had heard rumors that soldiers, in retaliation for the raids of the year before, were planning to invade central Rumyad and arrest them, much as they had done 13 years before in 1940.

While Tukbaw was away trading with lowlanders on the north-western margin, his wife, Yennaw, repeatedly visited the house of Tawad; her excuse was that he was making her a hooked chain belt and she needed to be fitted. Midalya, Tukbaw's usually accommodating younger sister, became so livid at her sister-in-law's blatant deceptions that she threw the entrance ladder of their house to the ground and refused to allow Yennaw in. She then told her brother about his wife's widely noticed affair with Tawad. The divorce was traumatic because Yennaw had flaunted her adultery in public; thus Tukbaw had no cultural option but to display his anger.

Indeed, Tukbaw was beside himself with anger at the news, and he promptly gathered his belongings and returned to his former home near the present location of Pengegyaben. He stayed there and left Yennaw to her own devices in Lakay's home. Tukbaw remembered that at the time his heart was thumping with thoughts of homicide. In the end, however, his anger was dissipated through the gift of a valuable wide-mouthed metal cooking pan (like the two awarded to the Butags in 1969), because on reflection it simply was inconceivable for him to behead his own "sister," Yennaw, or his own "brother," Tawad.

In the third case, Wagat's divorce from her Bēnabē husband was the most directly intertwined with the shift of the Kakidugen inter-group alliances during 1952–54. To be intelligible, this divorce case requires what appears to be a series of digressions, including residential moves and ambushes of Huks, concerning the sequence of events in 1954.

In about January of that year, Lakay decided that if he and his daughter (Wagat) gardened in two separate places it was unlikely that they would both suffer crop failures, and hence he made an extraordinary arrangement. He told his daughter and son-in-law to leave him for the course of that annual horticultural cycle and to garden among the people of Wagat's husband on the northwestern margin. Meanwhile he and the other Kakidugen people, along with certain Pengegyabens, moved near the present location of Pengegyaben in central Rumyad. There they rejoined Tukbaw, who had returned during his divorce the year before.

The Kakidugens moved to central Rumyad in order to be closer to the interior and to increase their strength of numbers in the face of potential violence. Wagat said they made the move because they feared the Huks; her father claimed they had fled because of rumors that planes were about to bomb Ilongot territory in an attempt to kill the Huks believed to be hiding there; her younger brother, Insan, denied that he had ever feared the Huks and claimed instead that their mission in moving was to fend off Butag marauders from their attacks on the vulnerable Pengegyaben people, who still remained short of adult men after the 1940 arrests. All three versions had a ring of truth about them; they pointed to the need for defense against the Butags and the threat of violence from the lowlands. The major move to central Rumyad was clearly made in a climate of fear and in an attempt, like that of 1942–44, to gather together in the hope of fending off incursions from the perimeter.

After the Kakidugens moved to central Rumyad, Ta'at, the only remaining novice among the ten, took a head. In about May 1954 a group of Huk guerrillas fled through central Rumyad, moving from the southeast to the northwestern margin, where they would find friendly hosts among a number of lowlanders and Ilongots. The Huks were guided by Insan, chosen because he had become relatively fluent in Ilokano during his childhood on the northwestern margin and his months in the lowlands in 1945. In agreeing to serve as a guide, Insan had hidden designs. As he said, "We would have killed them except that we didn't have enough time to set up an ambush." In any case, that band of Huks reached its destination.

About a month or two later the Pugus and Dekrans guided another group of Huks, also moving from southeast to northwest. This time when the group reached central Rumyad the Ilongots were prepared to act quickly. Convincing in her fluent Ilokano,

Wagat (who was visiting her father, Lakay, at the time) told the Huks to wait a day because (she lied) there were BCTs in search of Huk guerrillas on the trail ahead. The next morning the Huks were guided northward toward Kakidugen by two Rumyad men, who led them up the Bukaw River into a canyon with sheer sides and rocks so slippery that even Ilongots had trouble keeping their footing. Along the canyon walls—hidden in silent ambush from dawn of that day—were upwards of 80 Ilongot men, a mixed group of Dekrans, Pugus, and Rumyads. As the guerrilla group reached the midpoint of the ambush, the two guides bolted from sight and the Rumyad "leadshot" opened fire, closing off the up-stream route of escape, at the same instant the Pugu "followup" did likewise, closing off the downstream route of escape. The Huks leapt for cover and the ensuing battle, people said, was "like war," as gunfire echoed through the canyon and bullets ricocheted from rock to rock. Some Huks escaped, but nine of them were killed and beheaded: two by Dekrans, two by Pugus, and five by Rumyads including Ta'at (then 23) and Maniling once again. None of the Ilongots was seriously injured, just as they had hoped.

It was no accident that the two guerrilla bands fled through Rum-yad territory in mid-1954. Having built his reputation from 1950 as Secretary of National Defense, Ramon Magsaysay had been in-augurated as President of the Philippines on December 30, 1953. Immediately thereafter he began his promised intensification of the anti-Huk campaign on all fronts, from agrarian reform to di-rect counterinsurgency. The urgency of Magsaysay's move against the Huks was also a product of the French humiliation at Dien-bienphu and the subsequent visit of U.S. Secretary of State John Foster Dulles to Manila in order to organize the Southeast Asian Treaty Organization (SEATO) against the perceived communist menace. In that year of increased anti-Huk activity, the noted guerrilla leader Luis Taruc surrendered, and a number of guerrilla units fled from the Sierra Madre Mountains south of the Baler re-gion (southeastern margin) in an attempt to regroup on the north-western margin of Ilongot territory.

That August and September the rice harvest was good, both in central Rumyad and on the northwestern margin. When he had left Wagat earlier in the year, Lakay's parting words had been, "If only we are in good health I will come for you." In other words, the expectation had been that if the rice harvest was good, as it in fact was, Wagat and her husband would return to live with Lakay in central Rumyad.

After the harvest, Wagat said to her husband, "Take me on the trail, for I'm going to see Father." But her husband, she told me, "did not want to go with me; he wanted us to remain [on the margin]." Wagat, whose tongue was sharp, insisted on going to central Rumyad. Her husband, Insan said, became so angry that he "beat her and nearly killed her." When they learned of the beating, Wagat's father, her stepmother, her sister, and two brothers— in all a dozen men and seven women from central Rumyad— walked together toward the northwestern margin in an attempt to bring their daughter/sister home. Their action was justified, in that the usual Ilongot practice when no bridewealth has been paid (and none had) is for daughters, after they marry, to reside with or near their parents. In this way they are at first cared for by their parents and later, as their parents age, the daughters care for them in turn. But Wagat's husband refused to move to central Rumyad because his people (the Bēnabēs) were so closely allied by marriage with the Butags that he feared—with some reason—that he might be beheaded by a volatile Ringen youth who was not close kin to Wagat and her family.

The day Wagat's people arrived at the northwestern margin was the day on which a fiesta was being celebrated there by the Huks. Wagat's husband leapt at this opportunity and went to tell the leader of the guerrillas that his wife's Rumyad relatives were the ones who had beheaded nine Huks about a month before. Fortunately for the Rumyads, another Bēnabē man (the widower of Lakay's classificatory sister [FZD] and the classificatory son [ZS] of Lakay's deceased first wife) was so eloquent in his defense of the Rumyads that he persuaded the Huks that the charges were false. Nonetheless, the Rumyads remained watchful, fearing treachery, and at dusk the next day they sneaked back home, taking Wagat with them.

Some time later that year, Wagat's Bēnabē husband arrived in central Rumyad along with his mother. He was told, Wagat said, the following by Lakay: "No, we will not let you sleep with your wife. You would only leave all over again." Lakay recalled the moment thus: "I no longer would let him sleep with Wagat. I told him, 'Don't come back here again; go away now.' He did not return." Insan said, "Had it been up to us children [he listed himself among five of the ten young men] we would have gone ahead and killed him, but luckily the older men admonished us over and over and told us not to do it."

The incident of Wagat's divorce brought the Bēnabēs and the Kakidugen people close to a beheading and the feud that certainly would have followed. Had the Huks, for instance, acted upon the testimony of Wagat's husband, they probably would have executed Lakay and his younger brother, his sons Insan and Tepeg, and the other men. Retaliation against the informer's people might well have been immediate because of the general violence of the times. Alternatively, vengeance could have been delayed until after the watchfulness of the Bēnabēs had dissipated. By then the son (then eight) of Lakay's younger brother would have come of age. Such hypothetical events aside, Insan and his youthful peers were so angry at the threat on their lives that only the forceful restraint of their elders kept them from beheading Wagat's husband.

As sides were taken in the process of Wagat's divorce, social and geographical distance became increasingly congruent, as is usual among the mobile Ilongots. The Kakidugens and Pengegyabens retreated into the center of Rumyad land and thus drew more distant from the Bēnabēs, who remained where they were on the northwestern margin, thereby drawing relatively closer to the Butags and the Huks. This change of allegiances among groups was as basic as it was abrupt; for the Kakidugen people had lived side by side with the Bēnabēs for the more than two decades since 1923, and during this time the two groups had systematically intermarried. What for so long was an enduring marital alliance based upon co-residence had in the brief time from 1952 to 1954 become stretched to the breaking point of beheading and open feuding. Through Wagat's divorce, all parties involved came to realize that intergroup relations had undergone a fundamental shift, effectively reorienting the Kakidugen people toward their Rumyad brethren and away from their Bēnabē affines.

CHAPTER SIX. THE POLITICS OF MARRIAGE, 1955–1960

Much of the previous two chapters, as is probably evident, was drawn from what the Ilongots conceive of as an event worthy of being told as a story. Among such events are headhunting raids, hunting forays, fishing expeditions, the flight from the Japanese, and such oratorical confrontations as bridewealth and covenants. These narratives—except the ones about oratory—usually take the form of a journey, a walk away from home and a return. During the journeys episodes are organized as points in space; they follow one upon the other as people move in succession from one place to another along a path. Each incident along the way is self-contained and can be elaborated or skipped over without affecting the rest of the story. In fact, what happens in one place is viewed neither as commentary on what came before nor as a foreshadowing of what is yet to come. Irony thus does not play a role in these narratives.

Though the elements of Ilongot stories are like modules in their autonomy, the overall shape of the action is often like that of foraging. Stories begin with a slow, step-by-step stalking movement toward the literal or figurative prey, then are (or are not) punctuated by a sudden capture, and finally end with a quick return home. On the 1950 raid, for instance, Insan and the others walked downstream in a "deliberate" manner—fishing here, bidding farewell there, and hunting over yonder—until they reached their victim, ambushed him, and rushed back upstream toward their homes. Stories of the Japanese told to me by the Kakidugen people followed events day by day—that is, place by place—from their initial flight until their safe arrival in the lowlands (in this case

An Ilongot meal: a woman serves bowls of rice and men arrange chunks of meat. Everyone present for the meal receives an equal portion.

there was no prey), and then their return homeward was reported without elaboration. The plot lines of these stories follow a circular path, leaving their point of departure in measured steps and rushing back in return, and as a result the episodes are told one after the other in a relentlessly chronological sequence.

On the other hand, topics most suited for telling as "gossip" grow out of domestic life and the world of women more generally. Sitting by the hearth, gathering firewood, fetching water, pounding rice, hoeing, planting, weeding, harvesting—these activities entail no long walks and no litanies of place names. Indeed, Ilongots say that men surpass women in their "knowledge" because their distant treks in hunting and raiding have taken them to see more places away from their homes and gardens.

In the case we are discussing here, the ten men who married in 1955–58 did so without oratory and bridewealth, hence virtually without stories to tell afterward. To review briefly, these ten young men, whose lives I have followed over the course of a decade, had by 1954 "arrived" and taken heads. Their coming of age during two moments of violence, the time of the Japanese and the time of the Huks, meant that they were able to put on red hornbill earrings as a prelude to their marriages. When they married they did so in quick succession. Their conduct, as will be seen, was guided by the cultural pattern of action energized by mutual envy among peers that shaped the rapid chain of beheadings in 1952 and that more broadly constitutes Ilongot historical consciousness. Through their marriages the young men crossed the cultural divide separating youth from adulthood. Whereas their youth had been energetic, vital, and packed with movement, their marriages were described as "stopping" or "sitting" a moment—like the years of 1946–49—when social action came to rest, motionless and silent. Like all moments when Ilongot social life becomes still, marriages without oratory, bridewealth, and the public politics of the senior generation are recounted in retrospect not as stories but as gossip.

ILONGOT TYPIFICATIONS OF THE DOMESTIC CYCLE

When Meyer Fortes attempted to introduce a historical dimension into the study of synchronic social structure, he proposed that ethnographers study the developmental cycle of domestic groups. In his view, the domestic cycle initially follows a waxing arc of increase from the time the couple marries until the birth of their last child; it follows a waning arc of decrease or dispersion as the children in turn marry and some or all leave their parental home (see Fortes 1958). The perception of a universal metabolic rhythm of increase and decrease, however, derives from the fact that Fortes saw the domestic cycle primarily from the perspective of the conjugal family, rather than of the multifamily or multihousehold domestic group. Moreover, he failed to see that the developmental processes of the domestic group were socially constructed and therefore should be understood, at least in the first instance, from the native viewpoint.

Ilongots describe the developmental cycles of their domestic groups as a journey with a long walk in one direction and a quicker return. The unfolding relations of domestic life are conceived in terms of shifts in who leads and who follows. Still suggesting movement loosely coordinated among people, the image of walking along a path no longer stresses unity and sameness, as it did for youthful age-mates, but emphasizes rather more the asymmetrical ties between men and women, youths and elders, those who marry in and those who stay home.

This process is initiated in marriage when the man moves into the home of the woman and her family of origin. Insan said that after marriage, "We don't have the woman move away." Tulbit from Tauyang said that when a man marries, he "stays with the woman at her place." A Kakidugen man spoke to me as if I were an inmarrying son-in-law and said, "You follow (*'unud*) the woman that you sat down with." Throughout this movement that constitutes and symbolizes the marital process, the man follows the woman.

Once married, the couple follows the wife's parents in what is regarded as a continuation of the movement of the marital process. The daughter, as she has done since birth, continues to follow her parents; the son-in-law, who once followed the woman, simply extends the walk along his path until he reaches her parents. As long as the wife's parents remain strong and in good health their married daughters continue to follow them, the youngest one or two residing in the same house and the others living nearby.

As time passes decline sets in, and the wife's mother, according to Insan, "no longer is able to work and her father also may happen to have grown old." At that point, Insan went on, "things turn around," and the wife's parents in turn begin to follow their married children as "now the two of them lead" (*bukur*). In the end the direction of movement is inverted, as aging parents turn around and no longer lead but now follow their fully adult children.

The man moves toward the woman. The beginning of the developmental cycle of domestic groups is conceived as a man's movement toward a woman in marriage. Culturally, this period of entry is regarded both as a continuous process and also—like another beginning, infancy in the life cycle—as a series of segmented units. This significant moment of marriage is pivotal for the members of the household because, from the wife's parents' viewpoint, it initiates the phase of decrease or dispersion of their family, while, from the children's viewpoint, it begins the phase of increase of their family.

The direction of movement in marriage, that of the man toward the woman, is viewed as a unitary action from the moment the man initiates courtship through marriage to conception and beyond. "The man," Insan said, "is truly the source [*rapu*] of courtship." The two ends of the continuum, courtship and postmarital residence, are conceptually collapsed into a unified totality of conduct during which the man "goes into" the house of the woman. "The man," Maniling said, "walks [toward the woman] because it is truly the man who goes to court" (*ramak*, literally, desire). The fact that initial postmarital residence is uxorilocal by household Ilongots see as following directly from the normative view that courtship is initiated by men and not women. Initially moved by his desire, the man simply keeps on walking into the house of the woman.

Though the residence rule is followed without exception, the normative force of the notion that men take the initiative in courtship is revealed most clearly through those rare instances of its violation. The strength of the norm was tellingly revealed in the aftermath of Tukbaw's 1953 divorce from Yennaw (see Chapter 5). Recall that the precipitating cause of the divorce was that Yennaw initiated sexual relations with Tawad; later she married his younger brother Adēlpig. Midalya, Tukbaw's younger sister, told me that Yennaw "wanted to collect ['*upug*] men," and that she acted more like a man than a woman by taking the initiative in her sexual pursuits. On another occasion she said that the origin of Yennaw's marriage to Adēlpig had set an enduring deviant pattern of female initiative and dominance in domestic affairs. Midalya said, "Yennaw is deeply lazy; she bosses Adēlpig around and Adēlpig pounds their rice [a woman's chore]." Still speaking of Yennaw, she asked rhetorically, "What about the way she had her hair curled?"—referring to the fact that a number of teenage girls had recently had their hair curled and Yennaw was the only older woman who had done likewise. Midalya was suggesting (not so obliquely) that Yennaw still aspired to attract men other than her husband,

Adēlpig. Such was the strength of her feelings about what had happened over 20 years before.

In a revealing hypothetical instance, Duman spoke about a rather different example of the norm's inversion. Suppose, Duman said, that a daughter actually did the unthinkable and abandoned her aging parents. In such a case gossips would surely say, "Why did the woman so thoughtlessly go and leave her parents? So, it looks as if she went into the man's house." People would infer, in other words, that the woman had originated relations with the man—that she had gone into his house—and as an eventual result she had left her parents. In Duman's hypothetical case the long-term direction of movement was irrevocably set in the first moment of courtship.

When the man approaches the women in his initial desire—and on through the ordeals her kin will set him to—he should move slowly, ever so slowly, thus demonstrating that his "knowledge" is the true guide of his "passion, energy, anger" (liget). The movement of courtship not only sets an enduring direction, but it is also distinctive in its manner, as it moves step by step through a series of phases that are studiously delicate, gradual, and deliberate.

The marital process is the example par excellence of that range of situations where Ilongots proceed with caution, attempting to excite neither their own apprehension nor that of the others in certain human encounters. In entries and greetings the underlying notion of decorum is one of slow movement that assiduously avoids abrupt acts. It was this idea of decorum that was enacted during the 1969 covenant when the Rumyads walked—elegantly dressed, unarmed, and in single file—slowly toward vigilant Butags, who awaited their arrival with loaded weapons. More casual greetings on a path or in a house are similarly protracted; they begin with a period of motionless silence, then proceed slowly through exchanges of betel, and conclude with the first words of conversation.

The significance of greeting etiquette became clearer to me in 1974 when I mindlessly entered Tukbaw's home in quick strides. The children inside were so startled by my uncouth act that they jumped out a window to the ground in fear and screamed, "Uncle Natu is angry." In such a situation, as I should have known, to move slowly is to show respect and good intentions, whereas to move abruptly is to show anger and hostile purposes. From the children's viewpoint my abrupt entrance was of the same conceptual family as those sudden appearances of soldiers or raiders—the arresting soldiers in 1923 and 1940, the Japanese, the Huks, the Butags—that had so deeply threatened, indeed taken, the lives of their elders and were still invoked in 1974 as bogeymen in order to frighten them and thereby silence their crying.

Like other Ilongot beginnings, entries, and greetings, courtship is divided into a progression of steplike phases that are as uniform in their general segmented shape as they are flexible in their particulars. In this sense the movement of courtship is endowed with cultural form, at the same time that it permits leeway for various personal styles and the myriad contingencies of complex human relations.

Through the course of its overall process, courtship widens in social scope, moving from a private matter between the man and woman, through its gradual revelation before the wife's family, to its full public display during an assembly in which the man's people confront the woman's people.

A private matter between the man and woman. When the man first makes his desire known to the woman, perhaps on a visit to her home, he does so discreetly, only by the look in his eyes. After time passes, perhaps on another visit, the man takes another step. He may, for instance, give the woman a betel quid to see if she will give one in return and thus indicate that their hearts may someday "follow" one another. At this stage the two lovers still conceal their passion; Maniling said, they "do not reveal it to other people; it is there, only with the two of them, that those thoughts exist."

While the woman simply remains "still" (*pedeg*), the man makes his advances toward her through as gradual a sequence of gestures as his desire tempered by shyness will allow. Apart from its general character as a beginning, the initiation of relations between the lovers is designed to allow time for their hearts to "grow fond of" one another. This notion of *tagdē*, at once to "grow fond of" and "become accustomed to," was used to speak of our becoming accustomed to life among the Ilongots, as well as of our special friendships with Insan, Duman, and Tukbaw, among others. In a related sense of the term, people said that their 1928 move toward a schoolhouse was a means by which they were supposed to have become accustomed to lowland law and order. For the two lovers, the process of becoming fond of one another is said to grow out of their visible actions, usually their initial shy exchanges of betel.

Maniling compared the man's conduct in this early phase with the extreme patience required with a newly purchased domesticated pig. At first, he said, food is placed on the ground; thus enticed, the pig draws near, retreats, and draws near again until eventually it becomes accustomed to the scent of its new caretaker. Later on, the affection between the two lovers develops more deeply through the less visible actions of their thoughts and dreams. "If you think of him," Yennaw said, "he'll dream of you." Maniling elaborated: a lover "calls you by name" and "sighs over you" and in so doing induces you to dream of him or her. And dreams themselves, rememberd the morning after, in turn lead to more sighs, naming the lover; and so matters spiral onward. Desire, as Ilongots say, is the matter of the heart.

The gradual revelation before the wife's family. Sometime later the man tells the woman to go and fetch (*tuydek*) something (for example, a drink of water) because, Maniling said, "this way the woman's heart [*rinawa*] becomes known." If she does as asked, clearly "their two hearts follow ['unud] one another," for she has shown that she will care for (*saysay*) the man. At about the same time, the man comes to work (usually to help clear a first-year swidden) and thus demonstrates his energy to the wife's family, for he hopes that eventually they will "eat his hand" as they consume the product of his labor. About this time, the man lies next to the woman and they talk. Maniling said that the woman speaks first, saying, "See that your heart is not deceitful," and the man replies, "My desire has not been a lie." So the relationship is tested by the woman's family even as the lovers test their increasing affection for one another.

In their complementary ways the man and the woman display their "ability to work hard." The woman, for her part, moves quickly when her suitor makes a request of her. As the intruder, relative to the woman's family, the man struggles to achieve a delicate balance between asserting his prowess in labor and maintaining the pretense (a public fiction that fools nobody) that he has no amorous aspirations toward their daughter/sister. The man's hard work, Maniling said, is "the source of his coming to enter the house" of the woman; yet his approach must be "gradual and slow," lest the woman's family "take offense and answer back in anger." Room for the lovers to make their desires known to one another is provided by the expectations about how youths should conduct themselves when they move beyond their closely woven world of peers. Culturally, the two "quick ones" are cast in the role of workers endowed with speed, energy, and grace—the valued beauty and vital intensity of youth—at the same time that they are obliged to act shy and silly, blushing and giggling because they do not yet know what to say in public situations.

The suitor fears the woman's men, her father and brothers, because, Talikaw from Tauyang said, speaking as a suitor, "we take their sister" (*bēkur,* literally, woman). The woman's men take this opportunity to test the mettle of her suitor; they insist that he neither act abruptly in his movements nor answer back in his speech during this period, while they decide whether he is hard working or lazy. The woman's father, Talikaw said, warns her suitor to conduct himself properly in the present and to plan to work hard in the future; he says, "Now if you quarrel with me, you will not come to me." And, "Do not come to me unless you plan to care for me in my old age."

The suitor is put through ordeals of varying severity by the woman's father and brothers. In the most extreme case I heard, a Rumyad suitor went to pollard trees for the woman's family. When he was high in the air—possibly more than a hundred feet—and tightrope walking along a rattan vine thrown slack between two trees, the woman's brother on the ground below opened fire, shooting not to kill, but just above his head. This chilling episode was widely celebrated because the suitor lost neither his nerve nor his life, he neither moved abruptly nor answered back. Instead, they say, he simply kept on working as he blithely called out, "Halloo, brother-in-law." Though the woman's brother nearly

A man moving along a slack rattan vine between two tall trees: he is pollarding the living branches from the trees, so that sunlight can reach the rice in the garden below.

went too far, the suitor's cool courage was just as it should have been. Similarly, if less convincingly, a downstream youth told me that his parents just had advised him to pursue the woman he desired even if her brothers and father tried to stop him with crossed bolos, "because nobody is ever killed over a woman"—at least not during the process of courtship.

The very severity of the ordeals that the suitor undergoes lends further support to the notion that in courtship the man moves toward the woman rather than the reverse. When I asked him to imagine the consequences should the woman move toward the man, Maniling immediately said the woman's fear would prevent her from confronting the anger of the man's parents. More obliquely, Tepeg said that a husband may answer back when his wife becomes too demanding in telling him to do chores by saying, "Go and tell my father what chores to do." His wife, in other words, could not face up to the anger of his father. That men's anger is greater and their fear lesser than that of women, Maniling explained, is because men walk further than women in their respective workaday lives as hunters and gardeners. To know distant places and people is to lose one's fear of them, hence the particular sense in which the social construction of gender differences underlies the process of movement through courtship.

Public display during an assembly. At this point the degree of variation in how matters may progress increases markedly. Whether there is to be a public assembly, and if so whether bridewealth is to be given, are questions for discussion and debate. The extent to which ceremonies and payments are elaborated depends roughly on several factors: whether it is a first or later marriage; the closeness of kinship; geographical distance; whether the lovers are from distinct bērtan; the nature of prior grudges between the families; whether—least predictable of all—a brother or father of a woman becomes angry. At the most formal extreme might be the first marriage between once-hostile groups; in that case premarital bride-service would be prolonged, its ordeals severe, and bridewealth payments would be demanded over a series of occasions.

At the opposite extreme were the marriages of the 20 Rumyad men and women during 1955–58, when the close ties of kinship and residence and the prevailing mood of amity precluded the need for any assembly at all. Then, as Tukbaw said, the men simply took the women by stealth and neither held public assemblies nor paid bridewealth. Instead, their period of bride-service gradually merged into their residence in the homes of the women, without crossing any line of demarcation. At midpoint between the two extremes stand those marriages that demand public assemblies but no bridewealth payments. In these cases the man and his father come to the woman's parents and formally tell them of the man's intentions. Together they discuss the date of their coming public assemply and what the man should give, and affirm that the gifts will not constitute a bridewealth payment.

Assemblies normally open on a coy note. The man's party, Maniling said, arrives at the woman's house and enters with high decorum, slowly, in order not to offend anyone inside. Yet somebody inside the house often breaks the silence of greeting by saying, "Go and give a betel quid to those who have come to see you." The speaker means that the guests have surely come to see somebody other than himself, even if he happens to be the woman's father or brother. Often the woman's party pretends not to know why their guests have arrived, saying, "No, I don't know why you have come." In one of the cases I witnessed, the man's side tried to reveal its intentions, speaking obliquely, not abruptly ("We have come to look at the blossoming flowers," that is, the woman). The woman's side acted perplexed and refused to understand ("Perhaps the flowers are in bloom at your place, but here they are not"). This tactic of deliberate obtuseness was carried on from midmorning until nearly dusk. Maniling explained that their willful failure to understand the suitor's intentions was designed to preclude such possible insults as "The woman might as well have a penis"—had they failed to resist so adamantly, members of the man's party might think that the woman had initiated courtship. Thus ritualized in its initial phase, the very process of disclosing the purpose of the assembly takes the form of a re-enactment—or at any rate what Pierre Bourdieu has aptly called an official version—of the inception of courtship when the man made his first move toward the woman of his desires.

Once the purpose of the assembly has been revealed, the father or brother of the man presents the woman's family with the first gift, a piece of cloth, "so that," Maniling said, "when they see it their anger will be gone." The idea of giving the cloth, they say, is to "medicate" the heart of the woman's father and brothers so that their anger will be snapped in two. When I suggested that the gift was perhaps empty ritual because the two families would surely grow used to one another with the passage of time, their anger gradually dissipating, Maniling denied emphatically that that was possible. Such fondness might grow and flourish in private relations between people, but once matters had been cast as a public oratorical confrontation between two groups the gift had become obligatory. Maniling compared the gift of cloth to the indemnities given in convenants: in both cases the goods must be displayed and handed over to dissipate anger before all else.

After the opening gift is accepted there is a lull. Those assembled, Maniling said, then want to "know how quick the man is." Just as the man and woman had displayed their quickness by working hard during the period of bride-service, so now the liquor and game presented by the man and his family are viewed as a visible sign of his "quickness, speed, energy" ('awet). Food and drink are given so that those assembled may "eat the hand" of the man. And "if the man," Maniling said bluntly, "is not able to provide enough, he is depyang" (incompetent).

Though courtship may have originated in the private desires of two hearts, by this point in the assembly what has been enacted and thus made real is the conception that marriage is a relation, not simply between a young man and a young woman, but also between two circles of relatives differentiated by sex and generation. This shift in the underlying shape of social relations was most vividly brought home to me during another 1974 assembly that I attended. On that occasion the relation between the lovers was likened to hunting. Tukbaw, the main orator for the man's side, compared himself to the man who guides the dogs in collective hunts. No longer a simple affair between a man and a woman, the patient caretaker and the domesticated pig, the public assembly demanded a metaphor that suggested more differentiated social relations—hunters, dogs, a man guiding the dogs, and game.

Maniling later explained that in the trope the suitor "counted as if he were a dog," and Tukbaw, as the suitor's spokesman, was like the guide for the dog because he "leads [*bukur*] him forcefully into the house." Tukbaw grinned as Maniling interjected that dogs indeed need guides, for no dog is a worse dog than a dog on the loose. He was referring to the one case I know of where the hunting metaphor was literally acted out in an especially revealing way. During the 1974 public assembly the suitor became so drunk that he was, he later claimed, overwhelmed by the force of his desire and passionately leapt upon his wife-to-be. She was furious and demanded compensation because, she said, he had treated her as if she were a wild pig. The story was told and retold, and each time people laughed without stopping until tears came to their eyes. Both the imaginative power and the practical limits of metaphor became apparent as people invented other kinds of things that any man so foolish as to confuse a woman with a wild pig might as well have done while he was at it.

The witty contesting orators with their riddle-like tropes usually go on—talking, drinking, eating—through the night and into the early afternoon of the next day. While the others gradually disperse, returning homeward, the suitor remains in the woman's house, where he becomes one of their people. His father-in-law, Maniling said with a wink, "no longer releases him to run unleashed." For that first night the suitor's father also remains in the woman's house because he cannot bear the sadness, the pain in his heart, at losing his son from his home.

The couple follows the wife's parents. After the man moves in, sometimes before, the woman may become pregnant in what is as much a continuation of the movement through courtship as it is the beginning of their family of marriage. During courtship the man followed the woman, who at once waited for him—that is, did not move toward him—and also followed her parents, as she had done since birth. Once married, the woman maintains the direction of her movement, while the man simply extends his as the couple now follows the wife's parents.

In its cultural imagery, conception often resembles the beginnings of courtship, in that it highlights the way in which things originate with the man. Duman said to me that men evidently make babies because no woman has ever given birth without having had intercourse with a man. Her brother Maniling agreed that the man is the source of conception, and he compared the woman's womb with a hollow gourd into which "the man puts water." Others disagreed and thought, rather vaguely, that the source of the fetus was blood and seminal discharge from both the man and the woman, mixed together. Yennaw, for instance, was often said never to have conceived a child with Adēlpig "because their two bloods never met." In any case, the fetus is said by all to grow and develop, not of its own accord, but through repeated intercourse. Consistent with Ilongot ideas about anger and strength, Disa and Sawad put forth the view that it is because a man's sperm "collects" ('upug) inside the woman that the fetus is able to "become a person." If the man were to ejaculate only a few times, Maniling said, his sperm would simply "drop, drop, dribble, and disperse" (siwak, the opposite of 'upug), with no result at all. Conception and pregnancy are thus viewed as a unitary process of growth that requires a continuation of the male initiative in courtship for its fruition.

When I asked why the man follows the woman and then her parents, people replied in terms that I thought were transparent. An older man from Kakidugen said that people follow the wife's parents because it was painful and difficult for them to raise their daughter from infancy. Tukbaw and Wagat spelled matters out more fully and said that the wife's parents "eat the hand" of their son-in-law to "replace" their having cared for (saysay) their daughter. That uxorilocality by household was regarded as a continuation of premarital bride-service and a form of compensation for the labor involved in raising a daughter seemed nothing more than a homespun version of social exchange theory. But then I reflected on the obvious fact that, for Ilongots at any rate, sons were as painful to bring up as daughters, and long-term reciprocity for child care could justify virilocality as easily as uxorilocality.

Ilongot conceptions of postmarital residence, I realized, should be unpacked into notions about direction and duration. Whereas statements about direction explain why married children live with the wife's rather than the husband's parents, statements about duration explain why they reside with or near their parents at all

A man tying a bundle of herbs for use in hunting magic.

A woman using halved pieces of bamboo to clear a thin layer of topsoil from her garden. The topsoil, which contains weed seeds, is scraped into narrow ridges as a means of confining the growth of weeds before planting rice.

rather than anywhere they please. Ilongot ideas of direction emerge from their conceptions of gender, particularly the notion that women are more fearful because they have walked less far and hence have less knowledge of men. Because they have less fear and more knowledge, men are expected to take the initiative in courtship, and uxorilocality is seen as but a continuation of the direction of movement already set during courtship.

Ilongot ideas of duration, on the other hand, grow out of the lifetime familial obligation that parents and children provide for one another during their respective phases of dependency: old age for parents and early childhood for children. Just as the notion of equality in hunting ability was tied to the long-range phases of the life cycle, so the notion of mutual caretaking is linked to a long-range view of the domestic cycle. The idiom of providing for one another is connected less with whether the daughter, rather than the son, remains at home than with the way that parents and children are obliged to follow one another for the duration of their lives.

Although the topic of courtship elicited extended conversations

A woman digging sweet potatoes and collecting them in her rattan carrying basket.

Two men dueling on the banks of the Kasiknan in the early light of dawn, April 1968.

about strategies over a series of phases, the incremental process of increase and then decrease in the number of conjugal families in the household was well known but not a matter for much comment. Culturally, courtship was like other Ilongot beginnings in that it was relatively differentiated, compared with the later less-broken flow of action. Regarding the subsequent phase of postmarital residence, what people stressed was simply that married daughters follow their parents.

What is implied in saying that married daughters follow their parents is that after the first daughter marries and brings her husband home, a second daughter may marry and do likewise. At this point the household will consist of three conjugal families: the parents and two married daughters. Households of more than three conjugal families are said usually to become too crowded. "The children then are like worms," Kadēng explained, referring to their wriggling numbers. "They make us deaf," Lakay said, repeating a phrase he used to shout often to the children of his youngest daughter, Sawad. Hence in subsequent marriages the youngest one or two married daughters remain in the parental household, while their older sisters reside nearby in single or dual-family homes. Indeed, this general pattern accounted for all four of the household types found during 1967–69 in Kakidugen, Pengegyaben, Kēyat, and Tauyang. These household types were distributed as follows: (1) single conjugal family (6, or 26 percent); (2) parents and one married daughter (10, or 43 percent); (3) parents and two married daughters (5, or 22 percent); and (4) two married sisters (2, or 9 percent). That these types are predominant derives from their providing maternal support for newly married daughters, as well as later support for the aging parents from their married daughters, especially their youngest co-resident daughter.

Two of the most strictly followed structural principles in Ilongot social life are, first, that initial postmarital residence is uxorilocal by household and, second, that marital relations are rarely terminated by divorce. Nonetheless, the local landscape no more than *tends* to be divided into discrete two- and three-generation matri-filial clusters. Surely nothing human—certainly nothing Ilongot— could be so free from life contingencies and whims of the heart as to result in such a crystalline settlement pattern. Complexities and exceptions usually enter in two broad situations. First, orphaned children are usually cared for by a sibling or parent of either of their parents; sometimes they are raised by a succession of two or more foster parents. How strongly and how long they will feel obliged to live with or near their foster parents varies a good deal more than with children of natural parents and depends in large measure on the age at which they were orphaned, the number of foster parents who cared for them, and the number of living natural daughters of the foster parents. Second, the woman's family in occasional cases moves to the man's local cluster, whereupon he moves into her family's home. Such unions thus are uxorilocal by household and virilocal by local cluster. Usually these cases arise in the context of direct exchange marriages between the two families; at times the shift in residence anticipates, indeed helps precipitate, further marriages between siblings.

The parents in turn follow their married daughters. In time the wife's parents become afflicted with the infirmities of age. Memory fades; hearing fails; eyesight grows dim; tendons lose their elastic strength. Now, as Insan said, "things turn around," and the wife's parents begin to follow their children. It is at this time, if ever, that siblings are able to move and join one another. Yet this period, the terminating episode in the developmental cycle of domestic groups, is culturally passed over in relative silence. The process of sibling reaggregation is not a matter for public confrontation and oratory, but for tactful conversation in private among the concerned parties. As with stories patterned after journeys, there is little to say about this parental "return" to the dependency of childhood.

This moment when things turn around, nonetheless, is the most critical of all for relations among the households of local clusters. The problem for the married couple moving toward the senior position within the household is to calibrate the multiple pulls among the households of the husband's sisters (who reside elsewhere), the wife's brothers (who live in yet another place), and the wife's sisters (who live in the same house or next door). Among the mobile Ilongots all possible strategies can be followed at once, as some local clusters split and others become unified. The original married couple, for instance, along with the wife's sisters, might move to the place of the husband's sisters and there perhaps be joined by the wife's brothers. How things actually turn out depends on the possibilities afforded by the prior pattern of marriages—intricately woven as they often are within the range of second or third cousins—in combination with the relative strength of the contending sibling sets (their numbers, their ages, their sexes, the astute persuasiveness of their older members). It is through these delicate negotiations that the solidarity of local clusters, such as it is, extends beyond its matrifilial units to a dominant sibling set in the senior generation.

When Ilongots describe the movement of a married couple through the phases of the developmental cycle of domestic groups, they, not unlike Meyer Fortes, conceal a central structural factor in the politics of marital alliances. Cast in the most general terms, the problem is that any linear model that is abstracted from synchronic observations will necessarily fail to show the high likelihood that two seemingly disconnected phases of the process may in fact normally overlap in time. More concretely, this cohort analysis enabled me to perceive that married children gradually replace the woman's parents as the dominant core of a local cluster at about the same time that their older children begin to marry. The time, in other words, of sibling reaggregation in the emerging senior generation of a local cluster usually coincides with the time when the oldest children of the emerging junior generation are about to marry.

The residential shifts of sibling reaggregation often bring groups of teenage children into close proximity with potential spouses, and matters follow from there. Parents, of course, rarely tell their children whom to marry, simply because they would probably fail in so directly imposing their will. Whether by design or not, a stimulus as well as a consequence of sibling reaggregation is to provide, not a particular partner, but a diffuse orientation for the direction of their children's future marriages.

A RESIDENTIAL MOVE AND MARRIAGES, 1955–58

Let us return now to the cohort analysis as we consider the interplay of generations, the reaggregation of siblings that coincided with the marriages of their children in 1955–58. In the case I shall discuss, the marital unions through which the children became adults overlapped historically with the residential reunion of their parents, the classificatory siblings Lakay and Baket. The emergence of these relations, their initiation for the children, and their renewal for the parents took place in characteristic Ilongot fashion. Gradually, step by step, these ties of kinship and marriage were interwoven as so many overlapping lines, not as discrete points in time.

The proximate origins of this process dated from shortly after the Pengegyaben people's move of 1936. It was then, the first time they had been in contact with one another since the Rumyad dispersal of 1923, that the people of Kakidugen and Pengegyaben began to visit and hunt together. Through these visits Lakay and Baket, the children of half-brothers, slowly began to renew, as they put it, the knowledge of their relatedness. In 1942 Baket's son by her first husband married Lakay's classificatory sister (FZD) and moved to the place of the Kakidugen people. But that marriage led to no further unions between the two groups until the marriage of Insan and Duman in 1955.

In 1945 the Kakidugens retreated toward the interior, where their hoped-for residential union with the Pengegyabens was aborted by the Japanese, who by then had penetrated the navel of Rumyad territory. As they fled through the forest, the two groups briefly joined together, as mentioned earlier, then went their separate ways.

After the war, Lakay and Baket once again tried to build on the marriage of 1942. At the same time, they cultivated relations with other groups and thus provided some maneuvering room for the direction of their children's marital unions. During those immediate postwar years Lakay and Baket encouraged their children, Wagat and Tukbaw respectively, to marry one another, but to no avail. Wagat told me that she had in fact intended to follow her father's wishes, but that she had been deceived by Yennaw, who said that she, not Wagat, was the woman Tukbaw truly desired. Thus Wagat married a Bēnabē in 1948 and Lakay became angry, Duman said, not because his daughter had a lover, but because the man from Bēnabē had grabbed her ahead of Tukbaw. Politically, this marriage constituted the ninth alliance between the Bēnabēs and the Kakidugens in the 25-year period 1923–48. Even as late as 1951, just before the Butag-Rumyad feud erupted, Lakay's children appeared more likely to marry Bēnabēs than the children of Baket.

Meanwhile, Tukbaw married Yennaw in 1948; their union can be construed as one between the Pengegyabens and Kakidugens (see Fig. 2). Certainly Yennaw had grown up among the Kakidugen people until 1945, when she was 19, for her maternal grandmother and Lakay's father, who were related as sister and brother, had resided together in an earlier moment of sibling reaggregation. In 1945 her family was decimated by the deaths of her mother's three siblings and her maternal grandparents. Early the following year Yennaw and the remaining members of her family, her three siblings, her parents, and her paternal grandfather, returned from the lowlands to Kakidugen ahead of the others. Shortly after they arrived, Yennaw's father died, while hunting with dogs; he was, Lakay said, cursed by the spirit of the forest.

The others had not yet arrived, and Yennaw's mother, who was afraid to remain in Kakidugen after such an uncanny death, had few places to turn. All her siblings were dead, and her husband's only sibling, a half-brother, was among those who had been arrested in 1940 (and had, though she did not know it then, already died in prison); hence she led her aging father-in-law (who until then had been following her) to Pengegyaben, because the old man had lived among those people while his first wife, the sister of Baket, was still living. Shortly after moving into the home of Tawad and his siblings (who were Yennaw's classificatory siblings because their maternal grandmother, the one shot by the Japanese sniper in 1945, was the sister of her paternal grandmother), Yennaw was definitively orphaned by her mother's death from illness in 1946. Two years later, when he married Yennaw, Tukbaw simply moved into what had by then become a neighboring Pengegyaben household.

That same year of 1948, Baket's daughter, the sister of Tukbaw, married a Ringen man. Their marriage was contested because the groom, among others, had "threatened the lives" of the Pengegyaben people in their vulnerable moment of 1942, two years after

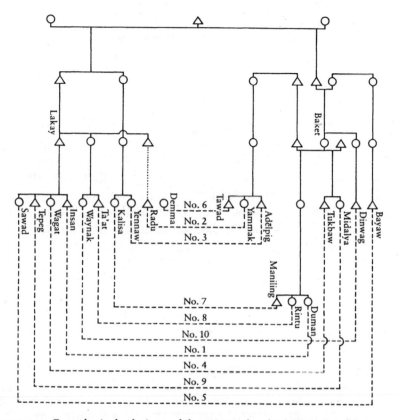

FIGURE 2. Genealogical relations of the 20 people who intermarried in 1955–58. (Marriage numbers refer to those in text. Dotted line represents relationship by adoption; dashed lines connect marriage partners.)

the arrests and immediately after they had moved into central Rumyad. The groom and the other Ringen people had set an ambush for Baket's children in the hope of beheading a Bēduk man among them, because he was then courting Dinwag's sister. They were retaliating for the Bēduk people's role in egging on the soldiers who had murdered Bayaw's brother earlier that year. The Ringen people claimed they did not know of their relatedness to Baket and did not abandon their plan of beheading her people until Lakay's father—whom they had gone to ask—told them, according to Maniling, that Baket was his daughter. He said, "If you are going to kill her people, begin with me."

These strong words put matters to rest until the Ringen man initiated his courtship with Baket's daughter. In the end the marriage took place only after major payments had been made (a blanket, a wooden chest, two bolos, brass wire, and a wide-mouthed metal cooking pan); these were viewed as compensation for the attempted ambush rather than as bridewealth. Not until a decade later did it become evident that this Ringen-Pengegyaben marital union would not be further built upon, and that instead a series of events would lead the children of Lakay and Baket to intermarry.

In 1949 Baket was, as Ilongots say, pulled in another direction. Her only brother beckoned her to Kēyat shortly after her second husband, Tukbaw's father, died of tuberculosis. Her brother had no daughters, so in his old age he had begun to follow his sons, who had married two sisters from Kēyat. It was in part because he was so poorly anchored in Kēyat that he was especially eager to be joined by his two living sisters from Pengegyaben. With a mischievous twinkle in her eyes, Baket said that she told her brother yes, but that she never really intended to move across the hill because she wanted more room to maneuver.

When Lakay's son Insan took a head in 1950, Baket's granddaughter (DD) Duman was among those women who pounded rice for the raiders. Some time after that Lakay, seeing that Duman was hard-working, said to Insan, "Marry that woman there." Insan agreed with his father's choice, and in 1951 he came to Pengegyaben, where he pollarded the tall trees for Duman and her mother (her father, Kadēng, was still in prison). Later that year he brought gifts of meat and betel nut from the forest and gave them to Duman's family. It was not until a return visit, Duman recalled, that Insan spoke with her, his eyes sparkling as he made his heart known to her. And it was on yet a later visit that they said yes to one another and lay down together, talking of how their desire was true, not a lie, until their hearts followed one another. Their courtship continued even past the year 1954, when Lakay's family moved to Pengegyaben and stayed initially in a single house with Baket, her children, and her grandchildren, including Duman. During their period of co-residence Insan gave Duman a blouse, a cotton blanket, and a piece of cloth, but they were not regarded as having married until the following year, after Kadēng returned from prison.

Among those arrested in 1940, Kadēng was the first to be released. He had earned time off for good behavior because he had served as a guide for the incoming American troops in 1945. At that time, incidentally, he had also seized the opportunity, provided at last—long after his marriage and the birth of his four children—to take a head, that of a Japanese soldier given him by an American soldier. The term of his incarceration had been 14 years by the time he was freed, late in 1954, from Iwahig Penal Colony in Palawan.

Kadēng sailed from the southern island of Palawan to Manila and then rode by bus along Highway 5 to the home of a lowland compadre near Bambang, where the Kakidugen people had stayed for a short time during their nomadic year of 1945. Unfortunately for Kadēng, Ilongots at that moment rarely walked to the lowlands because they feared violence from the Huks or the BCTs. After waiting for a couple of months, Kadēng finally spoke with an Ilongot and asked him, "Where are you from?"

"Kabean," the man replied.

"What is your bērtan?" Kadēng asked.

"Why do you seek it?" the man responded. "All of us are Payupays."

"Do you know," Kadēng kept questioning, "the man whose name is Dalawen?"

"He's my uncle," the man replied.

"He's also my uncle," Kadēng said. "He married my aunt."

The two men wept because they had discovered their relatedness. And, Kadēng said, "He wept and I wept because he told me about how they were wiped out when the Japanese went up" into the Ilongot hills.

The Payupay man in turn told a Bēnabē youth about the arrival of Kadēng. Shortly afterward the youth walked to the lowlands and told Kadēng the news of his family. Kadēng's son, his third child, had been lost when the spirit of the forest seized his heart and led him away with such cunning that his footprints became the tracks of a deer and then vanished over a rocky stretch. He was never seen again. His two daughters, Duman and Rintu, had become young women, and his son, Maniling, the youth went on, "knows how to hunt by himself. Your oldest daughter is being courted by Insan, but they haven't yet set up house together." The Bēnabē youth then agreed to ask Kadēng's children to walk up to the lowlands and guide their father back to his home in Pengegyaben.

Kadēng described his time of waiting as follows: "I grew impatient and over and over again I went out and looked down the road. When the setting sun drew low in the sky I said to myself, 'Are they never going to arrive?' I wept and my tears fell to the ground."

When, at last, the people from central Rumyad did arrive, Kadēng was overwhelmed by his emotions. "When I was in Palawan," he explained to me, "I remembered my daughters as children. I returned and they were grown, even though in my dreams they had been the size of children, my children. I never dreamed of them as grown women."

In another of his four verbatim texts (and in his frequent conversations) about his return from prison, Kadēng recalled his feelings at the moment of reunion: "My breath died; I was struck speechless by the barbed feeling of seeing my brethren. Surely all our hearts are like that, when you haven't seen your own children for 15 years." The Bēnabē youth who had returned with his children said to Kadēng, "I'll point out Duman for you. Over there, that's Duman; over there, that's Insan; over there, that's Rintu." All three of them had grown and changed beyond recognition, for at the time of Kadēng's arrest Duman had been nine, Insan eight, and Rintu newborn. The youths explained their delay, saying, "We did not hasten more because we killed some Huks on the Bukaw and we now are afraid of them."

On their return homeward, up into the hills, they stopped and spent the night at the house of a Bēnabē man who had been Kadēng's friend. As he greeted Kadēng, the Bēnabē waxed eloquent: "Friend [kabuintaw, literally, fellow unmarried young man], we should thank the one who created us because the two of us are now here to look at one another. Let us thank god [diyut, from the Spanish dios] for your return to your place, your true birthplace. Now, I'll give you a betel chew. What will follow after

I hand you the betel chew are my tears shed for the days of old before our lives were cut off by the arrival of the Japanese, who wiped us out. Alongside the arrival of the Japanese, the people in Ilongot country were wiped out by the starvation and the disease that came hand in hand."

"What can be done about that now?" Kadēng replied. "In truth, we people are not like the highest hills, unchanging and forever undiminished. It is up to those of us who have been passed over not to be contrary and not to come to hate one another. I have now finished what I have to say to you, my friend from the days of old."

The following day, Kadēng said, "I arrived at Pengegyaben. I no longer recognized Tukbaw. They said, 'Over there, that's Tukbaw.' That's all. I then became Ilongot."

Much had changed during the 15 years since Kadēng had been torn from his world. His children had grown beyond recognition; the paths he had walked were now covered with vegetation, and others had come into use. The watershed that was "the time of the Japanese" had been reached and left behind; the violent tenor of the time of the Huks had enabled Maniling, unlike his father, to take a head before he married. Moreover, marriages were clearly in the air, as a number of children had come of age. All of the ten unmarried young men had already succeeded in taking heads—unlike four of their eight fathers, who were not able to do so in the earlier era of peacetime—and were thus prepared to answer back throughout the ordeals of courtship.

The decisive step in setting the direction of the ten intermarriages of 1955–58 had been taken just the year before Kadēng's return. In that year Lakay and his younger brother had grown apprehensive about the increasing climate of violence—the Huks, the BCTs, the Butags, and rumors of war planes bearing bombs—and had decided in Ilongot fashion to increase their strength by moving further toward the interior and gathering together with their classificatory sister, Baket, and the people of Pengegyaben. Seen from another perspective, this move was an instance of sibling reaggregation; at once reactive and proactive, it was stimulated by the courtship of Insan and Duman at the same time that it resulted in a further succession of marriages. The series of marriages developed as they did, Maniling said, because the people from the two local clusters found themselves living together for the first time in over 30 years, and then said, "good," and leapt upon the opportunity to marry their classificatory siblings.

And leap they did, in the major succession of marriages for the people of Kakidugen and Pengegyaben during the post-1945 era. To review the data decade by decade, there were five marriages in 1945–54 (all in 1947–48); there were 13 marriages in 1955–64 (ten from 1955 to 1958); and there were five marriages in 1965–74 (four in 1970–71). Three clusters of years thus account for 19 of the 23 marriages during this 30-year period; to put it another way, more than 80 percent of the marriages occurred in less than 30 percent of the time period. This cultural pattern, an integral part of the Ilongot sense of history, in which youths followed one another in marriage, much as they had in taking heads, was manifested most clearly over the course of the ten marriages that occurred from 1955 to 1958.

The first four marriages were based on co-residence, not as mere neighbors, but as members of the same household. Lakay moved into the home of Baket in 1954, and the following year his son Insan and Baket's granddaughter Duman, who had been courting since 1951, were married; in this case co-residence simply solidified an already existing relationship. Also in 1954, Lakay's younger brother moved into the house of Yennaw, and the next year his adopted son, Radu, married her classificatory sister, Yammak; they had started their relatively brief courtship as housemates. In 1956 Yennaw married her classificatory brother, Adēlpig; the two of them had lived in the same household for a decade. Later that year came the marriage of Lakay's daughter Wagat and Baket's son Tukbaw; they too had begun their courtship as housemates. Whatever the results of living together in the same home from birth, it is clear that, among Ilongots, co-residence starting from the years of youth is more likely to breed desire than contempt.

By the end of 1956, the direction of intermarriages had built up enough momentum so that the remaining youths in the two now-united local clusters would follow the ones who had gone before. The progression of the ten marriages, as they unfolded case by case, was as follows (see also Fig. 2):

1. In 1955 Insan (age 23) from Kakidugen married his "niece"

(FFFSDDD) Duman (age 24) from Pengegyaben. They courted from 1951 at the suggestion of Insan's father, Lakay; they lived in the same house during 1954; they married after Duman's father, Kadēng had returned from prison.

2. In 1955 Radu (age 24) from Kakidugen married his "distant sibling" Yammak (age 25) from Pengegyaben. They began to court after living together in the same house during 1954; they both had been orphaned in 1945, and hence there was no possibility of parental arrangement for their union.

3. In 1956 Adēlpig (age 28) from Pengegyaben married his "sister" (MFZDD) Yennaw (age 30) from Kakidugen. While Yennaw was still married to Tukbaw, her first husband, she had an affair with Adēlpig's older brother, Tawad. Later the two brothers fought one another with heavy sticks over who should pursue Yennaw. Adēlpig won. This was Adēlpig's first marriage.

4. In 1956 Tukbaw (age 33) from Pengegyaben married his "sister" (MFFSSD) Wagat (age 31) from Kakidugen. Their marriage was originally promoted by their parents, Baket and Lakay, just after 1945, but at that time they each married other people. This was the second marriage for both of them, and their union grew out of their becoming housemates after Wagat's 1954 divorce.

5. In 1957 Bayaw (age 28) from Bēawet married his "distant sibling" (FFMZDSD) Sawad (age 29) from Kakidugen. Bayaw was closely identified with the Pengegyaben people because his mother was Baket's classificatory sister (MZD) and his family had lived with Baket's older sister in 1952–54. Lakay opposed this marriage primarily because Bayaw was doubly related, as classificatory brother (MZS) and brother-in-law (WB), to the Aymuyu man whose firearm had accidentally killed Lakay's father in 1952.

6. In 1957 Tawad (age 32) from Pengegyaben married his "distant sibling" (FMFBSDD) Demma (age 25) from Bēnabē. Demma was closely identified with the Kakidugens because her family had resided with them until she was orphaned in 1945. After 1945 she was raised by a Bēnabē woman, though she often spent long periods at the home of Dilya, her classificatory sister (FBD) and the wife of Lakay's younger brother. Tawad's marriage was slightly off the path of the others because he wanted to flee the scene of his quarrel with his younger brother, Adēlpig, over Yennaw.

7. In 1957 Maniling (age 22) from Pengegyaben married his "aunt" (MMFFDDD) Kalisa (age 26) from Kakidugen. This marital union was regarded by many as an "exchange" (*tubrat*, also "retaliation") for the 1955 marriage of Duman, Maniling's sister, and Insan, Kalisa's classificatory brother (MMBSS).

8. In 1958 Ta'at (age 27) from Kakidugen married his "niece" (MFFSDDD) Rintu (age 18) from Pengegyaben. Kadēng opposed this marriage because, Sawad said, he wanted to "watch Rintu grow older" and have her do chores only for him. His time in prison had evidently deepened and complicated his feelings toward his daughters, whom he had dreamed of as children and returned in 1955 to find as attractive maturing women. Furthermore, Kadēng objected because his daughters' marriages would be tilted to one side, as Ilongots say, if they married two such close classificatory brothers (Ta'at was Insan's FZS). Lakay said that Kadēng told Ta'at, "You may not come to me because Insan has already come to me." Once Rintu was pregnant, Ta'at gave her father a flannel blanket and some shotgun shells, not as bridewealth, but in order to soothe his wrath.

9. In 1958 Tepeg (age 24) from Kakidugen married his "sister" (FFFSDD) Midalya (age 29) from Pengegyaben. Tepeg, Lakay's son, and Midalya, Baket's daughter, had lived in the same household in 1954. Bangkiwa from Ringen was the first to court Midalya, but they never reached the point of lying down together. Baket had objected that, among other things, Bangkiwa (then 42) was too old for her daughter. Both Lakay and Sawad felt that Tepeg was too young to marry, especially a woman five years his senior, but they were ashamed to become angry and oppose the marriage because Midalya was Lakay's classificatory daughter (FFSDD). By 1974 Midalya worried that she, her husband's mother (her ironic way of saying that she was much older than he), might become dependent in her old age on his caretaking, and that he in turn might look to younger women for his sexual pleasure.

10. In 1958 Dinwag (age 40) from Pengegyaben married his "sister" (MFFSDD) Waynak (age 25) from Kakidugen. In this case they simply married; nobody became angry, nor was any compensation given.

The cumulative impact of the progression of marriages over

1955–58 was especially evident in the relative ages of the spouses. The difference in age between the spouses was 1.4 years for the first five marriages, as contrasted with 8 years for the last five. This progressive increase in the age difference between husband and wife can also be seen to increase stepwise from one year to the next as follows: one year in 1955; two years in 1956; four years in 1957; ten years in 1958. In addition, six of the ten women married men younger than they were; whereas in the other 13 post-1945 marriages from the two local clusters, only one woman married a man younger than she. It is apparent that those who came later in the chain of intermarriages seized the opportunity for marriage that had already been set in motion. The point by then was to marry and become the same as one's fellow young men. As more and more of their actual or classificatory brothers were married, those of the ten men who remained single grew increasingly envious and sought women who were markedly younger or older than themselves.

After the union of Insan and Duman, the young men were impelled onward through the subsequent marriages by what, Insan said, "was in their own hearts [rinawa]; it was truly in their hearts." He then invoked the cultural conception that youths moving toward marriage, like people on the quest for food, become mutually energized through their collective pursuit of a goal that they all hope to reach at about the same time. Speaking of the 1955–58 marriages, he said, "They all finished at once in a tie. It happened because envy made them want to marry, and besides it came from each of their hearts." Since, he added, "the man is really the source [rapu] of courtship," each of the other nine said to himself, "I'm not the same [in marital status as my age-mates], so I'll go find out how that woman feels toward me." The young men, in other words, initiated courtship in accordance with the desire of their hearts; but as the progression of marriages developed, their desire increasingly originated as much from envy of the other young men who had immediately preceded them in marriage as from the attraction of the young women.

This view that emulation among men was the dynamic force in building the momentum of the marriages—much in the way that it is in headhunting—was carried one step further by an outsider who was Tukbaw's classificatory son (MBSS) from Kēyat. "They exchanged like that," he said, "not because anybody told them to, but rather because they said to themselves, 'Since he came for my sister, I'll go there and we'll both have drawn our bolos.' " Here the bolo, a machete or long knife, is a metaphor for the man's penis, and it is associated with both sexuality and the anger involved in courtship. In less metaphorical terms, the outsider said that the momentum of the marriages was built up through mutual envy among men. When one young man learned that another young man had had sexual intercourse with his sister, he became angry and wished to retaliate. Therefore he in turn had sexual intercourse with the sister of the man who initially had done so with his own sister.

The densely interconnected marriages of 1955–58 were too complex to be viewed in terms of such a single pattern. Some of the unions surely did have their source in anger over a sister taken by another man who should be dealt with in kind. Yet this motivational pattern of marriage as retribution—however apt it may or may not be as a description of the initiation of any particular courtship—only becomes enshrined as an official version of the entire process through the oratory of public assemblies, especially those concerning direct exchange marriages between members of two distinct bērtan.

The Ilongot conception of marriage as retribution results in a high frequency of what might be classed as direct exchange marriages, both within and between bērtan. But my point is that Ilongots engage in so-called sister exchange marriage, not because (as many exchange theorists would suppose) they value exchange itself, but out of an urge to retaliate. Indeed, it is surely because of the diffuse enduring solidarity that unites bērtan members that Ilongots often claim that the term tubrat (exchange, retaliation) never applies to marriages within a bērtan. After all, how could a man retaliate against his own kinsman? Although the sense that all bērtan members are related as kin mutes the cultural idiom of retaliation, there still is a good deal of direct exchange marriage within bērtan.

Consider the case at hand. The marriages of 1955–58 united two historically separated local clusters and in this sense resembled the politics, not only of consolidation among kin, but also of exchange and alliance between distinct groups. Hence, Maniling said that these marriages were similar to, but not really the same as, tubrat. As an insider, one of those who married, he acknowledged the outsider's version of retaliatory motives in the same instant that he denied their applicability to the Kakidugen-Pengegyaben marriages. In true tubrat, he said, one man becomes angry because another man has taken his sister, indicating scorn for him as a man; the angry man then goes to court the sister of his future brother-in-law. True tubrat between distinct groups is at once an "exchange" and a form of "retaliation" (hence it becomes intelligible that tubrat also applies to the retaliatory killings of a feud). Thus tubrat could not describe the marriages between the children of Lakay and Baket, because retaliatory anger is incompatible with their close ties of kinship.

In retrospect, these marriages were regarded as "unions among themselves" ('uneng), where the women were taken, as Tukbaw said, by stealth, and no public assemblies were held afterwards. Among such close kin neither the oratory of public confrontation nor the remembrance of retaliatory anger in taking another's sister would have been appropriate. In characterizing the complex web of kin connections crisscrossing among those who intermarried, Ta'at said, "Our hearts [rinawa] were as much as woven together." Much in the way that people claimed (despite their awareness of a few exceptions) that because the man had entered the woman's house after marriage he must also have initiated their relationship, so in this case the marriages were usually interpreted by looking backwards from a known public ending along a continuum toward a consistent private beginning.

What was seized upon in 1955–58 was more than the global opportunity to marry anybody; it was more particularly the chance to marry within an in-group (see Fig. 2, p. 199). Nine of the ten marriages at that time fell within the genealogical range of second to third cousins in the following manner:

a. Four marriages (numbers, 3, 4, 9, 10) were between classificatory siblings whose grandparents had been siblings (half-siblings are equated with full siblings in specifying genealogical connections).

b. Three marriages (1, 7, 8) were between people of adjacent generations where the grandparent of one had been the sibling of the great-grandparent of the other. Although usually made uneasy by intergenerational marriages, in this case, Ta'at said, people had never addressed one another as "aunt" or "uncle" because, first, they had not grown up together in the same place, and, second, they were approximate age-mates.

c. Three marriages (2, 5, 6) were between people who were distantly related (kinship is said to branch off as it moves beyond the point where two people's grandparents were siblings), even though in two cases their great-grandparents had been siblings. (This I discovered not from those who married—for specifiable genealogical memory rarely extends beyond three ascending generations—but only by piecing together the accounts of Lakay, Baket, and others of their age.)

It should be kept in mind that in a loose sense all the Rumyad people are kin, as Disa said, "because we hook together in so many ways." In this broader sense, of course, all intra-Rumyad marriages are in-group unions.

This pattern of close marriages, more often attempted than successfully carried out, was often justified as a means whereby all neighbors could be one's children and all one's children neighbors. Bangkiwa from Ringen, for instance, told me that his elders also had favored close marriages because "it was good when their children did not move away; it was good when we married ourselves and when we did not lose our men." The older people, said Tulbit from Tauyang, used to try to gather all of their own in one place. Had they uttered their thoughts, he said, they might have spoken as follows: "You children, let us fill this place of ours with our siblings, so that we who are alike will cluster in one place and none will go and mix with enemies. In that way our children once again will be siblings and we will have nothing to fear in our place." Close marriage thus affords safety in the local cluster, enables sons and parents to reside nearby, and renews ties of kinship that otherwise would lapse between members of succeeding generations.

This cultural conception of close marriage was applied both to those who married and to their parents in the ten cases. Speaking from the viewpoint of those who married, Maniling said, "We did not want to go and marry at a distance because we found it painful to leave our parents." Insan, who had followed his father's suggestion in marriage, viewed the alliances as a realization of the hopes held in "the heart of our grandfather [Lakay's father, who died in 1952] because he did not want us to move far away and go to another place. Because we were their children, we married ourselves." On the other hand, Tukbaw stressed the autonomy of those who married and said that the later marriages "had their source in the quick ones who desired their own kin [betrang, literally, body]; nobody told them what to do." On another occasion, Tukbaw agreed that Lakay and Baket had hoped their children would marry among themselves, but he reiterated that the parents' desires were expressed only obliquely through the oratory of public assemblies. Their children, it turned out in this case, overheard and took to heart the hopes of their parents.

Close marriage, however, was never regarded as an enduring preference, suited for all times and all places. Instead, Ilongots perceive that each historical generation of peers has followed its own distinctive path in marriage. Speaking as a resident of Kakidugen, which he was in 1974, Talikaw from Tauyang conceived of the local marital patterns as a shifting process, a moving back and forth between the two poles of close marriages among themselves and more distant marriages in exchange between distinct groups. He began his story of how people marry by alluding to a version of the Ilongot origin tale: "Those whose source was Simad [a mountain] married their own. Had the sister of one [of the two original brother-sister pairs] not had ringworm the two sibling pairs would have exchanged with one another and they would not have married their own." Originally, then, a brother married his sister and another did likewise in the epitome of close marriage.

His narrative then jumped, in Ilongot fashion, from origins in mythical time to what came next, the earliest moment of his remembered past. Since he was born in 1934, he spoke next of the tubrat unions of 1923–48 between the Rumyads of Kakidugen and the Bēnabēs. "Those in the middle," he said, "married outsiders, for their elders wanted them to marry another bērtan, like the Rumyads and the Bēnabēs." The tale was then brought up to the present, the years after 1945: "We at the bottom went back and married like those at Simad." That is, they once again married close rather than in exchange and at a distance. Each generation was seen, not as acting on a given pattern in a mechanical way, but as forging its own marital destiny in contesting interaction with peers and seniors alike. Parents might have tried to dictate their children's marital choices, Tukbaw said, "if only it had been possible, if it were not for the fact that the hearts of those who newly emerged were so different." Through shifting historical circumstances and quiet changes in the hearts of youths, successive generations of children found themselves in the midst of life chances unknown to their parents.

Ilongot marital alliances, as ideals at least, oscillate between two extremes: marrying close and marrying at a distance—'uneng, marrying one's own, and tubrat, exchange, retaliation. On a more formal plane, however, the two poles can be seen as manifestations of a single underlying paradigm: that of reuniting through a series of marriages back and forth, two groups who were once closely related. The close Kakidugen-Pengegyaben marriages of 1955–58, for example, reunited the children of Lakay and Baket; and the distant Rumyad-Bēnabē marriages of 1923–48 reunited the descendants of a nineteenth-century marital union. Where the two marital poles diverge, despite their formal resemblances, is in the extent to which the retaliatory anger of youths and the knowledgeable oratorical discourse of elders are necessarily part of their unfolding negotiations. In distinguishing 'uneng and tubrat, Ilongots call attention not to the unifying configuration of genealogical space, but to the polar political processes through which they attempt to construct their social worlds.

THE POLITICAL REALIGNMENTS OF 1959–60

The initial realignment of northern Rumyad intergroup relations during the 1950's was reflected, first, in the increase in distance separating the Kakidugens, who moved toward the interior, from the Bēnabēs and, second, in the residential and marital union that joined Kakidugen and Pengegyaben. As they grew more distant from the Bēnabēs, the people of Kakidugen drew closer to those from Pengegyaben.

The next major shift of the decade was the increasing distance, emotional and geographical, that separated the Kakidugen-Pengeg-yaben people from those in Ringen. The proximate source of tension was Luku's beheading of the Butag huntsman in 1952. But this intra-Rumyad hostility did not become manifest in a long-distance move until 1958, when Bangkiwa, his two brothers, his two sisters, and their families—the dominant senior sibling set of Ringen at the time—moved south across the Bukaw River, close to their 1960–74 location.

Bangkiwa and his siblings made their sudden dramatic move in a burst of anger because Tepeg had "stepped ahead" of the Ringen man when he married Midalya (marriage number 9, above). Their marriage was interpreted by Bangkiwa as a personal "insult" and therefore provided the rationale for his later retaliatory acts. The plausibility of this view was confirmed by Tepeg, who said that had Bangkiwa gone ahead and married Midalya he, Tepeg, would not have become angry, because the other man had come before him to court her.

Midalya said that her mother, Baket, had opposed her union with Bangkiwa for three reasons: first, Bangkiwa (then 42) was too old for her (then 29); second, his family and Baket's had been enemies in the days of old; third, "those Rumyads are so bad tempered that they won't take care of you when you're sick." Above all, Baket was still angry because Bangkiwa's people, among others, had beheaded her relatives in 1921. Had the Ringen man married her daughter, she would have been obliged to accept indemnity for the beheadings and thus her anger would have been snapped in two. But she absolutely refused to accept the suitor, and that was that.

When Bangkiwa asked Tepeg for compensation because the latter had stepped ahead of him in marriage, the answer this time again was no. Tepeg insisted that Midalya had never agreed to marry the Ringen man, and hence there were no grounds for payment.

The anger of Bangkiwa was simply awesome. Shortly after moving across the river in 1958, he returned and sneaked up on Midalya while she was working in her garden. His planned decapitation became a lesser "murderous threat" (*kaniyaw*) only because his prey was forewarned by the click that sounded when he loaded his Japanese firearm. Later that year he also threatened the life of a Kēyat man, for the same reason. The following year he prevented his classificatory daughter in Kēyat from marrying a Kakidugen, again for the same reason.

Thus in 1959 the Kakidugen people moved north to their former 1945–53 location, where they were to remain through 1974. Their move carried them to the opposite end of Rumyad territory from that inhabited by the Ringens, who had been their neighbors in 1954–56.

The next year Bangkiwa carried his anger, as Ilongots say, in another direction: he organized a raid against the Aymuyu people, among whom lived the classificatory siblings of Tepeg (his grandmother was the sister of their grandmother). Though it turned out that none of the three victims was related to Tepeg, the intention behind the beheadings had its impact on all concerned. The idea of beheading someone other than the actual target of one's anger, as Tepeg said, is to ensure that "the others see what has been severed in two so they will be frightened."

Tepeg said that through his actions Bangkiwa had shown that he "did not think of me as a man." These incidents and what had led up to them were the sources of the grudge that kept Tepeg from attending the 1969 covenant (Chapter 3). Rather than become afraid, for no Ilongot man cares to admit his fear of another, Tepeg decided to nurture his grudge and make it known, for the time being, more through obstinate noncompliance than through overt hostility. The situation would remain unresolved and prickly in its ambiguities.

The reunion among the twenty who went back and forth in marriage between the co-resident pair of local clusters, tightening their already close ties of kinship, was so successful, so closed in on itself, that it left little room for other relations of alliance. The perfect coordination between (a) marriage alliance among youths and (b) sibling aggregation among their parents created a relatively self-contained local cluster, where kin were neighbors and neighbors were kin. Thus those whose hearts were so artfully woven together by 1958 found themselves closer than ever to one another—at the same time that they had grown undeniably more distant, both socially and spatially in that characteristic Ilongot congruence, from the Bēnabēs to the northwest and the people of Ringen across the Kanuwap River to the south.

SIBLING REUNIONS AND MARRIAGES OF CHILDREN, 1974

To summarize briefly, Ilongot local clusters are composed of two main structural units above the level of the household: sibling sets in the senior generation and uxorilocal clusters in the junior generation (composed of married daughters who reside with or near their parents). My analysis of the developmental cycle of domestic groups has pointed to the central import of the overlap in time between the processes of sibling reaggregation in the senior generation and marriage in the junior generation. In the following section I shall describe how I learned first-hand about the earliest phases of sibling reunions, in order to show aspects of this critical process that are not so apparent in people's later recollections.

On March 28, 1974, Tepeg and Midalya came to visit the home of Tepeg's father, Lakay, where we were staying. They had ostensibly arrived to witness the celebration for the last day of the school year, but we were surprised to discover that their drawn-out visit became a permanent move; indeed, by June we had taken up residence in a new household with them. Tukbaw, it turned out, had persuaded his sister, Midalya, and her husband, his wife's brother, Tepeg, to move to Kakidugen—among other reasons, to care for us. Baket was even more surprised than we at the realization that her youngest daughter had moved without telling her. Midalya, then frail with a difficult pregnancy, felt that it had simply become too much of a burden to carry rice down the steep hill of Pengegyaben for her three children in school at Kakidugen. The plan, though it did not materialize that year, was for Midalya to return and bring Baket (then 92) to her new home in Kakidugen. What had been left ambiguous for some years without major moves was suddenly made clear: Baket was now following her daughter and son-in-law, not the other way around.

When the rice was nearly harvested, people began to discuss where they might clear their gardens for the following year. This was the transitional season of the annual cycle, with marriages and moves in the air. On October 25 we spent the night at Tukbaw's house. After we all lay down to sleep, Kadēng began to speak, formally and in low tones, with his half-brother, Tukbaw. Speaking obliquely, Kadēng asked what his children were thinking. His arthritic legs made it painful for him to walk; his recent separation from his wife, Baket's daughter by her first marriage, had brought him to Kakidugen, where he wanted them to move because he could no longer walk to their place. "Maniling," Kadēng asked his son, "are you awake?" Then he told Maniling how worried he had become because his infirmity made it difficult for him to care for his children. Maniling, then 39, replied that he no longer was nursing at his mother's breast; that as he had grown older he had acquired knowledge, including the understanding that he too had older ones to care for; that he would visit his father, though he was not a woman and hence could not come and pound rice for him. Diplomatic in his reply, Maniling pledged his loyalty as a son while skirting the issue of moving to Kakidugen.

While we were in Pengegyaben on November 17, bidding farewell to Baket (who died the following year), Maniling and his mother began to talk in the intimacy of the firelight after the evening meal. Maniling's mother said (without meaning it) that she wanted the Pengegyabens to move to Kakidugen so that they could better provide for their children in school there. Maniling replied that he had already cleared a garden in the flatland two hours to the west, because squatters had tried earlier that year to settle there and both he and Ta'at were determined to move there and defend their land. That flatland was a place where they had hunted as long as they could remember, and they had always hoped to garden there. This was what Maniling's mother had wanted all along to hear, for she was obliquely seeking assurance that nobody else would sneak off, perhaps to join her husband, to Kakidugen, as Tepeg and Midalya had already done.

This complex and delicate situation, the unfolding phase of sibling reaggregation, poses issues to be negotiated in the privacy of one's home after dark, rather than in public assemblies. Appropriately enough, such moves are gradual in their negotiations; they take place with as many options kept open as possible; and they are cast in an idiom of "holding hands," "pulling," "trying out," and "beckoning." Those who move together in loose coordination, whether uxorilocal clusters or sets of brothers and sisters, are said to "hold one another's hands." The still active older siblings among them are said to "pull" the younger ones and their children. As they consider moving, people in other local clusters "beckon" them, and they in turn "try out" a place where they expect to be well received. In this case Tukbaw had pulled his sister, Midalya, to Kakidugen and was beckoning his wife's brother Insan. At the same time, an abrupt move to Kakidugen would surely worsen the already strained relations with the people of Kēyat, who had become more distant because most of them by then attended Sunday chapel, in contrast to their Pengegyaben brethren. Indeed, another sister of Tukbaw (the one who had married the Ringen man in 1948) had converted to the new religion after the death of her teen-age daughter and would be pulled with difficulty, if at all, even two hours to the west of Pengegyaben. Beckoning her, yet knowing how slim his chances were of pulling her to Kakidugen, Tukbaw thought he would probably entrust her care to her brother-in-law Insan.

Although the complex negotiations—the chain of contingencies being weighed, the differing directional pulls on the various actors, and the ways in which decisions of one would affect the others and vice versa—could be much further unraveled, there remains another as yet unmentioned cluster of factors. Where would the children of the ten couples marry? And how would these future marriages interact with, both influencing and being influenced by, the process of sibling reaggregation among their parents?

Insan's oldest daughter was 18. The oldest daughter of Rintu was 16, and the oldest son of Bayaw 17. All that was certain was that the hearts of the new ones, the children of the people who married in 1955–58, would be unlike those of their parents. As schoolchildren coming of age in the era of martial law, the young men, perhaps in this respect more like their grandfathers than their fathers, would probably marry without taking heads. Moreover, the new generation had grown up in the same place together and felt too close to marry one another; hence they would surely marry in directions different from those of their parents.

The Ilongot sense that in marriage and residential moves children probably will not follow in the footsteps of their parents is central to their consciousness of society and history. Where the young people would marry, and who would come to marry their sisters, was a matter neither they nor their parents would even speculate about. Would they marry close or far, 'uneng or tubrat? In a single direction or dispersed among diverse groups? Both the directions of the children's marriages and the possible pathways of sibling reaggregation among their parents were living proof that, among Ilongots, social life is improvised as people go along. Whereas youths move impulsively, out of the desire and anger in their hearts, older people—especially their parents—attempt to unite knowledge and anger as they negotiate the multiple ties that might pull them in different directions. Indeed, few have the good fortune to concentrate the direction of their movements in raiding, marriage, and residence as much as did the people who were united in 1955–58.

PART III. THE DECONSTRUCTION OF COLLECTIVE IDENTITY

CHAPTER SEVEN. RUMYAD IN
HISTORICAL PERSPECTIVE, 1883-1905

The purpose of Part III is to extend my historical analysis so that the bērtan and the feud can be set in motion. In Chapters 2 and 3 the bērtan, Rumyad, and the feud, seen as a social process, appeared to be the invariant reference points of my analysis. The point in what follows will be to specify certain of the ways in which the bērtan and the feud, far from being a timeless bedrock of synchronic social structure, are historically conditioned and socially constructed.

Though the history of Rumyad that is developed in this chapter provides a broader context for the Butag-Rumyad feud, it also makes the very nature of Rumyad more problematic than it seemed before. The problem of discovering Rumyad, so to speak, arises from the contradiction between Ilongot views as they are articulated in the celebration of a covenant, and a more historical perspective based not on a single unified story, but on what one can piece together from a number of accounts by various people. As a cultural construct, Rumyad, like all bērtan, is viewed as an enduring unit of persons who trace their ancestry to an original co-resident group. On the other hand, all bērtan, and Rumyad is no exception, undergo certain changes through time, both in their developmental processes and in the particularities of their histories. The peculiarity of bērtan is that their historical vicissitudes, fluctuations in their salience and boundaries, do not prevent people from speaking of them as though they were unchanging, and as clearly demarcated in boundaries as an individual household.

BĒRTAN AS CLASSIFIER AND NAME

The word bērtan ranges in meaning from an all-purpose classifier to a designation for groups of people. In its broadest sense bērtan is a classifier par excellence. It can apply to virtually anything that can be enumerated. Most things in this world, including animals, people, and words, are said in their diversity to be of many bērtan. People thus can be classified, among other ways, as tall/short, stingy/generous, and thin/thick at the waist. And plants can be divided into bērtan along such dimensions as habitat, use, and mode of reproduction, or shape, texture, and color of leaf. (Portions of this section and the next are taken from R. Rosaldo 1975.)

The Ilongot classifier is all-purpose not only in the diversity of its possible referents, but also in its range of classificatory principles. Thus bērtan can be as discrete as natural species (wild pig, deer), or they can overlap (groups of plants, as described above). Perhaps the clearest example of how the classifier can refer to kinds constructed by human beings is provided by a derivative form of bērtan. When men describe the division into shares of meat from a hunt, they can call the shares either *bēet* or *binartan*. *Binartan* comes from bērtan, the infix and the vowel change giving the perfective sense, "divided into shares, made into kinds." Used in its widest sense, bērtan can classify innumerable objects in myriad ways.

In a narrower yet related sense, the term bērtan can be used as a category of affiliation to designate a group of people. Ilongots usually use the plural form in speaking of "our" bērtan (including or excluding the hearer) or "your" or "their" bērtan. The term so employed refers to a particular kind of people, especially as contrasted with another such kind. Those of a single kind resemble one another not only in their common name but also in their shared food prohibitions, among which are monkeys, pythons, eels, and civet cats. Whereas people I talked with resisted the attribution of character traits to individuals, Tukbaw was willing to repeat what he called the "gossip" about different bērtan. The true

Rumyads, he said, are fierce; the Peknars are fine gardeners and huntsmen; the Bēsilids marry among themselves; the Bēnabēs are preoccupied with courtship. And when his wife, Wagat, spent the night under her granary after having been gashed across the head by her father, Tukbaw wryly said, "She is like the Payupay people, who make homes of their rice granaries."

Above all, however, bērtan members share a common name. I once asked Insan about the bērtan of a woman from Tauyang, and he replied, "They have a name. Eh . . . they are from Rebugen." In this sense people say that a bērtan, a category of affiliation, is just that, a name. It might seem that as names for groups "bērtan" presents the simplest case of meaning: a perfect correspondence between word and object. What better basis for the sense that bērtan are, literally, kinds of people?

Though their original locations are rarely known to those living in the present, the names of bērtan are most often said to have been place names with no other significance. Even the most imaginative Ilongot folk etymologists, who claim to discover meaning in sound associations, usually reveal that the names suggest geographical features. Talikaw from Tauyang said that *rebugen* means *rebeng*, "deep water," and (less plausibly) that *rumyad* means *kinaduyar*, "the other side of a hill." Insofar as the more usual responses were concerned, of 67 such names that I collected in 1967–69 (virtually a complete list of those current in the Ilongot region), 45 in their folk etymologies were simply place names, nine were words for such prominent geographical features as hill, nine were plant names, and the remaining four were "game, edible wild animal," "pot," "white," and "black." The meaning of these names suggests a strong association between groups with a certain name and a particular locality.

It is worth reflecting a moment on the fact that bērtan, local clusters, and households are alike in that their names may be modified by the prefix *'i-* or "from." Thus the people in Lakay's 1974 house were called *'i'atanay*, "from Atanay," after the name of the stream where they got their drinking water. Those who resided in Lakay's local cluster of Kakidugen were called *'ikakidugen*, "from Kakidugen," after the name of the river that runs through their local cluster. The Rumyad people as a whole were called, *'irumyad,* "from Rumyad," after the name of the now-un-known place where their bērtan is said to have originated.

Although bērtan names and place names are similar in that they can designate human groups, they differ markedly in the duration with which they are attached to people. Whenever people move they retain their bērtan names, but the names of their local clusters and households are dropped and replaced in the new location by the name of a nearby river, hill, or craggy rock or grassy area. The local cluster that I have called, for clarity of exposition, the Ka-kidugen people has actually had the following series of names: Sinarewitan, 1923–26; Demug, 1927–34; Sinaben, 1935–36; Tegē, 1937–44; Kakidugen, 1945—53; Pakdut, 1954–58; and Kakidugen, 1959–74. What endures is the fact that both local clusters and households are named; but their names change every time their houses move.

In contrast, a bērtan name can be associated with a succession of places. Dekran, for example, is a bērtan name for a group of people who have resided in the following series of places: the east-ern fringes of Rumyad; the hills farther east by the Kasiknan Riv-er; the flatlands down on the southeastern margin; the hills up by the Kasiknan; and finally, in 1974, a site just over the hill to the east of Ringen. The various places that have been called Dekran are united, not by a shared feature given in nature, but by their common association with a group of people who have stopped to reside at each place as they collectively move their homes in loose coordination.

When asked about the source of their bērtan names, Ilongots consistently give a readily available cultural cliché in response. In a word, primal co-residence is the source from which shared names in the present are derived. When I asked him about the bērtan name *bēsilid* (hill), Tukbaw replied, "The hill people once lived on a hill." The source of *biaw,* "runo grass" (*Miscanthus*), Talikaw said, is this: "They made their homes near a large stand of runo grass." Even in the least plausible cases the cliché remained the same. The source of *budēk* (white), Talikaw said, was that "they made their homes near white rocks." In this case, another man re-tained the form of the standard reply but altered its content, saying that the Budēk people derived their name from a long-past co-residential group of light-skinned people. However persistent my efforts to clarify the meaning of this pithy reply, I found it to be self-contained, almost proverbial, and apparently self-evident. And when I asked, for instance, which hill the Bēsilids once lived on, people looked as surprised at my question as I was puzzled that they had no answer. None of my questions about origins uncovered any further evidence—mythical, historical, or other.

Although the folk etymologies of bērtan names appear culturally thin, they suggest that the meaning of such names rests in their location within a historical chain of reference.* It is by virtue of shared putative origins, plus the knowledge of later interconnections, that people who share a bērtan name are said to "hook into one another," that is, to be related as kin. Bērtan names, people say, are remembrances that have been handed down from parent to child over the generations. But the tracing of ancestry among Ilongots rarely reaches past the grandparental generation, for the names of the dead are rarely mentioned except to those who were acquainted with them. My genealogical inquiries usually reached their vertical stopping points when I was told, "I did not see that person. How could I know his name?"

Thus these lines into the past extend back from oneself through one's parents, to one's grandparents, and on into the forgotten past until they reach that primal co-residential group living on a hill, by runo grass, in a now-unknown place named Rumyad or whatever. Like many origin tales, the Ilongot view of bērtan names suggests that the essence of things was revealed in their primordial beginnings somewhere in the unknown past. Thus stable forms of bērtan are thought to have come before the succession of contingencies that pervades the remembered past and the immediate present.

A DIACHRONIC ACCOUNT OF BĒRTAN CONCENTRATION AND DISPERSAL

Bērtan names are all alike in their putative origins, the kinds of meanings attributed to them, and their modification by personal

---

*I have in mind the "causal theory of meaning" put forth by Saul Kripke and others. A useful collection of papers on this topic is Schwartz 1977.

possessives, as well as by the prefix 'i- or "from." They differ significantly, however, in their use, for some apply to present-day groups that are residentially concentrated and others do not.

In operational terms, the difference between residentially concentrated and dispersed bērtan is readily evidenced by seeing which names can be substituted in this sentence: "I am going to _____." One could use the name of any residentially concentrated bērtan and say, for instance, 'ungkita'ak di rumyad, "I am going to Rumyad," referring to any destination in the continuous expanse of territory from Kakidugen to Ringen. On the other hand, no residentially dispersed bērtan name can be used in the sentence, thus 'ungkita'ak di biaw, "I am going to Biaw,' is never said because the Biaw people are scattered among various places. Indeed, only 13 of the 67 names for bērtan known to me in 1967–69 were residentially concentrated and could be identified as one's destination.

The 13 residentially concentrated bērtan are listed below with their population figures for 1967–69 (see Map 1, p. 34):*

Abēka	251	Dekran	212	Sinebran	104
Aymuyu	68	Kebinangan	664	Taang	257
Bēlansi	?	Payupay	?	Tamsi	225
Bēnabē	?	Pugu	103		
Bē'nad	216	Rumyad	307		

Each of these bērtan names can be used in at least three senses. First, and most strictly speaking, they can designate the members of a bērtan as legitimately claimed only through ties of filiation, excluding those who have married in but including those who have married out into other areas. Second, and more loosely speaking, they can designate all the people who reside in an area dominated by a particular bērtan at a given moment in time. Third, and perhaps in a derived sense, they can designate the area where the people so named currently reside, as in the phrase "I am going to Rumyad."

The sense of collective identity shared by residentially concen-

*The reader should note that Butag is a dispersed bērtan name partially assimilated within the concentrated bērtan of Bēlansi. In this respect, it is analogous to the position of Peknar relative to Rumyad. But my remarks here should be taken more as an informed guess than an ethnographic fact, because hostilities prevented our visiting the Bēlansi area.

trated bērtan members derives less from co-residence at a particular moment in time than from their continuity over a series of residential moves. Concentrated bērtan are united by the diffuse enduring solidarity that grows among those who, as Ilongots say, hold hands and follow one another. Not their common roots in a particular place, but rather their shared histories of living together as they have moved together lend people like those from Rumyad an enduring sense of collective identity.

Beyond having moved together, residentially concentrated bērtan are united by virtue of their members' having married among themselves. My census figures indicate that about four of every five marriages are endogamous within such bērtan; in part, of course, this is a matter of definition, for a high proportion of exogamous marriages would lead to the dispersal rather than the concentration of members of particular bērtan. Marital histories collected in Rumyad north of the Kanuwap River during 1967–69 indicate that endogamous unions comprised 33 of 38 marriages for men and 33 of 39 marriages for women, that is, 87 and 85 percent, respectively. Since residentially concentrated bērtan (for the 10 of 13 cases where my census figures are reliable) average 181 in population, the tendency toward endogamy in combination with size produces a realistic conviction that all who share a category name "hook" together in their known or unknown ancestry and thus are of one "body" (betrang) in their shared substance of kinship.

So closely linked are the members of relatively concentrated bērtan that their speech is often distinctive in dialect. These differences in dialect range from intonation and speed of speech to distinct lexical items and features of grammatical form. Aware of these bērtan-specific varieties of speech, Ilongots delight in imitating the speech of other bērtan. Our companions from Kakidugen strutted and talked "tough" in the distinctive accent of Kama and the others from Butag for weeks after the 1969 covenant.

Dispersed bērtan names, on the other hand, refer to groups of people who currently share neither residence histories of coordinated movement nor a unifying pattern of endogamous marriage; nor do they have in common a distinctive manner of speech. Names designating dispersed bērtan are ambilaterally claimed and relatively unrestricted. Particular people can claim multiple dispersed bērtan names, provided they are traced through either or both of their parents and any of their four grandparents.

In many cases, dispersed bērtan names tend to be associated with a particular residentially concentrated bērtan. Thus Tabaku is associated with Bēnabē, and a number of names—Bēsilid, Peknar, "true" Rumyad, and Yamu—are associated with Rumyad. Other dispersed bērtan names are associated with two or more concentrated bērtan. Biaw, for example, is linked with both Rumyad and Tamsi; Pasigiyan is connected with Rumyad and Abēka. And the more widely dispersed Kidmays are found in Bē'nad, Taang, Abēka, Rumyad, and Bēnabē. Individuals describe their multiple bērtan affiliations in the following manner: because he claimed two dispersed bērtan (Tabaku and Peknar), Ta'at traced an imaginary line from his nose to his navel as he said, "Our bodies are cut in two." Because he claimed three dispersed bērtan (Tabaku, Peknar, and Pasigiyan), Insan said, "Our bodies are cut into pieces."

What matters most, for both concentrated and dispersed bērtan, is the social recognition that people share a name, and that they share a common origin when, once upon a time, they were residentially concentrated in one place. Although in a particular context it may be politic to prefer one bērtan name over another, these preferences fluctuate. Adults tend to use more and more bērtan names as they grow older and enter into more widespread relations, exchanging pots and raiding together. As people expand their net of social relations over time, including more diverse people from different bērtan, they come to activate more of their potential bērtan names. People claim that no one ever loses a bērtan name; changing social contexts may lead one to invoke previously held, but never publicly asserted, bērtan names. In practice, however, people rarely have recognized claims to more than five such names.

In the Ilongot view, the multiplicity of bērtan names has resulted from the process of gradual diffusion that bērtan usually undergo. In primordial time, bērtan are said to have been residentially compact. Subsequently, certain of them have become less compact though still relatively concentrated (the 13 cases, including Rumyad, enumerated above). In time, other bērtan have become even more dispersed (54 of the 67 bērtan fall into this loose category). Dispersed bērtan usually become assimilated, to varying degrees, within one or more of the residentially concentrated bērtan, and eventually their names may become lost to memory and simply vanish.

Once concentrated, now dispersed, that in a word is the Ilongot notion of the developmental process of bērtan formation and eventual dissolution. Indeed, the perceived long-term trend toward bērtan dispersal constitutes yet another illustration of the more general cultural conception that strength inheres in focus, "gathering together, concentration" ('upug), whereas weakness lies in diffusion, "scattering, dispersal" (siwak).

RUMYADS THROUGH THEIR HISTORIES, 1883–1905

By exploring now the early history of Rumyad, I hope to elucidate the nature of relations between dispersed and concentrated bērtan as they move through time. In particular, the stories I discuss make up the historical reference points for a problem that arose, only to be covered over during the 1969 Butag-Rumyad covenant. In preparing for a critical moment of the covenant, the sworn oath by salt, people initially proposed that the salt be held in hand by one person each from Bēsilid, Yamu, Peknar, Pasigiyan, and true Rumyad, thereby implicating the members of each bērtan in the dissolution that, should the oath be violated, would follow as certainly as salt dissolves in water. But in the end they discarded that plan because, they said, the summation of all the other bērtan was the name Rumyad. Their actions at the time—foremost among other things—perplexed me enough to inquire into the historical problem of whether (and if so, when, for how long, and in what way) the Bēsilids, Yamus, Peknars, Pasigiyans, and true Rumyads had actually differed from one another.

The reader who wishes to follow Rumyad history in detail should know that, in the present, the dispersed bērtan names I discuss have the following loose association with the six Rumyad local clusters:

Kakidugen	Peknar, Tabaku, Biaw
Pengegyaben	Peknar
Kēyat	Peknar, true Rumyad, Biaw
Tauyang	Bēsilid, Yamu
Ringen	true Rumyad, Pasigiyan
Bēawet	Bēsilid, Yamu

The associations of dispersed bērtan and local clusters listed above are more a useful simplification than an exact correlation. In the first place, dispersed bērtan names and local clusters only tend to correspond with one another. Often only a plurality of the people in a certain place can claim the dominant dispersed bērtan name, hence the sense that each local cluster can have several bērtan and each bērtan can reside in several local clusters. Second, certain dispersed bērtan names are equally or more strongly associated with residentially concentrated bērtan other than Rumyad. Thus the Tabakus (associated with Kakidugen) are primarily connected with the residentially concentrated bērtan of Bēnabē, the Pasigiyans (associated with Ringen) are equally closely connected with the residentially concentrated bērtan of Abēka, and the Biaws (associated with Kakidugen and Kēyat) are equally closely connected with the residentially concentrated bērtan of Tamsi.

The reason I must shift from the idiom of local clusters to that of dispersed bērtan is twofold. First, Ilongots encode their recollections of population movements prior to the time of their births with the enduring continuity of bērtan names, rather than with the ever-changing place names of local clusters. Thus, for example, older Ilongots can say where the Peknars, but not the Kakidugens, were living in the nineteenth century. Second, I shall argue that present-day dispersed bērtan, especially Bēsilid, Pasigiyan, Peknar, true Rumyad, and Yamu, were once more concentrated than at present and therefore more autonomous as actors in feuds. My argument should deepen our understanding of the sense in which bērtan are socially constructed, and reveal the historical sources of conflicts within Rumyad that surfaced during the 1969 Butag-Rumyad covenant.

My reconstruction of the Rumyad early past, including that of the Bēsilids, Pasigiyans, Peknars, true Rumyads, Tabakus, and

Yamus, is based primarily on stories that were told to the oldest
people I knew during 1967–74.* Handed down to Baket, Lakay,
and their age-mates, these received memories reach back into the
unseen past like so many separate wandering vines. There were
stories naming the places where long-dead women had cultivated
their gardens, tales about the sources of marriage alliances, and
histories of feuds with their back-and-forth movement of retaliatory beheadings. Each of these—gardening, alliance, and enmity—was its own story and had to be learned before I could
pull the various strands together and inquire into their overlapping connections.

The reader should bear in mind that my spadeless archaeologi-
cal expedition beyond what Ilongots have seen in their lifetimes is
based on convergent stories about the period, open-ended interviews through which I attempted to link and locate the various
events, and the testimony (in itself as mute as it was incontrovertible for Lakay and the others) of living cultivated plants from that
era, which were pointed out to me on one walk or another. In my
reconstruction there remains, of course, a degree of uncertainty.
Though the relative sequence of events within a larger story is usually reliable, connections between stories are often less so, and
dates for this period are only approximate, accurate within a range
of five or ten years. Nonetheless, this, the early horizon of what
might be called the usable past, is indispensable in my effort to elucidate Ilongot historical consciousness. Episodes from the time of
the Spanish, especially those that were remembered and retold,
have shaped the course of events when people have based their
conduct on their recollection of things past.

The period known as *kakastila*, "the time of the Spanish," refers
to the colonial regime that lasted until 1898, when the United

---

*The name Rumyad first appears in a number of reports by Spanish friars in the eigh-
teenth century. Usually located on the left bank of the Kanuwap River, near the present site
of Tauyang, the continuity of the name suggests considerable time depth for the true Rumyads as a collective entity. The location of the Bēsilids, Peknars, and Yamus on the Kakidugen-Tubu drainage system during the 1860's suggests that they probably were not part of
the eighteenth-century grouping. And since the Pasigiyans came from Abēka, on the southwestern margin, they probably were not part of eighteenth-century Rumyad either. In this
sense, living memories seem more reliable then documents written by missionary friars as a
means of reconstructing the early Rumyad past; and the period before the 1860's seems
simply beyond recovery for bērtan histories.

States took the Philippine Islands from Spain. I should stress that most of the people I knew during the research period 1967–69 were born after the nineteenth century. Even Baket, who was born about 1882, could no longer portray that distant epoch because her memory had so failed that her stories were confused.

Unlike the distinct versions of peacetime described earlier, it is generally agreed that the time of the Spanish was an era high in violence. The full bloom of headhunting is key in the characterization of this period.

Pangpang, who was born about 1895, characterized the time of the Spanish in an idiom resembling the manner in which Tukbaw and Kadēng, using the image of wild pigs, described how people were living shortly before their births (see Chapter 1). "Our houses were scattered about, here and there," he said, "and all we did was follow ['unud] wherever we happened to garden." The waning time of the Spanish was typified for Pangpang by its violent tenor. "Now these old ones," he went on, "they never fled from anyone, and soldiers never used to come up into the hills. In the old days they killed one another. Even lowlanders, we killed them." Shifting from "we" to "they" as he spoke of his predecessors, Pangpang was not only following an Ilongot storytelling convention, he (a convert to the religion of the New Tribes Mission) was also expressing his simultaneous rejection of and nostalgia for bygone days.

Kadēng, who was born about 1909 and was not a convert, also described the time of the Spanish as a period of fear and violence. The old people, he said, were under no governmental jurisdiction; they were under no mayor and no councilmen. They respected only their elders and otherwise followed solely the dictates of their own hearts. So vigilant were they in that era, he concluded, that people carried shields, spears, and bolos wherever they visited; and out of fear for their lives they never allowed themselves to fall asleep in the homes of their hosts.

Marital alliance as reunion: Peknars and Tabakus. Lakay, who was born about 1894, told me that the Bēnabēs and the Rumyads (like the people of Kakidugen and Pengegyaben prior to their 1955–58 intermarriages) had already been related long before the marriages between them that began after his arrest in 1923. "It was our arrest," Lakay said, "that was the source of people's becoming related. Tuyadeng told the tale of Iddung, and that was the source of our becoming related." Dating from the time of the Spanish, the story Lakay alluded to, about a captured mother and her ransomed sons, was told and accepted as true by the Peknars (a now-dispersed bērtan linked to Rumyad) when Lakay was arrested and confined on the northwestern margin, where the Tabakus (a now-dispersed bērtan linked to Bēnabē) resided (see Fig. 3).

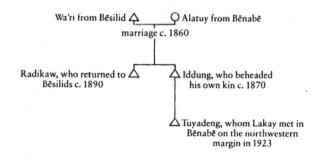

F I G U R E 3. Genealogical source of Bēnabē-Kakidugen marital alliance.

The story then became the charter for the subsequent intermarriages between the two groups.

Perhaps it was 1860 when a Tabaku woman, the story began, came to visit the Kakidugen River area where the Bēsilids and Yamus lived (both are now dispersed bērtan linked to Rumyad; see Map 2). In those days, for protection against marauders, their houses stood high on stilts. And when Alatuy, the Tabaku woman, climbed way up into one of these houses, a group of young men from Bēsilid kicked down the ladder, leaving her, Lakay said, "there like a prisoner. Then Wa'ri married her." For Lakay, the event that united Alatuy from Tabaku and Wa'ri from Bēsilid was evocative not of a classic marriage by capture, but of time spent behind bars.

Some years later, Lakay went on, the in-laws of Alatuy buried her dog alive because it had eaten their corn. Embittered, the woman took her two sons, Radikaw and Iddung, and returned to

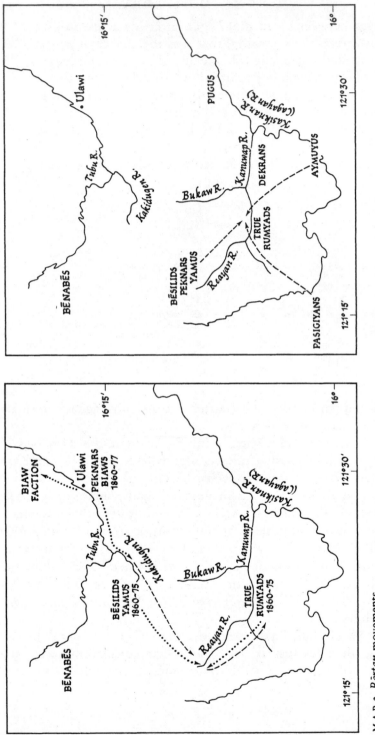

MAP 2. *Bērtan* movements.

Bēnabēs, Bēsilids-Yamus, Peknars-Biaws, and true Rumyads (1860–89). (Dotted lines indicate moves of 1875–83; dashed lines, those of 1883–89.)

Bēsilids-Peknars-Yamus, Aymuyus, true Rumyads, Dekrans, and Pugus (1890–1908).

her birthplace. Years passed; and in the late 1870's, when the two boys had become young men, their mother's people from Bēnabē made a demand as terrible as it was then normal in such situations: a human victim as what they called a covenant, to assuage their anger about the way the Bēsilids had simply grabbed Alatuy in marriage.

"If you do not lead us," the Bēnabēs told the youths, "we will kill you."

"Do not kill us," Iddung and Radikaw replied. Outsiders through their father, the two youths were being held as hostages with only themselves immediately available to pay the demanded ransom. "We will lead you," they told the Bēnabēs, "to the people in Binanag, those of our own body [betrang]."

The people in Binanag (on the Kakidugen River) were Peknars, who were related by marriage and kinship to at least some of the Bēsilids, who by then had moved to the Reayan River. The fact that they were of the same body in their relatedness surely appeared, then as now, to have been in the ancient nature of things, for their bērtan names are linked as follows: *bēsilid,* hill; *yamu,* uphill; and *peknar,* downhill. Indeed, basic spatial orientation for Ilongots is given neither by cardinal points nor by the path of the sun, but by two axes: uphill/downhill and upstream/downstream.

In the end, Lakay said, the two brothers led the Bēnabēs to Binanag, where they beheaded some children who had come to wash in the river. Thus the anger of the Bēnabēs was dissipated.

Lakay's son Insan embroidered the story in a way that was at once more fanciful and more revealing. Leading the Bēnabēs, he said, the two brothers reached Binanag. That night they prepared the way to the two houses there by removing the sharpened bamboo stakes hidden along the trail for protection. Then "the two brothers met and cried because they were going to kill their own bodies. At dawn they leaped into the houses and cut off the people's heads.

"The Bēnabēs said, 'That is enough.'

"The Bēnabēs were no longer angry at the two brothers. They had killed everybody in the two houses."

It was not until some four decades later that Lakay met Tuyadeng, the son of Iddung, one of the two brothers. The fact that

Lakay was a Peknar, like the people beheaded on the Kakidugen
River in Binanag, made the reunion problematic. Lakay had
grounds to retaliate against the two brothers, but he was also
linked to them, both through Peknar-Bēsilid ties of kinship and
marriage and through the more tenuous unity of Rumyad as a
whole. Lakay and his companions on the northwestern margin
embarked on a series of intermarriages (1923–48) that they regarded, at least in retrospect, as a Rumyad-Bēnabē reunion.

To conclude with a footnote, the other brother, Radikaw, returned to the Bēsilids, who then resided on the Reayan River, and
he married there. I saw his daughter as an enfeebled old woman
close to death. Her grandchildren, Radikaw's great-grandchildren,
were the core of Tauyang as I knew it.

Marital alliance as reunion: Peknars and Biaws. On May 2,
1974 I heard that a Tamsi man had arrived in Kēyat to ask a man
there for support in making his bridewealth payments. Like many
eruptions of the Ilongot past into the present, his request at first
seemed (both to me and to younger Ilongots) startling, abrupt, and
arbitrary. Yet, as I discovered when I unraveled the story, the request had an intelligible source.

In about 1860, a number of Peknars were interspersed among
the predominant Biaws at a place called Ulawi, located on the
Tubu River about a day's walk downstream from the fork of the
Kakidugen River (see Map 2). Ulawi was the birthplace of Lakay's
father; since Lakay was born about 1894, his father and his Peknar paternal grandparents probably resided on the Tubu River
during the 1860's.

One day the people in Ulawi, "fought over a woman and then
hit one another with sticks. That was the reason they separated."
In a livelier version of the story a Tamsi man, who once was a shaman and still possessed a vivid imagination, said that a man in a
drunken state killed his classificatory sister, the woman to whom
he was betrothed, and her brother retaliated by beating him with a
stick. Rather than initiate an escalating spiral of beheadings
among kin, the people of Ulawi, sometime in the period 1875–83,
split into two groups and went their separate ways, some moving
upstream and the others downstream. A bitter dispute over a

woman and a subsequent separation—all versions of the story make at least that much clear.

The group that went downstream consisted entirely of Biaws. Initially they stopped and resided in a place one day down the Tubu River. Some years later they moved onward, and climbed up along a stream on the right bank of the Tubu, continued over the top of the hill, and finally descended along another stream until they stopped in what from then to the present has been the Tamsi area. The descendants of the Biaws told me the name of the Tamsi man with whom they decided to reside, and the man's name was recorded in William Jones's census schedules. Since Jones estimated that the Tamsi man was about 40 when he knew him in 1908, I would infer that it was about 1900 when the Biaws joined the Tamsis. Indeed, I suspect that (much like the pattern of Rumyad moves in 1923–45; see Chapter 1) the final long-distance move of the Biaws was prompted by battles between Philippine patriots and American troops.

The group that moved upstream, on the other hand, was made up of Biaws and Peknars. They went to join another group of Peknars that had resided on the Kakidugen River from at least the 1860's. Sometime during the period of Biaw-Peknar co-residence (probably in Ulawi on the Tubu, but perhaps on the Kakidugen) two Peknar brothers, Sipdung and Kanedtung, married Biaw women (see Fig. 4). This was the basis for saying that the Biaws and Peknars were of a single ancestral source.

Kanu, the son of Sipdung, married the sister of Lakay's father.

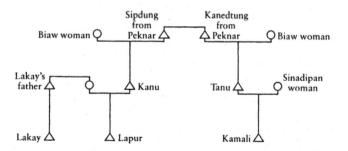

FIGURE 4. Genealogical source of marital alliance (1860's) between Tamsis and Peknars-Bēsilids-Rumyads through Biaw connection.

Among their children in turn was Lapur, the man from Kēyat whose support was being sought by the Tamsi man in 1974.

The source of the Tamsi man's Biaw connection, and the reason he felt he might seek the support of Lapur in Kēyat, is a much more involved story. Briefly, Tanu, the son of Kanedtung, married a woman from the downstream bērtan of Sinadipan. Shortly after Lakay's arrest in 1923, when the Sinadipan rice harvest was meager, Tanu took his family and went to live with Kanu (his FBS), who was residing with Lakay and the others on the northwestern margin.

Later that year (probably 1924 or 1925), the Sinadipans, who were vulnerable because their numbers had been depleted by raids and their rice harvest had been bad, became the targets of a Pugu raid. A Pugu man recalled the raid against the Sinadipans as follows: "After the Sinadipan people had fallen asleep and it was near dawn, a man from Pugu approached the house. The cock crowed. Then the men jumped into the house and killed two people inside. Only one man escaped, and he was later heard of in the lowlands." The only Sinadipans who remained alive were the man who escaped to the lowlands and Tanu's wife, who was with her husband in the northwest.

Tanu and his family knew nothing of the Pugu raid when they returned to Sinadipan, intending to reside there once again. As they approached the house they became suspicious because they heard no noise. Tanu went on ahead alone and found the decaying headless bodies of his wife's people. Tanu and his family fled immediately, returning to live with Lakay and the others, where they stayed for about a dozen years. Early in 1938, the year after Tanu's death, however, a group of Biaws who were residing in Tamsi arrived and took Kamali (Tanu's son) and his mother back to their home.

Up until the mid-1950's, about 70 years after the Biaws in Ulawi had split into two groups, the story of their single ancestral source continued to be known. But it had little social relevance, because Ilongots in the first half of this century rarely walked long distances, and there was little contact between the Tamsis and the Rumyads. The Peknars who raided with Insan in 1950, for example, said they walked in fear when they saw signs of the Tamsi people. After Insan's raid a number of men came from Tamsi to Pengegyaben; they appealed to Insan and the others not to raid in their direction. The Tamsis asserted that they all shared the bērtan name of Biaw. They also reminded the Pengegyaben people that all of their grandparents were Biaws who had once resided together in a single place, in Ulawi on the Tubu River. What the people from Tamsi were saying, of course, was that Insan and the others should be careful not to behead them, for they all were kin because they shared the bērtan name of Biaw. Nonetheless, the story of common origins in Ulawi was still not accepted as binding. Tukbaw told me that when he first heard it he thought the story of Ulawi on the Tubu River "was a lie because it did not make sense to us; we thought it was just a story, a mere story."

What transformed the story from a mere tale to an accepted charter was the process of renewed alliance, including a joint raid, a period of co-residence, and four intermarriages (between the Biaws in Tamsi and the Biaws in Kēyat) over the course of the late 1950's and early 1960's. Hand in hand, one supporting the other, the renewed alliance and the revitalized story grew stronger.

Thus the reunion of Lapur from Kēyat and Kamali from Tamsi was based in the politics of raiding and marriage. And Kamali's hope when he arrived in Kēyat on May, 2, 1974, was that he might complete his bridewealth payments and then move to Kēyat, where he would once again reside, as he had during his childhood, in the same place as Lapur. Though divided by residence and bērtan (Tamsi and Rumyad), Kamali and Lapur in 1974 started to affirm that they were united by what they shared—the name Biaw, their co-residence from about 1924 to 1938, and kinship, for their grandfathers, Kanedtung and Sipdung, were brothers. In fact, their kinship, if it was not renewed, was likely to be lost in the next generation because of the shallowness of Ilongot genealogical memory.

Demographic catastrophe and population movements, 1883–1905. When Lakay first told me the story of the woman who cursed her beheaders, I took it to be as mythical as the tales of weird beings who eat humans and humans who turn into birds. The story, which he first told me in 1969, was of a woman who just before her death cursed those about to behead her. In a few years the curse was fulfilled, and those who had beheaded her died, their bodies covered with sores, in an epidemic.

In 1974, five years later, I noticed that the woman in the story was named Madiya, a possible human name. Had the beheaded woman been alive, I asked, during the lifetime of Lakay's father? Lakay replied that she had been and that, furthermore, he knew the names of the raiders and their children, as well as their victims, the woman (who had no children) and her husband. The raiders were Yamus and the woman was a Peknar or a Biaw or both, who had lived in a now-cultivated spot on the Kakidugen River. It was in that spot, Lakay said, that she was beheaded. As her attackers drew near, she raised her bolo on high and cursed the Yamus, invoking her awesome spirit companion: "Now you, Gelutung, my spirit companion, kill them. Wipe them out, every last one, killed."

It was about 1875 or 1880 when the curse was uttered. Within less than a decade, in 1883 to be precise, the first of two major smallpox epidemics swept Ilongot territory. The second was in 1889. The Dominican missionary Fray Buenaventura Campa, who had contact with Ilongots between 1877 and 1891, testifed to the virulence of the epidemics. In his report on an 1891 visit up the Kasiknan River from the northeastern margin to the outlying Ilongot local clusters there (the route of entry into Ilongot country that William Jones followed some 17 years later), he said, "This race was once quite numerous, but with the epidemics suffered in 1883 and 1889 it has been decimated" (Campa 1891: 571). The woman's spirit companion (*gelutung*, smallpox), people said, had inflicted retribution against the raiders beyond all imagined proportions.

Baket told me that the Yamus who participated in the raid against the woman were later killed, in fulfillment of the curse, by the smallpox epidemic they suffered while living on the Reayan River. Lakay said the woman's spirit companion was so fierce that the affliction reached all bērtan—Yamus of course, Bēsilids perhaps by proximity, and even Biaws and Peknars who were brethren of the beheaded woman. Yammak's father, who was born about 1898, said that the reason the Yamus, Bēsilids, and Peknars were all equally hard hit was because they by then were residing together in the same general area along the Reayan. Whatever their relation to the beheaded woman and to stories of the awesome consequences of her curse, the two smallpox epidemics were clearly the greatest Ilongot demographic catastrophe within living memory prior to 1945.

The two epidemics also provide a known reference point for reconstructing population movements during the latter part of the nineteenth century. The wider picture, as best I can piece it together for the period, is clearer in its broad trajectories of population movement than in its absolute chronology. While the Bēnabēs remained in their present area on the northwestern margin, major moves were made during the late nineteenth century by the Yamus, Bēsilids, Peknars, and Biaws.

In the decade 1860-70 the Kakidugen River area, extending from the local cluster that is presently there to an hour upstream, was inhabited by the Yamus and Bēsilids. It was there, during that decade, that the Bēnabē woman Alatuy was seized by the Bēsilids and married by the one named Wa'ri. At the same time the Peknars were residing in two places, one an hour downstream from the Bēsilids-Yamus but still on the Kakidugen, the other a day's walk further downstream along the Tubu in Ulawi (see Map 2), where they were mixed with the Biaws. Thus in the period 1870-80 the following groups were distributed, from upstream to downstream, along the Kakidugen and Tubu rivers: Bēsilids-Yamus, Peknars, and Peknars-Biaws.

The initial moves from the above three locations took place during 1875-83. The Bēsilids and Yamus were probably the first to move, as they walked up the Kakidugen River, over a hill, and down into the Reayan River area. Their move may in part have been motivated by a desire to avoid the Bēnabēs (who probably were still angry at the seizing of Alatuy) when they made trading ventures toward the lowlands.

Probably a couple of years later the Biaws broke into two groups, one moving downstream and eventually joining the Tamsis and the other moving, along with the Peknars, upstream to the Kakidugen area recently abandoned by the Bēsilids-Yamus. The move by the Biaws and Peknars to the Kakidugen River was sudden, and the people must have been few in number and therefore vulnerable, for they were raided twice: first by the Bēnabēs, guided

by the two Bēsilid brothers Iddung and Radikaw; then by the Yamus, who killed the Peknar-Biaw woman whose curse reputedly
brought on the epidemics of 1883 and 1889. Thus by 1882 the
three residential groupings had become two, the Bēsilids-Yamus
on the Reayan River and the Peknars-Biaws on the Kakidugen
River.

What is most puzzling about the early Rumyad past, however, is
the next move that was made. A number of stories report that the
Peknars-Biaws and the Bēsilids-Yamus were residing in two separate places (the Kakidugen and Reayan rivers, respectively) at the
time of the epidemics. But other stories affirm that the Bēsilids-Yamus-Peknars-Biaws were living together on the Reayan
when the epidemic struck. Part of the puzzle, beyond the sheer
contradiction, is that the Bēsilids had aided in beheading the Peknars at Binanag on the Kakidugen, and the Yamus had decapitated
the Peknar woman of the curse. Why would the Peknars-Biaws go
and live with enemies? Perhaps the place to begin in reconstructing
these moves is that it is not clear whether the epidemic referred to
is the one of 1883 or 1889. Two accounts seem plausible, either or
both of which resolve the apparent historical anomaly.

First, the two epidemics could have been merged into one by
Lakay and the others who heard the story secondhand from their
parents and other eyewitnesses. Perhaps it was in the aftermath of
the 1883 epidemic, when people felt that the beheadings had been
avenged by the fatal illness, that the Peknars-Biaws and Bēsilids-Yamus, their populations much reduced, gathered in one
place on the Reayan River and attempted to confront the crisis.
Their notion of concentrating their strength of numbers would
have been consistent with Ilongot patterns during the catastrophic
period of 1942–45. Indeed, the Butag-Rumyad hostilities were
simply set aside during the severe crisis of 1945, and it is plausible
that a similar course was followed after the epidemic of 1883.
Then, six years later in 1889, the Bēsilids-Yamus-Peknars-Biaws
were all gathered together on the Reayan, where they were collectively afflicted by the second epidemic. Both versions of the story
could be true: the Bēsilids-Yamus and the Peknars-Biaws were residing both apart and together at the time of the epidemic, because
the two epidemics were conflated into one.

Second, historical memory of past population movements reifies bērtan by making them appear discrete, more residentially concentrated than they probably were. This exaggeration of past bērtan unity cannot be avoided in describing the paths of human movement during earlier times, because bērtan names (Peknar, Biaw, Bēsilid, and the rest) are the only culturally available labels for tracing the continuity of a group of persons. In contrast, residential groups ranging from single households to local clusters change their names every time they move. It makes no sense for Ilongots to speak, for example, of the Kakidugen people at the time that they resided in Tegē (for then they were the Tegē people), but it is perfectly intelligible to say that the Peknars (the dominant dispersed bērtan name among present-day Kakidugens) and the Tabakus resided together in Tegē before the time of the Japanese. At the same time, of course, the latter statement remains silent about both the density of Peknar-Tabaku marriages in 1923–48 and the fact that other Peknars, then residing in central Rumyad and on the Reayan River, had no connection through residence, marriage, or kinship with the Tabakus. To say, as Ilongots often do, that the Peknars and Tabakus were united through marriage alliances appears to imply what in practice it does not—that all the Peknars and all the Tabakus were so united. Though bērtan enjoy a certain solidarity, their names also gloss over internal divergences because they attribute characteristics of one or more of their parts to their collectivity. Possibly, therefore, certain Bēsilids-Yamus resided and married among the Biaws-Peknars during the 1880's while other Bēsilids-Yamus, who probably resided on the Reayan rather than on the Kakidugen, regarded themselves as separate and unrelated to the Biaws-Peknars.

Clearly, the four bērtan, Bēsilid, Biaw, Peknar, and Yamu, were engaged in relations of alliance and enmity with one another. Although the Bēsilids-Yamus beheaded some of the Peknars-Biaws at least twice before 1883, by the end of the 1880's the more salient pattern was the coordination of the broad arc of Bēsilid-Yamu and Peknar-Biaw residential moves. All four bērtan were neighbors along the Kakidugen-Tubu drainage system during the 1860's, and then they moved, stepwise, to the Reayan River, where they all resided by 1889. At the same time the Biaws, who were initially reduced in numbers when they split in half upon leaving Ulawi on the Tubu River, became even more dispersed and fewer in population as a result of the epidemics. Eventually the Biaws lost their autonomy as a concentrated bērtan and were assimilated as a dispersed bērtan, primarily within the Peknars. Thus by 1889 there was a loose unity between the Peknars and Bēsilids-Yamus.

The true Rumyads were rather more separate from the early net of bērtan relations. While the Bēsilids, Biaws, Peknars, and Yamus were residing along the Kakidugen-Tubu drainage system during the 1860's, the true Rumyads lived, at different times, on both sides of the Kanuwap River. Years later, toward the end of the 1870's, the true Rumyads began a very gradual series of moves upstream along the Kanuwap. Eventually, probably about 1883, they went further upstream along the Reayan, where they met the Bēsilids-Yamus who had arrived there shortly before from their former home along the Kakidugen.

The true Rumyads and Bēsilids-Yamus were nicely situated to begin a series of intermarriages. Like the people of Kakidugen-Pengegyaben in 1955–58 and the Peknars-Tabakus in 1923–48, the true Rumyads and Bēsilids-Yamus were in a position to legitimize marital unions between them by asserting their prior kinship. Some years before, one story had it, a true Rumyad man had married and paid bridewealth for a Bēsilid woman. Moreover, periods of co-residence initiated between Ilongot groups often derive from, or result in, an attempt to begin a number of marriages between them. The cultural expectation of marital unions between the true Rumyads and the Bēsilids-Yamus was ruptured when the daughter of the earlier Rumyad-Bēsilid marriage was sought after by two contesting suitors, a Yamu and a true Rumyad.

In the end, Pangpang said, the Yamu "grabbed" the woman from his true Rumyad competitor. Angered, in Ilongot fashion, because insulted by the loss of the woman to another man, the true Rumyads demanded that the Yamus return the bridewealth they had paid for the mother of the bride. Only if their relatively moderate demand was met would the anger of the true Rumyads be dissipated. But a Bēsilid man was drunk when the true Rumyads made their demand; and, heaping insult on insult, he replied, "Do not come to me for your bridewealth until after you have shattered the jar I am drinking from. That done, go and turn around the Kanuwap River until its mouth becomes its source. Then you may come to me." This probably was why the true Rumyads separated from the Bēsilids-Yamus without a single marriage having resulted from their period of co-residence. The true Rumyads returned to their former home on the right bank of the Kanuwap River, where, Pangpang said, they hoped to find refuge from the epidemic. The year of their return must have been 1889.

Some years later, probably in the 1890's, the true Rumyads were invited to Reayan, where a large feast, complete with sacrificial pigs, was to be held as a means by which the Bēsilids-Yamus hoped—they said—to dissipate the anger of their guests. The true Rumyads, willing to smooth things over, accepted the invitation. On their way to the feast, however, the true Rumyads spied their hosts, who awaited their arrival hidden in ambush. The guests fled homeward to the right bank of the Kanuwap and swore to reply to this treacherous threat on their lives by taking a Bēsilid-Yamu head.

During the years that followed, the true Rumyads visited and showed overt signs of friendship toward the Bēsilids-Yamus in order to lessen their vigilance. It was not until about 1905 that four unmarried young men from true Rumyad visited a Bēsilid home at the same time, as it happened, that a Peknar man was visiting there. The only adult man among the hosts remained vigilant throughout the night, despite earlier attempts to allay Bēsilid-Yamu suspicions. It was nearly dawn before their watchful host turned to one side, and in that instant the young true Rumyads hacked off his arms and then beheaded him and his guest from Peknar.

The chain of events between the true Rumyads and the Bēsilids-Yamus-Peknars was analogous to the near marriage alliance of 1958 between Midalya and Bangkiwa, that is, between the Peknars of Pengegyaben and the true Rumyads of Ringen. In both cases a true Rumyad man, who had initiated courtship, lost out and felt put down by a Bēsilid or Peknar who, as Ilongots say, stepped ahead of him and grabbed the woman. And on both occasions the immediate result was a sudden residential separation, in 1883 and 1958, respectively, plus later beheadings, one directly against the Bēsilids-Peknars in 1905 and the other against their

Aymuyu kin in 1960. Indeed, these two episodes, so widely separated in time, were more than parallel in how they were precipitated, for the beheadings of 1905 were also the earliest sources of Baket's unyielding refusal to allow her daughter Midalya to marry Bangkiwa, the true Rumyad man.

The Pasigiyans in the meantime resided at the turn of the century near the true Rumyads on the right bank of the Kanuwap River. Their relations with the Bēsilids, Peknars, and Yamus did not yet involve open hostilities, and they seem to have oriented primarily toward the true Rumyads, the Aymuyus to the south, and the Anunurs in Abēka on the southwestern margin.

In summary, during the period 1890–1905 the five dispersed bērtan (Bēsilids, Pasigiyans, Peknars, true Rumyads, and Yamus) that were most prominent on the Rumyad side at the time of the 1969 covenant with the Butags were all more numerous and residentially concentrated than they later became after the drastic depopulation of 1945. Indeed, perhaps the most significant index of their relative autonomy in that early era is that, aside from the Pasigiyans, heads were taken between all the four other bērtan except the Bēsilids and Yamus. And even in the latter instance, about 1905, a Yamu man, living on the Kasiknan River, fooled another Yamu man, then residing on the left bank of the Kanuwap, and beheaded him as the two of them walked along a path.

At the same time that their relations were often shifting and the autonomy of each was relatively great, the five bērtan by 1905 displayed a rather loose larger coordination. They tended to be divided, as the father of Yammak explained, into two broad groupings. First, there were the Pasigiyans and true Rumyads who resided along the Kanuwap River from 1889 to 1905. Second, there were the Bēsilids-Yamus and Peknars who resided initially in an arc along the Kakidugen and Tubu rivers (approximately 1860–85), later along the Reayan River (approximately 1885–1905), and finally on the left bank of the Kanuwap River (circa 1905). Thus, in about 1905 the true Rumyads-Pasigiyans were on the right bank of the Kanuwap, while the Peknars-Bēsilids-Yamus were on the left. Here, in characteristic Ilongot fashion, patterns of residential movement both reflected and promoted the loose political alignments between the two clusters of bērtan.

THE PAST IN THE RUMYAD PRESENT

My reconstitution of the Rumyad past before 1905 is based on what Lakay and his age-mates remembered of what their parents or grandparents had told them long ago. Usually these received memories were lists of place names where people had lived, stories about the sources of kinship between bērtan (later ratified through intermarriages), and episodes from feuds (later given canonical form in the celebration of covenants). Like Lakay and the others, I have no direct access to the early Rumyad past. Thus the early period of Rumyad history can be understood only through close attention to the conventions of Ilongot historical consciousness. For instance, the shape of stories and the ways of encoding place names or people's names constrain the kinds of things that can be said when people speak about their past. The further into the past one moves, the greater the salience given to bērtan because, once personal names are lost to memory, Ilongots use only the idiom of bērtan names to describe collective actions, ranging from residential movements to incidents in a feud.

What is most intriguing about early Rumyad history is that Rumyad itself, as a residentially concentrated bērtan, increasingly dissolves, the farther back in time one moves. Moving backward into the nineteenth century, Rumyad as a totality breaks down into Bēsilids, Pasigiyans, Peknars, true Rumyads, and Yamus, and all these bērtan become increasingly salient in what is clearly more than a simple artifact of the language for describing the past.

If 1880 is taken as a baseline, the pattern of residential movement over the preceding decade, and the epidemics suffered in 1883 and 1889, indicate that each one among the bērtan then salient—the Bēsilids, Pasigiyans, Peknars, true Rumyads, and Yamus—was more numerous, more autonomous, and more concentrated residentially then than at present. The subsequent long-term process involved was, first, the depopulation of the 1880's and the concomitant migration of the Peknars-Yamus-Bēsilids toward the homeland of the true Rumyads-Pasigiyans and, second, a gradual if incomplete assimilation of all five bērtan into one another through periods of co-residence and intermarriage.

The decimation of the Ilongot population in the 1880's and again in 1945 meant that the disparate bērtan that were eventually united in Rumyad as a totality became too few in numbers to be viable as groups engaged in feuding relations. Because it appears to be such a brute fact of life, the factor of severe depopulation is more likely to be given too much rather than too little weight. I should stress that the various bērtan need not have united, simply because they were depopulated, into the larger entity, Rumyad. The Peknars from Kakidugen, for instance, could have separated from their fellow Peknars and continued to orient toward Bēnabē rather than their former homeland. In addition, the critical mass for a viable bērtan appears to encompass a wide range. In 1967–69, the ten residentially concentrated bērtan for which I had gathered adequate census material ranged in size from 64 to 307 with a mean of 181. What was most striking was that Rumyad had a population nearly 20 percent larger than any of the other concentrated bērtan. Clearly, the solidarity of Rumyad seen in the 1969 Butag-Rumyad covenant was more than a simple reflex of depopulation.

What my reconstruction has revealed is that, during the early period of relative residential concentration that peaked by 1905, the elemental identities of the Bēsilids, Pasigiyans, Peknars, true Rumyads, and Yamus were still too sharply defined, as shown primarily by the beheadings among them, for them to be lumped together as a whole. The early period culminating in 1905, however, was but a loose precedent for a later reunion when, after nearly two decades of dispersal (1923–41), people gathered together by the Kanuwap River to face the Japanese threat of 1942–45. The wartime reunion was more or less repeated during the inward retreat from the Huks and Butags from 1954 to 1958. Thus the basis for the Rumyad unity expressed in the 1969 Butag-Rumyad covenant was a number of residential reunions, rather than a continuous period of co-residence.

In sum, the disparate bērtan that later became Rumyad were residentially concentrated, not once, as the elliptical Ilongot model would have it, but a number of times. Repeated residential gathering together, itself a protracted rite of intensification played out in slow motion, as contrasted with the condensed intensity of a covenant, produced solidarity among those in the co-residential group.* In becoming united during the wartime years people were repeating both a cultural form, the collective representation of focus and concentration, and an earlier moment in their collective biographies or those of their parents and grandparents. Cast in the timeless Ilongot cultural idiom of union, it was the repetition, the renewal of earlier ties with significant others, that enabled people to construct the deep solidarity of Rumyad during the process of feuding and making amends with the Butags. Indeed, it is to the relation of bērtan identity and the feud that I now turn.

*My remarks are an argument against the "presentism" of Emile Durkheim's model of rites of intensification, in which social solidarity is generated purely through ritual action in the present moment. The point is that the covenant, for Ilongots, both constructs solidarity in the present and re-enacts the more diffuse enduring solidarity of times when personal and collective biographies have been overlapped. Raising old grudges can mend fences, but it also invokes memories and strong feelings about certain moments in a collective past. Durkheim, to state my critique as a slogan, failed to recognize that people have memories, hence the sense in which his analyses lacked depth. To the extent that the discipline is heir to the Durkheimian legacy, a similar criticism could be extended to synchronic studies in anthropology more generally.

CHAPTER EIGHT. THE FEUD IN
HISTORICAL PERSPECTIVE, 1890-1928

Thus far I have discussed bērtan formation in terms of the collective identity construction of covenants (Chapter 3) and the interaction between demographic history and phases of population dispersal and concentration (Chapter 7). Through the celebration of covenants the solidarity of residentially concentrated bērtan becomes at once most real, because enacted by the collectivity, and most problematic, because grudges within the group are voiced as public issues. In addition, bērtan change in their degree of solidarity. On the one hand, they undergo demographic fluctuations that may lead to the amalgamation of a number of once-separate bērtan. On the other hand, they undergo alternations between phases of residential concentration and dispersal that correspond with a varying sense of the salience of collective bērtan identity. Thus seen in the long run, covenants are not mere enactments of solidarity in the present, but condensed reenactments of earlier periods of residential unity. Like marriages between groups, covenants are conceived more as reunions than as unions pure and simple.

This chapter concentrates on the connections between bērtan identity and the process of feuding. But the process of feuding is historically conditioned, and therefore its linkages with bērtan formation, though deep, are more a variable than a constant. Rather than document the full range of variation in Ilongot feuding, my approach to the problem will be to study a period of time (1905–28) when feuding reached an extreme, in both magnitude and character. By the end of this chapter it should become clear that the Butag-Rumyad feud, an enduring relation of mutual hostility, was a rather distinct, indeed relatively simple example of Ilongot headhunting.

BĒRTAN AND THE FEUD

In actual discourse among Ilongots, bērtan names are invoked by persons making a statement about their connectedness, especially in the contexts of oratory in public assemblies, ranging from redress for past beheadings to the regulation of minor disputes (see M. Rosaldo 1973). To claim a bērtan name is to affirm an allegiance. Bērtan names can be employed to assert strong opposition, in speaking, for instance, of "us" against "them" in the context of headhunting. Or they can be used to assert closeness, as when a gifted orator from a distant place is invited to speak at a public meeting and invokes a bērtan name that is shared by those who have invited him. A statement of bērtan affiliation is an assertion of solidarity with members of a bounded group that exists above all in relations of opposition to other like groups.

Bērtan names provide an idiom of alliance and enmity that becomes manifest throughout enduring relations of mutual hostility, that is, during the process of feuding. Whan an insult is to be avenged, by raiders who kill from ambush, the maximal unit that can be considered liable in direct retaliation is a residentially concentrated bērtan. In ongoing feuds between such groups the retributive infliction of death is not necessarily directed toward particular persons; that, as Insan said, is "the custom of those who arrest." Instead, anyone connected (sometimes by distant kinship, more often by sharing a bērtan name) with the person who is said to have incited the raid is vulnerable to beheading in retaliation. In practical terms, bērtan-wide liability is based on the fact that raiders walk toward a place where they either surprise the unseen people inside a house or ambush whoever happens along their path. Nobody I spoke with knew or cared whether the Butag huntsman beheaded in 1952 was a relative of those responsible for the arrests of 1940 or the murderous threat against Luku's father in the mid-1930's. The point was that their victim, like those against whom they held grudges, was from Butag.

Recruiting members for such a raiding party is another matter.

Apart from the fact that people come for different reasons, and some appear unaware of the precipitating source of a raid, the core of such groups can be built along various lines. Insan said that if he were beheaded by the Dekran people, the raid in retaliation would be initiated by his father, his brother, and his close kin, who would go and pick up the Tabakus on the northwestern margin (his mother's people) and the Peknars in Kakidugen, Pengegyaben, and Kēyat (his father's people). If Tukbaw were the victim, he said, retaliation would come from "us who are his body [*betrang*], the Peknars" (his mother's people), but not from the true Rumyads (his father's people), because his father had died some twenty years before.

If Bayaw were the victim, Insan said, his father was too old to raid; the source of retaliation would rest with his sons, who might perhaps seek out the Bēsilids (their father's people), but what would "encompass it all are the Peknars of their mother because that is where they reside." If Disa were the victim, he said, the source of retaliation would be "us, because her brothers are dead and we as much as became of the same body when she came to father" as Insan's step-mother. In this limiting case a retaliatory raid, if mounted at all, would be initiated by those Disa had married, the people where she had come to reside. Usually, as case histories confirm, the victim's father, sons, or brothers recruit raiders from their networks of kin combined with fellow bērtan members. The raiders are thus drawn from the personal networks of the man who initiates vengeance rather than of the victim.

Feuding in the beheading phase, as is probably clear by now, does not always involve groups with rigid boundaries; and the determination of who is a friend and who is an enemy is not strictly defined at every moment. When the Payupays and Peknars met on their way to a fishing trip in 1969, for example, the Payupays immediately mentioned an earlier beheading of one of their members by a Peknar man. The Peknars rose to the occasion, ingenious in their use of the unrestricted modes of category name transmission. Tukbaw said that he had only one category name, true Rumyad, handed down from his father—hence he denied any connection with the killers, who were identified as Peknars (his mother's name). Kadēng, on the other hand, invoked his mother's name, Payupay, in order to affirm his kinship with those who had confronted them. As for the rest from Kakidugen, Pengegyaben, and Kēyat, they simply stood beside their two spokesmen and maintained a discreet silence. Though nobody was fooled, the issued was aired and then dropped so that they could cooperate during the fishing trip. Ilongots thus use the idiom of dispersed bērtan names to engage in dialogue with their enemies, perhaps eventually leading to the celebration of a covenant between the two groups.

When people feud it can be a matter of life itself to muddle things, claiming to be a little on this side and a little on that, somewhat attached to both parties but not necessarily and unambiguously involved. The upper limit on the number of bērtan names that one can claim (five) is probably set by the range of social obligations to which any one person can potentially be committed; in such circumstances, to have too many allies can be to place oneself in a cross fire. At the same time, people who are enemies on one basis can claim to be friends on another. Cultural recognition of relatively unrestricted rules of transmission provides a ready-made means to contract or expand the category names claimed in any given situation. Hence conflicting loyalties and potentially shifting bērtan names promote multiple, crosscutting claims of affiliation and provide a degree of flexibility in social intercourse.

RUMYAD, THE FEUD, AND THE COLONIAL PRESENCE, 1890–1918

The personal recollections of Lakay, who was born about 1894, about the period of 1890–1905 date from his childhood, and hence, as he said, they are like a dream. When he spoke of the feuds from that epoch his stories derived more from hearsay, the tales of his elders that were usually told to him in the context of later covenants, than from his own lived experiences. Indeed, in general, Ilongot accounts of feuds from that period usually follow the canonical form in which they are rendered during a covenant; that is, they depict a chain of beheadings that move back and forth between two mutually hostile groups. Thus viewed from the perspective of later covenants, each feud is characterized as an autonomous chain of events that is so self-contained as to be unrelated to other feuds. Although the links among feuds are difficult to reconstruct for this early period, it is possible to show the relations between wider feuds and the shifting political alignments among the Bēsilids, Pasigiyans, Peknars, true Rumyads, and Yamus.

While the Bēsilids-Yamus were living on the Reayan River in the 1890's, a raiding party of Bēnabēs and Butags came from the west and attacked the house where Dinwag's father was born. It was dawn when the raiders rushed the house, but only one man was able to enter before the doors and windows were covered over. Those inside fought back with their bolos and forced out the intruder, but not before one of their own, an old man, lay dead with a gaping throat wound that had nearly severed his head from his body. The Bēsilids from that house and that of their neighbors chased, shot, and beheaded a Bēnabē woman, who had slowed the flight of the raiders. Another of the raiders, a Bēnabē man, was then "trapped," the father of Yammak said, "against the rocky face of a cliff." There, as he drew his bow, the Bēsilid killer of the trapped man shouted, "Now, friend, feel the tearing pain of this, my arrow," and beheaded him. In retrospect this beheading was viewed as retaliation, Lakay said, for the Peknar victims from Binanag on the Kakidugen River, where the two brothers Iddung and Radikaw had been compelled by the Bēnabēs to lead a raid against their own kin.

At the beginning of the same decade, in about 1890, a group of Yamus, Peknars, and Anunurs (from Abēka, on the southwestern margin) raided against the Payupays in Tau to the north (see Map 2, p. 234). Their victims were four women and children, who were alone at home while their men were out hunting with a large net, as they did in those days, into which the game was driven by dogs. Among the four men who took heads was Lakay's father. The composition of the raiding party reflected a tightening of the bonds between the Yamus and the Peknars, who had shortly before (perhaps in 1884) joined in residing on the Reayan River.

In the meantime, again in the 1890's, a Dekran raiding party happened upon a true Rumyad man and his young son who had gone fishing together on the Kanuwap River. The son, who saw the approaching raiders, was unable to rouse his father, who was debilitated at the time by malarial fevers. Thus the two were beheaded. The victims had two relevant identities for what was to follow. First, they were true Rumyads. Second, they were the maternal grandfather and maternal uncle of Lakay from Peknar.

The true Rumyads lost little time in letting the Dekrans see their wrath, as Ilongots say. They, along with some Bēsilids and Peknars, attacked a Dekran house and beheaded everyone inside. One of the raiders took two heads, his brother another, his brother's son another, and a Bēsilid man (Radikaw, since returned from Bēnabē) yet another.

The Peknars and some Bēsilids were drawn closer to the true Rumyads because of their joint participation in the raid and the resulting common antagonism against the Dekrans. In this case, even more than usual among Ilongots, having a shared enemy was enough to make closer the ties among the Rumyads-Pasigiyans and the Bēsilids-Yamus-Peknars.

Thus the Bēsilids-Yamus-Peknars moved from the Reayan River to a site on the left bank of the Kanuwap, just across from the true Rumyads and Pasigiyans on the right bank. There the Bēsilids-Yamus-Peknars purposely established a nucleated settlement in order to discourage, by concentrating their strength, expected predawn attacks by Dekran raiders. In their new site they were defended by a sheer cliff of white rock that extended in a semicircle to the Kanuwap and left only the flat grassland downstream, along which humans could be spied from a great distance, as a possible approach to their houses.

While the Peknars-Bēsilids-Yamus were on the left bank, they were joined by a group of Aymuyus who also sought a place of refuge. As so often happens in such moments of initial co-residence, the newly united groups sought to affirm their allegiance by raiding together as a possible prelude to intermarriage. This time an Aymuyu-Bēsilid-Yamu-Peknar raiding party was mounted, including a number of the Yamus and Peknars who had gone together some years before when the four Payupays were beheaded. Lakay's maternal uncle (a brother of the youth beheaded by the Dekrans) was also among them, along with two Aymuyus who later married his sisters, Lakay's maternal aunts. This raid and the

marriages that followed were the source of the kin connection between Lakay and the Aymuyus. So it was that over half a century
later, in 1960, Bangkiwa from Ringen let Lakay's son, Tepeg, see
his anger by leading a raid against the latter's "body," his Aymuyu
relatives (see Chapter 6).

The raiding party headed east toward the Kasiknan River in the
direction of the Pugus and Dekrans. They happened upon and attacked a Pugu woman who was working alone in her garden, and
she was beheaded by one of the Aymuyu men who later married
Lakay's maternal aunt. This beheading both drew the Peknars-
Yamus-Bēsilids closer to the Aymuyus and created a breach between them and the Pugus.

The long-term movement, from 1883 to 1905, was toward increasing interaction among the Bēsilids, Pasigiyans, Peknars, true
Rumyads, and Yamus. Though the five bērtan could be grouped
into two loose clusters—the true Rumyads-Pasigiyans and the Bēsilids-Yamus-Peknars—each of them was relatively autonomous
(compared with the period of 1967–74) even as they had reached
a point, by 1905, where they were all relatively concentrated residentially on either side of the Kanuwap. They had gathered together to better defend themselves against the retaliatory raids that
they had ample reason to anticipate from the Dekrans and Pugus
to the east.

The Pugu response to the Peknar-Yamu-Aymuyu raid was startling. In former times, it could have been anticipated that retaliation by the Pugus would take the form either of a raid (*ngayu*) or
of a killing by deception (*ka'abung*). Had the Pugus raided, they
might either have waited in ambush (*ta'neb*) or perhaps rushed
upon the house in the first light of dawn (*bēgbēg*). Had they killed
by stealth, on the other hand, they might have used any of a number of ruses, chief among which would be to spend the night at a
house and pretend friendship in order to catch those inside off
guard and behead them. Any other form of retaliation would have
been beyond classification in Ilongot terms.

But times had changed; and in about 1905 the Pugus, along with
some men from the northeastern margin, openly walked up to the
Kanuwap River leading an escort of soldiers from the lowlands.
When they neared the homes on the left bank of the Kanuwap, the

soldiers opened fire; they shot at Lakay's father as he fled, then killed a less fleet-footed old man who was beheaded by a man from the northeastern margin. This was the first time, in the remembered past at any rate, that people from the margins had used troops to settle their scores with those living further toward the interior.*

What had changed, of course, was that the Spanish had been replaced by the American colonial regime over the course of a violent decade that spanned the turn of the century. By 1896 the Philippine Revolution had entered a phase of open combat, and by 1898 only Manila and its environs remained in Spanish hands. A year later, however, the Americans—impelled, as historian Richard Hofstadter has said, by Duty and Destiny—had succeeded the Spaniards in their colonial venture. Philippine resistance to their new invaders continued steadily until 1902 and more sporadically until 1910. No doubt the apparent increase in Ilongot headhunting during the 1890's and early 1900's was the by-product of an increase not simply in the number of feuds available to historical memory, but also in the general level of chaos and violence in the surrounding lowlands (as was the case during the Huk period after 1950).

The cluster of incidents from about 1905 indicates that beheadings were reaching a high point of intensity. These decapitations, both killings by deception and raids, penetrated the inner sphere of common co-residence and shared bērtan membership more than they did immediately before or after this time. In the first episode, there were the four Rumyads who slept at a house and before the night was over had taken their Bēsilid host by surprise and beheaded him and his Peknar guest. And there was the Yamu who, while they walked together along a trail, beheaded his fellow Yamu. Finally, an Aymuyu man living on the left bank of the Kanuwap was walking with two Bēsilid young men, novices who were beside themselves with envy of his glittering red hornbill earrings. The Aymuyu was abruptly beheaded.

---

*A similar pattern probably obtained during the eighteenth century, when the Spanish mounted a number of punitive expeditions against the Ilongots. Dominican and Franciscan archival documents contain reports of these expeditions, but it is impossible to reconstruct the Ilongot viewpoint on this early period.

The successful raids after about 1905 were two. First, Lakay's father, a Peknar, with a Yamu and two Bēsilids beheaded two Bēnabēs who were hunting with dogs in the last light of dusk. Second, a year or so later, a Bēsilid-Yamu-Pasigiyan raiding party beheaded three more people from the same place in Bēnabē. The source of these raids, even in retrospect, remains obscure, and Lakay could only offer the cultural cliché that "the old ones had been killed and now their children retaliated" (*tubrat*).

Yet, this new savage burst did not last. It was 1908 or so when a group of Dekrans, out hunting with dogs, happened upon a Peknar-Bēsilid-Yamu hunting party. Tense and dramatic, the story of their encounter and subsequent covenants is still often told today. As the two groups stood poised, brought face to face by chance, a young man from either side came forward to exchange chews of betel in greeting. Their every step was watched by some of the older men, who stood with bows drawn taut and arrows full against their cheeks. The instant they were within arm's reach of one another, the Dekran youth grabbed the other's foot. The Yamu slapped his hand over the Dekran's bolo and said, "Friend, let's just sit down together and chew betel, for I am holding your bolo." A stalemate thus reached, they agreed to talk again, along with the true Rumyads, on a later date in the hopes of celebrating a covenant. In time—about 1911—the Dekrans hosted a covenant still remembered for the ferocity with which men beat one another with sticks as they performed their customary dancelike duels.

After the initial confrontation between the Dekrans and the Peknars-Bēsilids-Yamus, events tumbled one on the other, reflecting the crisscrossing reverberations of the new social forces unleashed on the Ilongot region. With the Dekran threat lessened, the Peknars-Bēsilids-Yamus left their fortified site and in about 1908 moved a short distance uphill, still on the left bank of the Kanuwap. There the true Rumyads came from the other side of the river and joined them. This was a fine moment for marital union between the two groups.

The marital alliance, like the one that had been available between the two groups in the 1880's on the Reayan River, was aborted. This time the disruption was due to the members of the Philippine constabulary who arrived and arrested Baket's father (who died in a Bayombong jail). Like the Pugus before them, the Bēnabēs acted as informers to the troops, because they sought vengeance for the beheading of their people by Peknars-Bēsilids-Yamus a short time before.

On the heels of this incursion, the Yamus called in the constabulary once again to avenge the earlier intra-Yamu decapitation by requesting the arrest of their fellow Yamu. (He later died in Bilibid prison, confirming the view of Secretary of the Interior Dean Worcester in 1908, who said that "the sending of wild men from the Luzon highlands to Bilibid prison at Manila was, in most instances, equivalent to a death sentence" [Worcester 1908: pt. 2, p. 14].) In fear of yet other incursions of troops, the people who were gathered on the left bank of the Kanuwap fled in about 1910, in different directions. The Peknars-Bēsilids-Yamus went into hiding downstream on the left bank, while the true Rumyads sought refuge opposite them on the right bank.

What is most puzzling about Ilongot accounts of these events is that the actions of the arresting troops were, as Kadēng remarked, relatively restrained compared with the later incursions of the 1920's and early 1940's. During the two arrests in about 1909 only the allegedly guilty individual who had been named by Ilongots on the margin was arrested. Neither houses nor gardens were put to the torch; nobody was punched out, strung up, or shot on the spot. Why, then, did people fear worse to come and disperse into hiding after the arrests?

Part of the context of the seeming over-reaction in central Rumyad was the murder of William Jones on March 28, 1909. In a letter of February 25 Jones said, "The military haven't subdued this neck of the woods yet" (Rideout 1912: 199); ironically, his own death the following month brought reprisals so harsh upon the Ilongots (especially those along the lower Kasiknan) that the region was pacified before the year was out.

The process of pacification was described in detail in a report of November 1, 1909, by Lt. Wilfrid Turnbull, of the Philippine constabulary. Turnbull's report tells of how in April he burned Ilongot houses and crops in reprisal for Jones's murder in March. The three Ilongot men (from the bērtan of Keradingan) who were arrested and charged with the murder had succeeded in escaping from prison, and the mission of the constabulary expedition was to search for the "escaped convicts." Turnbull was unable to apprehend the fugitives, but he ordered other Ilongots to track them down, and he conducted a census as he walked upstream along the Kasiknan from the northwestern margin through Tamsi and Pugu to Dekran (from which point he returned downstream).*

At a meeting of August 31 with so-called *cabecillas,* or headmen, from the bērtan of Peniperan, Tamsi, Aliked, and Pugu, the Governor of their province, Nueva Vizcaya, told those gathered before him "to find the *escaped convicts* and deliver same dead or alive, and the reward for so doing was properly explained" (Turnbull 1909: 6; his italics). In fact, by that time of the year, "those rancherias implicated in the Jones murder had lost what small supply of rice they had on hand in April, as also their fishing nets, and were practically upon the verge of starvation" (pp. 6–7). The burning and destruction that resulted from the April raids by the constabulary bred further violence, and by September 1909 other Ilongots brought Turnbull seven human heads (taken, they claimed, from the guilty bērtan of Keradingan). The Pugus were the first to deliver a head to Turnbull. Then four more heads were handed over by the Peniperans, because "losing houses and crops at the hands of the constabulary, so incensed them at the Cadadiangan [Keradingan] people (the really guilty ones) that they took the heads of four of the latter. These heads were turned over to me on the 22nd of August" (p. 4). So angered, in other words, were the Peniperans at those who had murdered Jones and thereby incited the troops to burn their houses and crops, bringing them to the edge of starvation, that they retaliated by taking four Keradingan heads.

Shortly afterward, Turnbull gave rations to the peoples of Tamsi and Peniperan and told them to return with the three escaped convicts. On September 8 the Tamsis and Peniperans "returned with two heads, claiming that they were unable to find any but

---

*There in Dekran, Turnbull found that the houses were arranged in a natural fortress on a steep hill, where there was "but one steep and narrow approach, bristling with 'doldols [sharpened bamboo stakes]," so that the Dekrans might "feel comparatively safe from their worst enemy, Gumian [Rumyad]" (Turnbull 1909: 32). Thus the Dekrans, like the people on the left bank of the Kanuwap, had hidden in a place that afforded natural protection during the most intense period of their feud.

these, who showed fight and could not be captured" (p. 8). This constabulary practice of collecting Ilongot heads was probably introduced by veterans of the Indian wars in the American west; it unwittingly followed the practices of eighteenth-century Spaniards in their campaigns against Ilongots who had raided mission settlements.

During 1909 the news of incursions by constabulary troops, who burned as they went and collected heads (unlike Ilongots, who threw them away) along the lower Kasiknan River surely reached the people who were living along the Kanuwap. It is little wonder, in this context, that the relatively benign intrusion of troops on the left bank of the Kanuwap in about 1909 produced the degree of panic that it did, for people had a firm basis from which to imagine worse invasions that might follow. Turnbull was correct when he said, "I believe that head-hunting between the river rancherias has been stopped *for the present*" (p. 13; his italics). Constabulary actions, it would seem, had for the time being clamped down the lid with one hand, while the other hand fanned the flame of feuds yet to come.

The consequences of Jones's murder should also be understood in the wider context of pan-Philippine plans by the American colonial administration to bring under their control the people who were then called non-Christian tribes. It was while Jones was among the Ilongots in 1908 that Secretary of the Interior Dean Worcester announced in his annual report the creation of the non-Christian provinces in the Islands and the "transfer of Ilongot country to Nueva Vizcaya." Prior to Worcester's decision to grant exclusive control over the area to Nueva Vizcaya, jurisdiction over the Ilongots had been fragmented among five different provinces. He granted jurisdiction as he did because "only in Nueva Vizcaya has any effort been made to bring these very troublesome wards of the government [the Ilongots] under control" (Worcester 1908: pt. 2, p. 14).

By 1909 American colonial policy toward the Ilongots was more sharply defined with respect to both goals and limits. As planned, Nueva Vizcaya had undergone what Worcester called a very radical change in its boundaries, thereby in effect becoming the Ilongot territory. The concerted effort to pacify Ilongot country after

Jones's murder derived in part from a systematic policy, announced in 1908, to intensify the pacification and education of the so-called non-Christian tribes throughout the Philippine Islands.

In the years immediately following the murder of Jones, the Ilongots initiated a series of covenants to mend the ruptures between them, as will be recalled. First, in about 1911 the Dekrans and the Peknars-Bēsilids-Yamus-true Rumyads celebrated reciprocal covenants. Next, the Dekrans served as mediators when the Pugus and Peknars-Bēsilids-Yamus celebrated their covenants. Third, the Peknars-Yamus hosted the Payupays, who even by then (about 1912) dared arrive on the left bank of the Kanuwap only in the company of soldiers. (The soldiers, Lakay recalled, ate the choice liver of the sacrificial pig.) Finally, the Peknars-Bēsilids-Yamus hosted the Bēnabēs for a covenant in about 1918. In the period 1910–18 headhunting was rapidly becoming a thing of the past, and in this era most feuds were brought to a truce through the celebration of covenants.

Yet government control over Ilongot territory clearly had its limitations, and the peace did not last the decade. The difficulties of the pacification policy were evident even in 1909. Dean Worcester, for example, mingled colonial policies of control, the threat posed by the murder of Jones, and racial views of that imperialist period when he gave the following rather pessimistic assessment of the situation: "The establishment of governmental control over the Ilongots presents very serious difficulties ... Many of them show a large amount of Negrito blood, and as might be anticipated, they are an irresponsible, treacherous, and somewhat murderous lot, as demonstrated by the recent unprovoked murder of Dr. William Jones, of the Field Natural History Museum" (1909: 131). In Worcester's eyes the chief obstacle to the extension of administrative control over the Ilongot population was that the opening of good, low-grade horse trails (which had proved effective in the pacification of the Mountain Province to the northwest) was deemed impossible in upland Nueva Vizcaya. The low population density meant that, Worcester said, "sufficient labor for trail construction, or even for the maintenance of trails when constructed, is lacking in the Ilongot territory" (1909: 131).

In summary, the panic experienced by the people who fled from their homes along the Kanuwap River was probably a result of hearing about severe reprisals directed at the people who lived along the lower Kasiknan in the aftermath of William Jones's murder. At the same time, Turnbull's concerted efforts to pacify the region were part of a much broader intensification of the effort to pacify and civilize "non-Christian tribes" throughout the Philippines. And indeed, the policy worked for a period. Lakay, Baket, and their age-mates recall the years from 1910 to 1918 as a time of comparative tranquillity, punctuated more often by covenants than by killings. Despites its flaws, which were evident from the beginning, the program of pacification worked well for a while (1910–18), then sputtered badly (1919–26), and finally fell apart altogether (1927–28).

THE MARGIN, THE CENTER, AND THE COLONIAL PRESENCE, 1919–28

In 1919 the resurgence of Ilongot headhunting began. In his "Special Memorandum on the Ilongots" of August 10, 1919, Governor Lope K. Santos of Nueva Vizcaya described his shock and alarm over the sudden rash of headhunting incidents during that year, on March 29, April 1, April 14, May 4, June 24, and July 21. This rupture was as abrupt as it was unexpected, for during the previous year the Ilongot region "could be characterized," he said, "by a total tranquility, which might be called an 'Octavian Peace' " (Santos 1919: 1).

After recounting the incidents and the measures taken by the constabulary, Santos described Ilongot territory as divided into an outer ring of loyal groups (the Payupays and Bēnabēs, among others) that surrounded an inner circle of rebellious infidels (among whom were the Tamsis, Pugus, Dekrans, and Rumyads). More than a simple fiction (though it was also that), the distinction drawn by Santos pointed to the newly emergent articulation between Ilongot feuding and colonial mechanisms of control over subject populations. As became particularly clear over the course of the following decade (1919–28), those on the margins were becoming less inclined to engage in headhunting raids. Instead, they were relying more and more on opportunities to lead punitive expeditions of government troops as a means of venting their anger against those who lived further in the interior. Hence the Bēnabēs and Payupays, who rarely raided in this period and willingly informed on their fellow Ilongots, were regarded by government officials as exemplary in their loyalty. The distinction drawn between loyal and rebellious Ilongots was thus not only a central construct for, but also a direct product of, the implementation of colonial policies.

It was in the context of a broader resurgence of Ilongot headhunting that, in 1920, Singep from Yamu was deceived and beheaded by his hosts in Tau, the home of the Payupay people where he had taken a head in about 1890. The historical sources of this incident are somewhat involved and require a brief synopsis.

After taking the head of the Payupay from Tau, Singep (a few years later, in about 1895) married a Payupay woman from Didipyu, a place where the people were said, by the Yamus and Peknars at any rate, to be unrelated to those residing farther upstream in Tau. Some years after his marriage Singep completed his bridewealth payments and returned to his fellow Yamus, who then, in about 1908, were residing with the Bēsilids and Peknars on the left bank of the Kanuwap River. Along with Singep came his Payupay wife, his three children, and two more children whom his wife had adopted after her sister's death (see Fig. 5). Later, in what seemed to be a nicely developing marital alliance, one of the adopted children—the niece of Singep's wife (ZD)—married Singep's nephew (ZS) in what was construed as another Payupay-Yamu union. Among the four children to whom they gave birth was

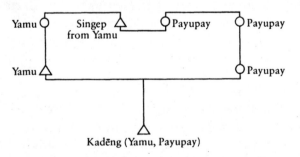

FIGURE 5. Genealogical source of Yamu-Payupay marital alliance (1890's).

Kadēng. (Decades later, in 1955, the first Ilongot encountered by Kadēng upon his release from prison was a relative from Payupay.)

In 1920, Singep's wife from Payupay was dead, and he was having an affair with another man's wife. To escape the anger of the woman's husband, the lovers fled to the home of Singep's deceased wife in Didipyu. In Didipyu the Payupays warned Singep not to visit the Payupays in Tau, because the young novices there might not feel constrained by the oath by salt sworn at the covenant of about 1912. The man who tried to warn Singep, Lakay said, urged him to stay, saying, "Why do you want to go there and visit? Think about the unmarried young men there." But this good advice went unheeded. And the Payupay youths who lived in Tau in fact leapt at the chance to behead Singep, a vulnerable fugitive who long before had beheaded their elders.

A year later, the true Rumyads also seized an opportunity that came their way, and they invited the Pugus to join them in beheading their relatively easy prey. The people who had happened along were a Peknar-Yamu group from the upper Kasiknan River; they had come to the Kanuwap River in a moment of need in order to ask their Yamu kin for food and shelter. After beheading a lowland couple on the western margin, they had been informed on— much as Governor Santos would have anticipated—by one of the so-called loyal groups of Ilongots. This catastrophe had left them hungry and homeless, for constabulary troops had quickly mounted a punitive expedition and burned their homes and crops. This Peknar-Yamu local cluster was then terribly vulnerable, at once wanted for murder in the lowlands and near starvation in the uplands. Worse yet, among the group was the Yamu man who about 15 years before had beheaded his fellow Yamu as they walked along a path together. The brother of the earlier victim was determined to take full advantage of the moment; he felt compelled to kill his own body, his fellow Yamus, as well as his more distant relatives from Peknar. Thus the dozen or so Yamu-Peknar refugees were received in a seemingly friendly home, fed heartily, and in the dim light of dawn the next morning beheaded at the hands of pent-up novices from true Rumyad, Pasigiyan, Pugu, Bēsilid, and Yamu.

Through their violent deed the true Rumyads solidified their relations with the Pugus in the same instant that they deepened the breach between themselves and the Peknars. In concluding his partisan Peknar version of the event, Lakay said, "If we were now really Ilongots, they [the close kin of the victims] would give the Rumyads their share (*bēet*) in return for having wiped us out." At the same time that he urged retaliation, Lakay also said that he could not retaliate against the true Rumyads because "our names are so very hooked together." Her feelings even stronger because her classificatory sister (MZD) was among the victims, Baket some 37 years later (in 1958) refused to allow her daughter, Midalya, to marry her Rumyad suitor, Bangkiwa. Most irate of all was Radu's father, who lost his brother in that massacre and told and retold the story to his son, instructing him to await the day that he or his son could let the true Rumyads see their Peknar wrath. This, of course, was the source of Radu's unbending stance against attending the 1969 covenant.

In 1923 the Payupays from Tau, the people who had beheaded Singep three years before, informed the constabulary that the Yamus-Peknars had beheaded two of their people (who in fact were beheaded by the Autuds to the west). Setting out on a horse trail that by then connected the three Ilongot schoolhouses along the northern sector of the western margin, the troops then had to hike the difficult footpaths from the Kasiknan River into the Kanuwap River area. In addition to the Payupay guides, other "non-Christian" tribesmen had by then become soldiers due to a deliberate shift in colonial policy. So it was that among the soldiers was a Bēnabē trooper who, despite the covenant of 1918, still bore a grudge against the Peknars-Bēsilids-Yamus for their two raids against his bērtan in about 1905.

Unlike their incursions of about 1909, the troops now were more punitive, burning houses and crops and beating up the men they arrested. Among the 11 men arrested in 1923 was Lakay, who was initially taken to Bayombong in the lowlands and then confined to the northwestern margin, where he later married.

Under the threat of further devastating incursions by troops, the people on the left bank of the Kanuwap scattered and sought haven in three dispersed places (see Map 3). First, the true Rumyads (who later became the Ringens) sought refuge among the Pa-

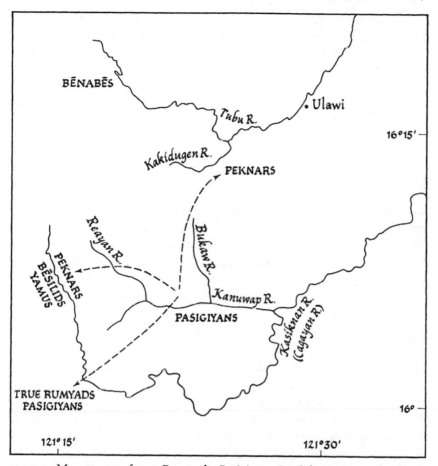

M A P 3. Movements of true Rumyads, Pasigiyans, Bēsilids-Yamus, and Peknars (1923).

sigiyans who lived in Abēka on the southwestern margin; two years later in 1925 they fled southeast to Baler; the next year they returned to Abēka. Second, the Peknars, who later became the Pengegyaben people, fled west to the upper Kasiknan, where they joined a group of Bēsilids-Yamus who lived there and later became the Tauyangs (it was there that Tukbaw was born). Third, the Peknars most closely related to the men arrested (who later became the people of Kakidugen and Kēyat) fled north to a site above the

Kakidugen River. The only people left along the Kanuwap after this terrible dispersal were the Pasigiyans, who remained on the right bank (and later joined the true Rumyads and became the Ringens).

In 1924, two true Rumyad men (one was a younger brother of Pangpang) spent the night at a house and beheaded two of their hosts, a Pasigiyan woman and her daughter. This beheading, to say the least, was problematic for the true Rumyads. Their deed had insulted not only the Pasigiyans in general, but Lakay (a Pasigiyan as well as a Peknar) in particular. Pangpang's younger brother had beheaded Lakay's classificatory sister (MZD), who was the daughter of one of his maternal aunts, who had married an Aymuyu man in the 1890's. Once again Lakay was caught in a dilemma. Though he acknowledged that young men were uncontainable in that epoch ("in the days when we really were Ilongots, those who had not yet taken heads used to be headstrong and kill by treachery"), he also said that, had it not been for a true Rumyad man who "came to us in marriage, I would have beheaded Pangpang's brother, for he killed my [classificatory] sister." Struck close to home, and still a novice at the time, the only indemnity that would suffice for Lakay was, not mere metal goods, but a person.

A year or two later, a raiding party composed of six men from Pasigiyan, true Rumyad, and Peknar attacked an Aymuyu-Pasigiyan household. It had been Pasigiyans who, for their own reasons, Pangpang said, had pointed the way to the true Rumyads, saying, "Behead the Pasigiyans in that place." The true Rumyads saw their opporunity to make amends with Lakay and his maternal uncle, and asked them both to join in the raid in the hope of giving Lakay his demanded covenant. The senior true Rumyad among the raiders was the man whom Lakay had described as the reason he never followed through on his impulse to behead Pangpang's younger brother. This true Rumyad man already had four children by his Peknar wife, who was the sister of Lakay's father. The raid, however, failed. The six men did attack the house in the darkness before dawn, and they killed one of those inside but were unable to enter and behead their victim.

In 1927, these internecine struggles spiraled through unheard-of reaches. True Rumyads, Peknars, Yamus, Bēnabēs—in all a group of about 25 men—decided to raid against the Payupays. This diverse group of raiders had gathered together from scattered places: from the northwestern margin came Lakay and other Peknars, as well as five of their Bēnabē companions and a Payupay man from Didipyu; from their hiding place on the hill above the Kakidugen River came four Peknars and Yamus, including the brother of Singep; and from a hill east of the Bukaw River on the left bank of the Kanuwap River came three Peknar men, who the year before had left the hill above the Kakidugen River, as well as a number of true Rumyads, including Pangpang, who the year before had been living in Abēka on the southwestern margin.

The raiders, as ever among Ilongots, traced their reasons for participation to multiple sources. Pangpang wanted to give Lakay a victim to behead as a form of covenant between them. At the same time, he hoped to make the Pasigiyans afraid to retaliate for the raid against one of their households a year or two before; he told me that he thought "it would be good if we went and killed elsewhere to make the Pasigiyans afraid." Lakay, of course, wanted to collect his indemnity from Pangpang as well as seize the chance to show his anger to those who had led the troops when he was arrested four years before. The Bēnabēs, including a grandson of Iddung (the one who had been compelled to kill his fellow Peknars in the late 1870s), were invited along as part of the incipient marital alliance between them and the Peknars (who later became the Kakidugens). The Payupay from Didipyu sought revenge because Singep, who had been beheaded by the Payupays from Tau in 1920, had been married to his maternal aunt. And Singep's brother was simply determined to make the Payupays from Tau feel the cutting edge of his bolo.

Once gathered near the Kakidugen River, this large raiding party listened for favorable calls from the omen birds and then departed northward to the place of the Payupays in Tau. When they reached a house in Tau, three members of the party entered, feigning friendship and bearing a gift of game they had bagged along the way. These three men, two of whom had been raised through early childhood by the Payupays in Didipyu, pretended to be on their way to visit their foster parents. The Payupay man inside the house was suspicious and vigilant; that evening he lay with his bolo by his side and remained awake throughout the night. After removing the sharpened bamboo stakes surrounding the house, the 22 men lying in wait outside began their approach in silence. Lakay began to take the lead and scout ahead, but Singep's brother insisted that he go first because the Payupays from Tau had beheaded his brother. The moment the three men inside caught their hosts off guard and started to slash furiously, those outside rushed to attack. Five men, including Lakay and the Payupay man from Didipyu, beheaded all the people inside the house.

The raiders rushed over the hill, down the Ulawi (the stream where the Peknars and Biaws had lived in the 1870's) up the Tubu, and up the Kakidugen until they reached the hill where Singep's brother lived. Together they sang the song of celebration, Lakay reported, until the house began to spin. Then they divided into two groups, one, including Lakay, heading for the northwestern margin and the other stopping at the hill east of the Bukaw River on the left bank of the Kanuwap to continue the song of celebration.

By the time the raiders reached the northwestern margin, they had been informed on by the Payupays from Tau. Unlike the time of his arrest four years before, however, Lakay now felt, with good reason, that he was safe "because even if we were informed on we lived where the soldiers came from." Indeed, the troops damaged neither their bodies nor their property; instead they simply arrested five people who lived there (among them Lakay's wife, his younger brother, and his maternal uncle) and ordered them to lead the way to the hideout of the remaining headhunters.

The raiders then on the hill east of the Bukaw were warned by two men who ran ahead of the soldiers, but they were too absorbed in their song of celebration to pay heed. When the soldiers drew near, one of the Ilongot guides purposely triggered a device hidden on the path that released a heavy stone that thudded on the floor of the house and warned those inside. As the celebrants bolted toward the forest, the soldiers arrived on the scene and opened fire. Two fleeing women were shot and fell dead in the forest and a third was captured and taken as a wife by one of the soldiers. A man who had just watched his mother die crept back and fired a bamboo-tipped arrow that glanced off the holster of the lieutenant who led the soldiers. Seriously wounded, the lieutenant was carried back to the northwestern margin on a stretcher.

Once again, people dispersed. Some sought refuge on the margins and others fled into the interior. The refugees from the hill above the Kakidugen assumed aliases (Turpag, for instance, became Usal) so that they could not be identified from the list of wanted persons given to the soldiers by the Payupay informers from Tau. They then joined Lakay and the others in the relative safety at the home of the soldiers on the northwestern margin. Pangpang and his Rumyad companions fled from the hill east of the Bukaw and returned to the southwestern margin, where they found a haven. The two groups that remained in the interior fared less well. The man who shot the lieutenant was afraid to appear on the margins; he and his companions went into hiding in the depths of the forest west of the Bukaw on the left bank of the Kanuwap, where they survived, they said, like homeless people lost in the forest.

Worse yet was the fate of a young true Rumyad who had just taken the head of a Payupay from Tau. He and his family (except his sister, who had been captured by the soldiers) crossed the Kanuwap and asked for food and shelter from the Pasigiyans then living on the right bank. The true Rumyad group, like the Yamu-Peknar group some six years before, was highly vulnerable; they were fugitives from lowland law and they had neither food nor shelter in the uplands. Overtly hospitable, their Pasigiyan hosts sneaked off in secret and told the nearby Dekrans how angry they were because their guests were stealing food. What the Dekrans heard, and they heard correctly, was an invitation to behead the true Rumyad fugitives. It was an offer they could not refuse, for the father of the young true Rumyad man had himself taken two Dekran heads on the raid in the 1890's. Time passed, until a young man from Dekran spent the night at the home of the true Rumyad refugees. In the familiar Ilongot pattern, the guest waited until about dawn before he began to slash at his hosts as he signaled his companions, poised to attack the house. The Rumyads were caught off guard because they thought the Dekrans would not dare violate their sworn oath by salt of about 1911. The true Rumyad father and three of his children were beheaded; the son who

had beheaded Payupay from Tau broke through the Dekran attackers, killing one as he went, and led his mother, two sisters, and
younger brother to safety.

That soldiers should arrive as they did soon afterward and arrest
three Dekran men was not an obvious conclusion. After all, the
groups involved—Dekrans, Pasigiyans, and true Rumyads—were
not among the so-called loyal Ilongots who could readily make the
soldiers listen when they informed on their brethren. This time, cu-
riously enough, Lakay guided the soldiers. His motives were twofold. First, he felt loyal to Pangpang from true Rumyad, with
whom he had just made his covenant during the raid against the
Payupays in Tau. Second, the true Rumyad father had been beheaded because in the 1890's he had taken two Dekran heads in
retaliation for the decapitation of Lakay's maternal uncle and
grandfather. It is therefore less remarkable that Lakay willingly
guided the soldiers than that the soldiers were willing to be guided
by him. Imprisoned only four years before for a crime he did not
commit, Lakay made the transition, simply by moving from the
center to the margin, from a so-called rebellious infidel to a "loyal" Ilongot.

In the meantime a violent struggle, precipitated by the beheading of a Payupay from Tau by the Payupay from Didipyu, erupted
within Payupay during 1927–28 as the Taus and Didipyus unleashed their mutual anger. To begin, the Didipyus raided and beheaded five from Tau. Then a Didipyu man who had married into
Tau was beheaded in his sleep by his brother-in-law as his wife
looked on, because his nephew, too young to know any better, had
unwittingly informed on him, saying, "Uncle just sang the song of
celebration at Didipyu." The Didipyu raiders were then imprisoned when people from Tau informed on them. Later a Didipyu
man guided a man, woman, and child from Tau into an ambush
and all three were beheaded. In retaliation a Tau man drowned
and beheaded a teenage girl from Didipyu. Her brother immediately vented his anger by chopping down the banana tree of the
Tau who had beheaded her. Taking no chances, that man from
Tau called in the soldiers, all of whom were Bēnabēs and Payupays
from Tau, and a constabulary trooper from Bēnabē beheaded the

irate but hapless brother.* Finally, a man from Didipyu visited the people in the forest west of the Bukaw on the left bank of the Kanuwap and was beheaded by the man whose mother had been killed by the soldiers. Things calmed down only after the Didipyus moved far downstream, allowing distance to bring peace to the Payupays in a way that troops could not.

Reflection on this awesome slaughter highlights the extraordinary optimism of Max Gluckman's (1956) functional view of the place of crisscrossing loyalties in the process of feuding. His generalization of earlier studies of the feud in stateless societies (especially the work of E. E. Evans-Pritchard on the Nuer) took as central the notion that human beings are often enmeshed in a web of conflicting, crosscutting loyalties that regulate the feud and produce social cohesion. The point is that when people belong to multiple, overlapping groups there will always be a number of them who are caught in the middle because they have ties to both sides. And the people caught in a conflict of loyalties are likely to work hard to end the feud because otherwise they might be attacked by either or both parties. Thus Gluckman spoke of the "peace in the feud," for in his view the feud contained the seeds of its own peaceful settlement, at least insofar as there were people who would mediate the dispute because of their strong allegiances to both sides.

It is instructive to recall that one source of the catastrophic chain of events in Ilongot country from 1919 to 1928 was Lakay's inability to resolve his conflicting loyalties: he wanted to behead Pangpang's younger brother, but he could not bring himself to do so because of his kinship with Pangpang through his true Rumyad maternal grandfather. The end result, far from a stalemate, was a raid in which the true Rumyads and Peknars resolved the differences between them by raiding against the Payupays in Tau. (For other instances of building alliances between bērtan by raiding against a third bērtan, see pp. 255–56, 265–66). In the raid against the Payupays from Tau, five people were beheaded; and as

---

*In this period American colonial policy encouraged members of the so-called non-Christian tribes to join the constabulary. The policy only tightened the connection between the actions of soldiers and the patterns of Ilongot feuding.

a further consequence there were six more deaths along the Kanu-wap River, and eleven more people from Payupay were beheaded (not to mention the wounded lieutenant, the captured woman, and the imprisoned men from Payupay and Dekran). Kadēng attributed the meandering lethal sweep of this flow of events, horrifying as it was by his standards and mine, to the Payupay violation (in 1920, when they beheaded Singep) of their sworn oath by salt of less than a decade before. This Payupay violation, I should add, in turn led indirectly to the Dekran violation of their oath in 1927. Surely in this case it would be more apt to invert Gluckman's slogan and speak of the "feud in the peace."

In the case of the Payupay man's beheading his sleeping brother-in-law, the Tau people said afterward (not unlike Gluckman) that the inmarried man from Didipyu should not have joined in singing the celebratory song, but should instead have urged his Didipyu brethren not to raid because he had married into Tau. At the same time, Kadēng told me that the victim's wife was incompetent because she should have retaliated for her husband's death by beheading her own brother. Conflicts of loyalties among Ilongots, in short, can produce the uneasy yet peaceful stalemate that Gluckman would anticipate. And then again, they often can and do not. Instead, contradictory allegiances among Ilongots can lead, for instance, to the beheading of a third party—mending relations tenuously on one front while creating a breach elsewhere—or to the venting of anger against a target close to home, as in the extreme case of the beheaded co-resident brother-in-law/husband.

When Ilongots take heads in such a wild fashion, they are most likely to do so in periods of widespread violence within and often beyond Ilongot country. It is during such periods of unbounded turbulence (for example in about 1905, in 1919–28, and in 1942–45) that novices are especially inclined to be carried away by passionate envy of their peers who have already taken heads.

REFLECTIONS ON THE FEUD

By now it is probably clear that the unity of Rumyad should be understood in the historical context of American colonial policies toward the Ilongots. Colonial policies were implemented through the practice of indirect rule, in which "loyal" Ilongots from the margins (including the Butags, Bēnabēs, and Payupays) were used as informers against "rebellious" Ilongots from the center (including the Bēsilids, Pasigiyans, Peknars, true Rumyads, and Yamus). But the colonial officials did not perceive that their policies were fused locally with Ilongot patterns and histories of feuding. Soldiers lent their firepower to bērtan on the margins and thereby escalated the intensity of feuding until it reached unheard-of proportions.

During the initial period of margin-center relations in the colonial context (1908–18), constabulary troops simply made arrests, and what disruption occurred resulted from the reputation that Turnbull and others had gained along the lower Kasiknan River in the aftermath of William Jones's death. Nonetheless, the new dynamic in which "loyal" Ilongots informed on their "rebellious" brethren was begun and then remained dormant during the process of pacification.

By the period of 1919–28, the troops often unwittingly lent their firepower to bērtan on the margin that continued or renewed their feuds with bērtan in the center. Indeed, the Rumyads were collectively lumped together by colonial officials who viewed them as particularly dangerous headhunters. At the same time, however, the incursion of troops in 1923, when Lakay was arrested, led to the dispersal of the Rumyads, who fled in different directions and sought haven toward the margins.

Eventually the Rumyads began to regroup by their homeland along the Kanuwap River. It was then, in 1940, that Kadēng and the others living in the interior were arrested by soldiers guided by Butags. These arrests, of course, were a primary source for the Butag-Rumyad feud—which itself should in part be understood in relation to the colonial presence and the division between loyal Ilongots of the margins and rebellious Ilongots of the center.

The compelling presence of Rumyad solidarity that I experienced in 1967–69 was thus as much inspired by the past, including both phases of residential concentration and the consequences of the colonial presence, as it was artfully forged in the present. In the 1969 confrontation with the Butags, multiple bygone fissures were mended, or at any rate covered over, as past moments of collective unity were made visibly present. Indeed, bērtan become more solidary through the social enactment of a covenant. During the celebration of covenants feuds are viewed as two-party relations of enduring hostility, in which one bērtan's solidarity becomes socially manifest in opposition to another's.

During the beheading phase of a feud, however, overlapping loyalties among the parties involved are critical, not so much because they either heighten or dampen violence (for they may do either, neither, or both), but rather because they provide multiple socially constructed vectors along which relations of alliance and enmity may develop.

The potential sources of a feud, the insults stored as grudges, are myriad; whether and how they surface depends in part on when and whether an opportune moment arrives for a beheading or a raid by soldiers. In some cases prior hostilities between two bērtan can lead them to make amends by joining to attack a third bērtan. Beginning with a beheading derived from a prior insult, the events of a feud can move like a chain reaction, cutting horizontally across groups. To simplify the events of 1927–28, for example, a Peknar grudge against the true Rumyads led them to band together in a joint raid against the Payupays in Tau, which resulted in a punitive incursion of troops and the beheading of true Rumyads at the hands of Dekrans. This step beyond functionalism suggests that the concept of the feud is a cultural construct used most often for looking back on events and making amends.

AFTERWORD

When we arrived in Kakidugen on October 27, 1967, we thought at first that the local cluster had felt relatively little outside influence, and we were pleased to find that people were dressed more or less as they had been in the time of William Jones. Clearly, Jones's sense that he was bearing witness to the end of an era had been mistaken. And yet, people's lives were changing.

At the time, the influence of the New Tribes Mission radiated outward from Ringen, where a Tagalog-speaking missionary had lived for some eight years. The influence of the mission was only beginning in Kēyat and had not yet extended farther north.

Shortly before our arrival, Ilongots had divided the land in Kakidugen into individual shares. Prior to that time, land had been public domain, and people had cleared gardens or hunted or fished wherever they pleased within the general area. Boundaries, as Tukbaw said, were unknown to them in the days when they lived as Ilongots.

This parceling of their common land was a last-ditch attempt to cope with the increasing encroachment of settlers, which had been rumored from 1959. When a band of squatters composed of Ibaloys, Kallahans, and Kankanays cleared land about an hour upstream in 1962, the Kakidugen men, Wagat said, talked about beheading them, but gave up their plan because they felt so outnumbered and feared retribution from the many children and siblings of their potential victims. In 1966, Ifugaos began to grab land about an hour downstream, leaving our companions wedged between the two points of population increase. This time Lakay, Tukbaw, and the other men tried to frighten the squatters away (as they heard that Kama from Butag had recently done): fully armed and wearing red hornbill earrings, they arrived as a group

Wagat planting rice in her garden.

and told their new neighbors to return to their homes. The Ifugaos replied that they were prepared to die on their new land.

The pain of even more routine transitions became clearer to us about a year after our arrival, on January 27, 1969, only a few days before we left for the Butag-Rumyad covenant. That afternoon Wagat told her stepmother, Disa, who was about to leave for her garden, that she should be sure to return early enough to prepare rice for the evening meal. The innuendo—that Disa was stingy with her rice and lazy about working around the house—was not lost on the target. Rather than argue back, Disa mumbled unintelligibly to herself as she picked up her things to leave. Wagat's sister, Sawad, then said, "That's enough." But Wagat, never one to mince words, shouted that Disa was at it again, mumbling, muttering, acting silly, just the way she had during the recent visit of her niece (ZD) from Ringen, when the two of them sat together and giggled, snubbing other people, and complaining about Wagat. She went on to say that Duman, who had just visited, had advised her and Tukbaw to move out of the house. Disa countered that she should be respected as an older person who had married Wagat's father, Lakay, through a public assembly with oratory. Wagat screamed back that there had been no oratory and that Disa had just got herself pregnant and come inside the house (suggesting that the woman, not the man, had taken the initiative in courtship).

Lakay could contain himself no longer. After threatening to throw her out the window, he began to beat his wife, Disa, with a stick of firewood. Stomping with rage, he stalked over to his daughter, Wagat, who tried to hide behind her husband, Tukbaw. Lakay then drew his bolo and gashed Wagat across the top of her head and said he was going from there to behead Disa. All the while Tukbaw sat still, silent, sharpening his bolo as he had been doing before the women began to yell, his eyes bloodshot and welling

Two Ilongot rice granaries.

with tears. Michelle and I looked on, shaken at the realization that our presence had surely added to the tensions of a household in transition.

That night Wagat took her adopted daughter and went to sleep beneath her granary, where Tukbaw brought her a meal of rice. Wagat told Michelle the next day that she had been raised, not by Disa, but by Lakay's father. Had Disa felt her "weight"—carried her through pregnancy, birth, and infancy—she would have been grateful for the opportunity to feed her in her old age. But as it was, this woman, Disa, had just up and entered her home (when she was 15) and deserved nothing in return. Not only that, she went on, when Disa had an affair with a man who later married into Ringen, just after the time of the Japanese, she cursed Lakay and wished him dead. And when Wagat's brother died in 1948, Disa said, "Don't be sad, it's just as well." Later, when Wagat was ill, Disa said, "If you pass away . . ." as if she were wishing for her death. Wagat insisted that she and Tukbaw would move out of the house immediately.

Disa said that she would simply remain in Ringen for an indefinite period after attending the covenant there. She would ask somebody to wind her a brass wire belt; then she would stay and hoe the garden of her niece, and she might even stay until the end of the year to harvest the rice. That would show Lakay, she said.

That night Tukbaw went hunting alone, to be by himself with his thoughts. When he returned the next morning he quietly said that he and Wagat would move out of the house. On January 30, the morning before we left for the Butag-Rumyad covenant, Tukbaw returned from having taken food to Wagat, and sobbed that she was living outside, alone like an animal. That night he asked Lakay to be patient and remember his love for his daughter. The old man was so embarrassed that he was only able to mumble that he could not speak.

As it turned out, Wagat went with us to the covenant and Disa remained at home. When we returned, Wagat began to eat and sleep inside the house, and Disa told Lakay he should give her something, indicating that she was willing to forget her anger. Though they decided, in part because of our presence, to remain together for the rest of the year, Tukbaw said that they were certain to separate in the near future. What had been revealed through this crisis was the ambivalent emotional tone of the shift from a three-family household to one where the youngest married daughter was to care for her aging father over his final years of dependency. The participants clearly felt the anguish of their coming separation even while they provided an impetus for the transition by airing the deep grudges and petty annoyances accumulated over most of a lifetime together.

As we prepared to leave Kakidugen in June 1969, we asked Lakay where he would be living in the years to come. He said that, were their lives as they once had been, they would now make a major move of about a two-hour walk either downstream or upstream. Indeed, the Kakidugens had resided at their present location for ten continuous years, and during 1923–69 they, like other Rumyad local clusters, had made a major move once every eight or nine years. It was time, by standards of the recent past, to move again. But now, even though their place no longer afforded what they considered good land for dry rice gardens, because the forest cover needed more time to regenerate itself, they planned to remain where they were, for their squatter neighbors had grabbed the land in the next places they might have gardened.

The Kakidugen people's strategy in the face of the encroaching settlers was the familiar one of attempting to hold their center and defend their perimeter. They had even tried to increase their strength of numbers by persuading kin from Kēyat and Pengegyaben to come and join them. That year three new places for gardens were cleared: first, Lakay went just across the river from our house; second, his younger brother went about 20 minutes downstream to join the other two families at that extremity; third, Tukbaw and Ta'at went about an hour upstream. The idea was to block both riverine directions, along which the squatters were certain to attempt further incursions. Yet at the same time, new gardens with their temporary field shelters are usually the first step toward the construction of more permanent homes on that site. Though people often say that they move their houses in order to follow their gardens, and in this case to fend off settlers, the new gardens also serve to excuse moves made because of social realignments, both separations and unions between conjugal families. In so moving, Tukbaw and Wagat clearly intended both to save their land and to distance themselves from Lakay and Disa by an hour-long walk.

Within a month after our departure, a number of men from Ka-kidugen and elsewhere set off on a raid toward some distant squatter settlements. One reason, among others, for this raid was the death in 1968 of Lakay's classificatory sister. Although we suspected that something like a raid was in the air, all our questions were met with flat denials. The obvious reasons for secrecy were there, but they were also shaped by the Ilongot pattern of social process as improvisation—of not saying, because they could not know, what would happen until it had happened. As Ilongots see it, human plans change, and other options, thus kept open, can be seized. Certainly this is the way with raiding and marriage, both fickle matters. That time in mid-1969 the raiders—perhaps showing wisdom of the cultural pattern—encountered bad omens along the trail and felt compelled to return home, not to set off again during that year.

By the time we reached Kakidugen on March 20, 1974, we had been in Ilongot country for about ten days, first at a mission station in the southern sector and then in Ringen, where we were met by Tepeg, Ta'at, Insan's eldest daughter, and Tukbaw's nephew (ZS). From there we walked to Pengegyaben, where we had a tearful reunion with Tukbaw, Insan, Duman, Baket, and others, who now regarded us, not as uninvited guests, but as the people they had "called" to return in a taped message Tukbaw sent us in 1971. Our ability in the language had improved, and on both sides we felt an increase in familiarity and trust. We had gradually, as Ilongots say, grown more used to one another.

Even before we reached Kakidugen, we learned much of what had come to pass during our absence of nearly five years. The New People's Army had been active, especially in 1969–70, on the southeastern and western margins, and one band had passed through Kakidugen on its way northeast. Martial law was declared in September 1972, and people, fearing rumors of firing squads, had come to regard headhunting as a thing of the past. Shortly after the declaration of martial law, a new leader—the son of a Ringen man, he said, long lost since 1945 and raised as a low-lander—had emerged in pan-Ilongot politics. He built his following along the lines of a network recently established through yearly conferences of the New Tribes Mission followers scattered throughout Ilongot country. The Ringen people, supported by their new leader, and those from Kakidugen-Pengegyaben had once again found themselves on opposite sides of the fence, this time in a dispute over land only days before our arrival.

In Pengegyaben, Tukbaw tried to persuade Insan and the others to move to Kakidugen. Their land, he said, was no longer good for dry rice; it had been cleared up a single hill for some 14 years. Further, it was hard for the women to walk the trail carrying heavy baskets of rice for their children who were attending school at Kakidugen. This merger had been proposed before, but Lakay had said he loved his place too much to move, and Baket could not bear to leave the expansive vistas of her hilltop home. Once again the proposal came to naught.

Along the trail to Kakidugen, Tukbaw saw no signs of game, and he remarked, joking half-heartedly, that the deer and wild pigs must have done some dreadful deed, otherwise they had no reason to be in hiding. Later he cautioned us, lest we be disappointed, that we should not expect to eat as much meat as before because the forest had become peopled with squatters and the game was depleted.

Once in Kakidugen, we found that a new primary school with grades one through four had opened in June 1972. By the time of our arrival, 26 of the 43 living children (19 had died) of the ten couples who had married in 1955–58 were enrolled in school: ten were in first grade, eight in second, seven in third, none yet in fourth, and Radu's oldest son (then 15) was a star fifth-grade pupil in a school on the northwestern margin. The only children who were unquestionably of school age and were not enrolled were the eldest daughters of Insan and Maniling, aged 18 and 17, respectively. Their labor was too valuable to give up, and in any case school seemed more important for boys than for girls.

The local cluster had changed in other ways that had seemed likely by the end of our previous stay. The newly cleared garden sites of 1969 had become the sites of permanent homes well before 1974. Lakay's younger brother had indeed moved downstream.

An Ilongot mother in her garden.

And when our former home was blown down in 1970 during a typhoon, this reason to build a new house (a common excuse in such cases) was seized to justify the upstream move of Tukbaw and Wagat as well as the move across the river by Lakay, Disa, Bayaw, and Sawad. The attempt to block the squatters by so moving, however, was as futile as my most pessimistic forecasts. Ibaloys, Kallahans, and Kankanays had become Tukbaw's neighbors upstream, and a few Ifugao families had managed to become interspersed among the Kakidugen households.

The only remaining hope of holding their land seemed to lie with mastering the alien techniques of permanent-field wet rice agriculture. The need for draft animals to pull plows was evident, but the acquisition of the 11 carabaos owned by the people of Kakidugen and Pengegyaben in 1974 had resulted more in the sale of land than in the harvest of wet rice. One wet rice field was working well, another was caving in at the sides, and two more had been abandoned. That year a member of Radu's household, in an act as self-defeating as it was desperate, invited a group of squatters from near Baguio, to the west, to settle on his land. The idea was that the Ilongots would gain draft animals, knowledge of wet rice agriculture, and further numbers in their support against the lethal witchcraft of the Ifugaos. It was a losing battle.

Dilya and others told me in hushed tones about what had happened farther toward the margin, where Ifugaos had approached, penetrated the Ilongot perimeter, and then used witchcraft to inflict a series of deaths until everybody there had either died or moved away. This clearly was not an idle tale, but the story of what was now happening to the people of Kakidugen. Perhaps the deaths of Yennaw's paternal grandfather and Baket's younger sister in 1970 had had other sources, she said, but what other than witchcraft could have killed Dinwag and the three children of Radu in 1971, as well as Dilya's husband, Lakay's younger brother, in 1972? The spiral had yet another turn, for the Ifugao shaman who was called in to combat the fatal illnesses—which he did in fact attribute to witchcraft of other Ifugaos—demanded the sacrifice of domesticated pigs. The purchase of these pigs, more than were owned by any single Ilongot, in turn led to the sale of more land to Ifugaos.

Let me use the case of Radu to illustrate the consciousness of Ilongots about how such diverse forces for change interpenetrate. The incident involves settlers, the mission, and the end of headhunting brought by martial law. Radu, the main protagonist, was 43 years of age; he was regarded as quiet, reliable, and little given to the banter and horseplay in which other men indulged. His wife, Yammak, had given birth to 11 children, of whom six had died; that was an inordinate number of deaths even by Ilongot standards. In fact, during the dry season of 1971 three of Radu's children died suddenly, one after the other in a matter of days. Radu was stricken beyond grief. These were not ordinary deaths. Seeking explanation, he consulted a nearby settler, an Ifugao shaman, and in exchange for a large domesticated pig he learned that his three children had been killed by another Ifugao settler's witchcraft. He was advised to abandon his house and move elsewhere. People speculated that the children's deaths were inflicted in retaliation for the deaths of settlers beheaded by Ilongots in the past. They told of a similar series of incidents between settlers and Ilongots to the northwest. Indeed, they feared Ifugao witchcraft.

In June 1974 Radu's six-month-old son became ill; we medicated the baby, who probably had pneumonia, but to no avail. Heaving and gasping loudly to the end, he died about dawn. We visited Radu that afternoon; he was sobbing and staring through glazed and bloodshot eyes at the cotton blanket covering his baby, the seventh he had lost. The baby's grandfather said they planned to confine themselves to the house for a day, or perhaps two, following the customary Ilongot prohibition. The baby's uncle by marriage was recounting his grudges against lowlanders, telling of how a soldier had beat him up; perhaps he was contemplating taking a head to rid himself of his grief, or maybe he was simply musing about the kinds of events that cause people grief. The baby's aunt by marriage, rather than airing her grudges, seized the moment to preach the word of God to all who would listen. That afternoon the situation was murky; just how the conflicting currents of opinion would resolve themselves was as yet unclear. Nevertheless, people in the neighboring houses had already made up their minds; they had decided to follow the customary display of sympathy by not working for two days.

What happened that next day was not anticipated. At Radu's request, recent New Tribes converts from downstream had come and dug a grave and buried the baby. But it was not that that had so surprised the people. Much more perplexing and gossiped about was what everybody could see before them: at the very time that they themselves had abandoned urgent work in their gardens as a way of making their sympathy public, certain members of Radu's household were laughing and playing volleyball on the cleared airstrip. I was as bewildered as they. I went over and asked the volleyball players what had happened: did they feel no sorrow? They explained that they had decided to follow the way of God and not the Ilongot way of mourning; they had deduced that American missionaries, because of their belief in everlasting life in heaven, were surely not in the least saddened by death in this

An Ilongot father holding his infant son.

world. The volleyball game was an attempt to emulate an only partially known religion.

A month later, I puzzled further over what had happened. By then it had become clear that Radu's household intended to convert to the new religion; a small Sunday service was conducted at his house by people who had been invited to come from the mission center. Radu's coming conversion, I was told, resulted directly from his son's death; as I had seen, the two events, the death and the conversion, did coincide in time, making the causal link plausible. What remained enigmatic to me was the nature of the connection between a baby's death and his family's conversion to evangelical Protestantism. One day, as I was discussing Radu's conversion with Tepeg, my "brother-in-law," I blurted out the conclusion I had reached: "Can anybody be so blind as to believe that their children will never die if they accept the new religion?" Tepeg, a reflective skeptic, told me I had missed the point: what Radu in fact sought in the new religion was not the denial of our inevitable deaths, but a means of coping with his grief. With the advent of martial law, headhunting was out of the question as a means of venting his wrath and thereby lessening his grief. Were he to remain in his Ilongot way of life, the pain of his sorrow would simply by too much to bear.

Thus I began to perceive the depth of the changes that were taking place as political control was extended to encompass most Ilongots. While the Ringens heaped scorn upon their Kakidugen brethren for selling land to Ifugao squatters, they were themselves receiving lowland government officials who flew directly to their airstrip and promoted talk of a pan-Ilongot federation. The new generation in Ringen, predominantly true Rumyads and Pasigiyans, had started to intermarry with distant bērtan in what seemed to be a diffusion of their larger Rumyad identity and in support of the coming pan-Ilongot federation; the new generation in Kakidugen and Pengegyaben, predominantly Peknars, appeared about to renew their former direction of marriage toward Bēnabē. And because the Butags were no longer the incessant topic of conversation, the split within Rumyad was all the more evident. The division between true Rumyads and Peknars was like a geological rupture along a fault line that dated from the 1860's. In the present, the line of fission manifested itself as an antagonism between the New Tribes converts in Ringen and the people of Kakidugen and Pengegyaben who (partly because we, as their companions, were Americans and clearly non-missionaries) had not yet converted.

On yet a deeper level, Kakidugen with its influx of settlers seemed on the way to becoming a place of the margins, and Ringen, the center, had come under the direct transforming influence of the lowlands. Just as Dean Worcester had anticipated in 1909, the Ilongot region had been neither crisscrossed by horsetrails nor permanently pacified by regular constabulary patrols. What he had never imagined was that the Piper Cub that reached Ringen in 1959 would virtually turn the Ilongot region inside out. Initially, only New Tribes missionaries and then we two anthropologists skipped the margins altogether and flew directly to the interior, bringing the mixed blessing of our commodities. By 1974 that same pathway, the direct nonstop route from the lowlands to Ringen, was being used by government officials.

Whether Ringen will become a lowland outpost, as seems likely, and the Kakidugen people will be dispossessed of their lands is for the future to determine. If the past is any guide, Ilongot society has followed not a straight-line progression, but an uneven motion, now starting, now stopping, then shifting direction. In reflecting upon their own social order, the Ilongots themselves confirm that it is ever improvised anew, as they follow one another along shifting paths, at times gathering together and at times dispersing. But the present period of transformation—however it turns out in the end—makes especially clear the wisdom and pain in the recognition by Ilongot parents that their children will walk different paths as they grow up into worlds unlike their own.

REFERENCES CITED

APPELL, G. N., ed.

1976 The Societies of Borneo: Explorations in the Theory of Cognatic Social Structure. Washington, D.C.: American Anthropological Association.

BARTON, R. F.

1919 Ifugao Law. University of California Publications in American Archaeology and Ethnology 15.1: 1–186.

1938 Philippine Pagans: The Autobiographies of Three Ifugaos. London: George Routledge.

1949 The Kalingas: Their Institutions and Custom Law. Chicago: University of Chicago Press.

BERNSTEIN, RICHARD

1976 The Restructuring of Social and Political Theory. New York: Harcourt Brace Jovanovich.

BOHANNAN, LAURA

1952 A Genealogical Character. Africa 22: 301–15.

BOHANNAN, PAUL

1953 Concepts of Time Among the Tiv of Nigeria. Southwestern Journal of Anthropology 9: 251–62.

BURLING, ROBBINS

1965 Hill Farms and Padi Fields. Englewood Cliffs, N.J.: Prentice-Hall.

CAMPA, FR. BUENAVENTURA

1891 Una visita a las rancherías de Ilongotes. El Correo Sino-Annamita 25: 563–646.

CAMPBELL, J. K.

1964 Honor, Family, and Patronage. Oxford: Oxford University Press.

CARMACK, R. M.

1972 Ethnohistory: A Review of Its Development, Definitions, Methods, and Aims. In Annual Review of Anthropology, pp. 227–46. Palo Alto, Calif.: Annual Reviews.

CRAPANZANO, VINCENT

1977 On the Writing of Ethnography. Dialectical Anthropology 2: 69–73.

CULLER, JONATHAN

1975 Structuralist Poetics. Ithaca, N.Y.: Cornell University Press.

DAVIS, NATALIE

1979 Les Conteurs de Montaillou. Annales, E.S.C. 34 (January–February): 61–73.

DYEN, ISIDORE
1965 A Lexicostatistical Classification of the Austronesian Languages. Indiana University Publications in Anthropology and Linguistics, Memoir 19. International Journal of Linguistics 31: 1–64.

EGGAN, FRED
1941 Some Aspects of Culture Change in the Northern Philippines. American Anthropologist 43: 11.–18.
1954 Some Social Institutions in the Mountain Province and Their Significance for Historical and Comparative Studies. Journal of East Asiatic Studies 3: 329–35.
1967 Some Aspects of Bilateral Social Systems in the Philippines. In Mario Zamora, ed., Studies in Philippie Anthropology, pp. 186–302. Quezon City, Philippines: Alemar.

ELIADE, MIRCEA
1971 The Myth of the Eternal Return: Or, Cosmos and History. Translated by Willard R. Trask. Princeton, N.J.: Princeton University Press.

EPSTEIN, A. L., ed.
1967 The Craft of Social Anthropology. London: Tavistock.

ERIKSON, ERIK
1975 Life History and the Historical Moment. New York: Norton.

ERRINGTON, SHELLY
1979 Some Comments on Style in the Meanings of the Past. Journal of Asian Studies 38: 231–44.
n.d. Genealogies and Society in Luwu. Typescript.

EVANS-PRITCHARD, E. E.
1941 The Nuer. Oxford: Oxford University Press.
1962 Anthropology and History. In E. E. Evans-Pritchard, Social Anthropology and Other Essays, pp. 172–91. New York: Free Press.

FERNÁNDEZ, PABLO, and JACINTO de JUAN
1969 The Social and Economic Development of Nueva Vizcaya, Philippines, 1571–1898. Acta Manilana, Ser. B, no. 1(8): 59–134.

FORTES, MEYER
1949 Time and Social Structure: An Ashanti Case Study. In Meyer Fortes, ed., Social Structure: Studies Presented to A. R. Radcliffe-Brown, pp. 54–84. New York: Russell & Russell.
1958 Introduction. In Jack Goody, ed., The Developmental Cycle in Domestic Groups, pp. 1–14. Cambridge, Eng.: Cambridge University Press.

FOX, JAMES
1971 A Rotinese Dynastic Genealogy: Structure and Event. In T. O. Beidelman, ed., The Translation of Culture, pp. 37–77. London: Tavistock.

FRANKEL, S. A.
1948 The 37th Infantry Division in World War II. Washington, D.C.: Infantry Journal Press.

FREEMAN, DEREK
1958 The Family System of the Iban of Borneo. In Jack Goody, ed., The Developmental Cycle in Domestic Groups, pp. 15–52. Cambridge, Eng.: Cambridge University Press.
1970 Report on the Iban. New York: Humanities Press.

FUSSELL, PAUL
  1975 The Great War and Modern Memory. Oxford: Oxford University Press.
GALLIE, W. B.
  1968 Philosophy and the Historical Understanding. New York: Schocken.
GEERTZ, CLIFFORD
  1965 The Social History of an Indonesian Town. Cambridge, Mass.: MIT Press.
GIDDENS, ANTHONY
  1976 New Rules of Sociological Method. New York: Basic Books.
GLUCKMAN, MAX
  1956 Custom and Conflict in Africa. Oxford: Basil Blackwell.
GUERRERO, AMADO
  1970 Philippine Society and Revolution. Hong Kong: Ta Kung Pao.
HAVILAND, JOHN
  1977 Gossip, Reputation, and Rumor in Zinacantan. Chicago: University of Chicago Press.
HEXTER, J. H.
  1971 Doing History. Bloomington: Indiana University Press.
ILETO, REYNALDO
  1975 Passion and the Interpretation of Change in Tagalog Society. Unpublished Ph.D. dissertation, Cornell University.
JENKS, A. E.
  1905 The Bontoc Igorot. Manila: Bureau of Printing.
JOCANO, F. L.
  1968 Sulod Society. Quezon City: University of Philippines Press.
JONES, WILLIAM
  1907-9 The Diary of William Jones. Typescript. Chicago: Field Museum of Natury History.
JORDANA Y MORERA, RAMÓN
  1885 Bosquejo geográfico e histórico-natural del Archipiélago Filipino. Madrid: Imprenta de Moreno y Rojas.
KEESING, F. M.
  1962 The Ethnohistory of Northern Luzon. Stanford, Calif.: Stanford University Press.
KLUCKHOHN, CLYDE
  1941 Patterning as Exemplified in Navaho Culture. In Leslie Spier, A. I. Hallowell, and S. S. Newman, eds., Language, Culture, and Personality, pp. 109-30. Menasha, Wis.: Sapir Memorial Publication Fund.
KNIGHT, L. K.
  1908 Report of the Governor of Nueva Vizcaya. In Annual Report of the Philippine Commission, 1908, Part 1, pp. 381-86. Washington, D.C.: Bureau of Printing.
KUHN, THOMAS
  1970 The Structure of Scientific Revolutions. Chicago: University of Chicago Press.
LACHICA, EDUARDO
  1971 Philippine Agrarian Society in Revolt. Manila: Solidaridad.

LARKIN, JOHN
1972 The Pampangans. Berkeley: University of California Press.
LEACH, EDMUND
1954 Political Systems of Highland Burma. Cambridge, Mass.: Harvard University Press.
1961 Two Essays Concerning the Symbolic Representation of Time. In Edmund Leach, Rethinking Anthropology, pp. 124–36. London: Athlone.
LÉVI-STRAUSS, CLAUDE
1966 The Savage Mind. Chicago: University of Chicago Press.
1969 The Elementary Structures of Kinship. Boston: Beacon.
LEWIS, I. M.
1968 Introduction. In I. M. Lewis, ed., History and Social Anthropology, pp. 9–28. London: Tavistock.
LISÓN-TOLOSANA, CARMELO
1966 Belmonte de los Caballeros: A Sociological Study of a Spanish Town. Oxford: Clarendon.
MACDONALD, CHARLES
1977 Une société simple: Parenté et résidence chez les Palawan (Philippines). Paris: Institut d'Ethnologie.
MACFARLANE, ALAN
1977 Reconstructing Historical Communities. New York: Cambridge University Press.
MALINOWSKI, BRONISLAW
1929 The Sexual Life of Savages. London: George Routledge.
MALUMBRES, JULIÁN
1918a Historia de Cagayan. Manila: Imprenta de Santo Tomás.
1918b Historia de la Isabela. Manila: Imprenta de Santo Tomás.
1919 Historia de Nueva Vizcaya y Provincia Montañosa. Manila: Imprenta de Santo Tomás.
MANNHEIM, KARL
1952 The Problem of Generations. In Paul Kecskemeti, ed., Essays on the Sociology of Knowledge, 2d ed., pp. 276–320. London: Routledge & Kegan Paul.
MARÍAS, JULIÁN
1970 Generations: A Historical Method. University: University of Alabama Press.
MINK, LOUIS
1965 The Autonomy of Historical Understanding. History and Theory 5: 24–47.
MURDOCK, G. P., ed.
1960 Social Structure in Southeast Asia. Chicago: Quadrangle.
ORTEGA Y GASSET, JOSÉ
1923 El Tema de nuestro tiempo. Madrid: Revista del Occidente.
OSSIO, JUAN
1977 Myth and History: The Seventeenth-Century Chronicle of Guaman Poma de Ayala. In Ravindra Jain, ed., Text and Context: The Social Anthropology of Tradition, pp. 51–93. Philadelphia: ISHI.
PETERSON, JEAN
1978 The Ecology of Social Boundaries. Champaign: University of Illinois Press.

POCOCK, DAVID
  1964 The Anthropology of Time-Reckoning. Contributions to Indian Sociology 7: 18–29.
RADCLIFFE-BROWN, A. R.
  1952 Structure and Function in Primitive Society. London: Cohen & West.
RIDEOUT, H. M.
  1912 William Jones: Indian, Cowboy, American Scholar, and Anthropologist in the Field. New York: Stokes.
ROSALDO, M. Z.
  1972 Metaphor and Folk Classification. Southwestern Journal of Anthropology 28: 83–99.
  1973 I Have Nothing to Hide: The Language of Ilongot Oratory. Language in Society 2(2): 193–223.
  1975 It's All Uphill: The Creative Metaphors of Ilongot Magical Spells. In M. Sanches and B. Bount, ed., Sociocultural Dimensions of Language Use, pp. 177–203. New York: Seminar.
  1980 Knowledge and Passion: Ilongot Conceptions of Self and Social Life. New York: Cambridge University Press.
ROSALDO, M. Z., and JANE ATKINSON
  1975 Man the Hunter and Woman. In Roy Willis, ed., The Interpretation of Symbolism, pp. 43–75. London: Malaby.
ROSALDO, RENATO
  1970 Ilongot Kin Terms: A Bilateral System of Northern Luzon, Philippines. Proceedings of the Eighth International Congress of Anthropological and Ethnological Sciences 2: 81–84.
  1975 Where Precision Lies: "The Hill People Once Lived on a Hill." In Roy Willis, ed., The Interpretation of Symbolism, pp. 1–22. London: Malaby.
  1976 The Story of Tukbaw: "They Listen as He Orates." In F. E. Reynolds and Donald Capps, eds., The Biographical Process: Studies in the History and Psychology of Religion, pp. 121–51. The Hague: Mouton.
  1978a The Rhetoric of Control: Ilongots Viewed as Natural Bandits and Wild Indians. In Barbara Babcock, ed., The Reversible World, pp. 240–52. Ithaca, N.Y.: Cornell University Press.
  1978b Lope as a Poet of History: History and Ritual in El testimonio vengado. In Alva Ebersole, ed., Perspectivas de la comedia. Colección siglo de oro, no. 6, pp. 9–32. Estudios de hispanófila.
  1978c Viewed from the Valleys: Five Names for Ilongots. In Mario Zamora, Donald Baxter, and Robert Lawless, eds., Social Change in Modern Philippines. Papers in Anthropology 19: 1–9.
  1979 The Social Relations of Ilongot Subsistence. In Harold Olofson, ed., Contributions to the Study of Philippine Shifting Cultivation (in press). Laguna, Philippines: Forest Research Institute.
RYDER, NORMAN
  1965 The Cohort as a Concept in the Study of Social Change. American Sociological Review 30: 843–61.
SAHLINS, MARSHALL
  1976 Culture and Practical Reason. Chicago: University of Chicago Press.

SANTAYANA, GEORGE
    1920 Character and Opinion in the United States. New York: George Braz-
          iller.
SANTOS, L. K.
    1919 Memorandum especial sobre los Ilongotes de Nueva Vizcaya al hon.
          secretario del interior. Typescript. Manila: National Library, Filipini-
          ana Division.
SAVAGE LANDOR, A. H.
    1904 The Gems of the East: Sixteen Thousand Miles of Research Travel
          Among Wild and Tame Tribes of Enchanting Islands. London: Macmil-
          lan.
SCHWARTZ, S. P., ed.
    1977 Naming, Necessity, and Natural Kinds. Ithaca, N.Y.: Cornell Univer-
          sity Press.
SCOTT, W. H.
    1974 The Discovery of the Igorots. Quezon City, Philippines: New Day.
    1975 History on the Cordillera. Baguio City, Philippines: Baguio Printing and
          Publishing.
SISON, TEOFILO
    1932 Annual Report of the Departments of the Interior and Labor. In Annual
          Report of the Governor General of the Philippines, 1932, pp. 167–69.
          Washington, D.C.: Bureau of Printing.
SMITH, R. R.
    1963 Triumph in the Philippines. Washington, D.C.: U.S. Government Print-
          ing Office.
SPITZER, ALAN
    1973 The Historical Problem of Generations. American Historical Review
          78: 1353–85.
STONER, BARBARA
    1971 Why Was William Jones Killed? Bulletin, Field Museum of Natural His-
          tory 42(8): 10–13.
THOMAS, DAVID, and ALAN HEALY
    1962 Some Philippine Language Subgroupings: A Lexicostatistical Study. An-
          thropological Linguistics 4(9): 22–33.
TURNBULL, WILFRID
    1909 Report of an Inspection Trip Through the Ilongot Rancherías and Coun-
          try on and near the Cagayan River. Typescript. Chicago: Philippine
          Studies Library.
TURNER, VICTOR
    1957 Schism and Continuity in an African Society. Manchester, Eng.: Man-
          chester University Press.
VANSINA, JAN
    1965 Oral Tradition. Chicago: Aldine.
WALLACE, BEN
    1970 Hill and Valley Farmers. Cambridge, Mass.: Schenkman.
WHITE, HAYDEN
    1973 Metahistory: The Historical Imagination in Nineteenth-Century Eu-
          rope. Baltimore: Johns Hopkins University Press.

WILLIAMS, RAYMOND
1977 Marxism and Literature. Oxford: Oxford University Press.
WORCESTER, D. C.
1908 Report of the Secretary of Interior. *In* Annual Report of the Philippine Commision, 1908, part 2, pp. 3–64. Washington, D.C.: Bureau of Printing.
1909 Report of the Secretary of Interior. *In* Annual Report of the Philippine Commission, 1909, pp. 97–132. Washington, D.C.: Bureau of Printing.
YENGOYAN, ARAM
1973 Kindreds and Task Groups in Mandaya Social Organization. Ethnology 12: 163–77.

CHRONOLOGICAL INDEX

Impact of American Colonial Administration

Presence of William Jones (1908–9), 1–9, 24–25, 149, 259–63, 275, 277; government reprisals after death of Jones, 259–63, 275; dislocation of Peknars-Bēsilids-Yamus, 259, 261–63

Pacification intensified (1908–10), 36, 259–68 *passim*, 274–75

Government troops involved in Ilongot feuding by making arrests (1923), 49–50, 69–70, 73, 118–19, 233, 266, 275, and (1927), 272

Effects of world economic depression (1931), 36, 48, 51

Lowland political tension (1935), 52

Arrests (1940), 18, 52–53, 71–73, 275

WARTIME (1941–45)

Fighting in the lowlands (1941–43): World War II, 48, 112–13; Japanese invasion of the Philippines, 36, 53, 84n, 120–22; establishment of "Anti-Japanese People's Army" (Hukbalahap Movement), 156

Population movements

Sudden return to central Rumyad (1942–44), 48, 53, 121–22, 171, 198–99, 242, 249

Inward retreat from Japanese (1945): Lakay's family to Kakidugen, 73, 79, 124–25, then joined by lowlanders, 125; Pasigiyans to Pengegyaben, in joint raid against Japanese, 123–24, 129, 155; Buwa people to Kakidugen, in joint raid against Japanese, 125, 127, 129; Butags and Tengas to Bēawet, 125–26, 129

Alliance and enmity: character of hostilities (1942–45), 48, 53, 58, 72–73, 84n, 122–23; Bēduks' involvement in murder of Bayaw's brother by soldiers (1942), 122, 199; threat to Pengegyabens by Ringens, 198–200, and by Butags, 72–73, 123; Rumyads' raid on Bēduk refugees, 122, and beheading of Aymuyus, 84, 102–3; cessation of intra-Ilongot raiding (1945), 113, 242

"Time of the Japanese" in central Rumyad (1945): stories about, 16, 18, 39–40, 126–34, 175–76; character of, 36, 112–13, 126–34, 181, 242, 248–49; Japanese forced into Ilongot interior by American troops, 123–27, 197; Ilongot decimation, 36, 40, 77, 112–18, 130–34, 158, 164–65, 198, 201–6 *passim*, 248; Bēawets' displacement and counterattack, 125–26, 156; Kakidugens' displacement, 127–28, 133, counterattack, 128–29, joining with Pengegyabens, 128–30, 197; Lakay's murder of soldier, 131, 154, 156, and flight to lowlands, 132, 171, 201; Pengegyabens' displacement, 130, wandering with Kakidugens, 128–30, 197, hiding in central Rumyad and return to home, 133–34; attack by Japanese sniper, 134, 158, 198; raid against Japanese, 117, 133–34, 156

CONTEMPORARY PERIOD (1946–74)

Population movements and alliances

Postwar return to homelands, recovery and restoration (1946–49), 36, 132, 153, 155, 164–65, 177

Kakidugen-Bēnabē divorces and residential separation (1952–54), 168–74, 212, 214–15

GENERAL INDEX